NOTTS COUNTY

The Tommy Lawton Era

DESERT ISLAND SPORTS HISTORIES BY EDDIE GILES

FOOTBALL

Derby County: Champions of England 1972 & 1975	978-1-874287-98-8
Bristol Rovers: The Bert Tann Era	978-1-905328-37-6
Bristol City: From Atyeo to Dicks	978-1-905328-67-3
Billy Walker: Once, Twice, Three Times a Winner	978-1-905328-42-0
Notts County: The Tommy Lawton Era	978-1-874287-79-1

CRICKET

The Derbyshire Chronicles:	978-1-905328-25-3

NOTTS COUNTY
The Tommy Lawton Era

Series editor: Clive Leatherdale

Edward Giles

DESERT ISLAND BOOKS

First published in 2010
by
DESERT ISLAND BOOKS LIMITED
7 Clarence Road, Southend on Sea, Essex SS1 1AN
United Kingdom
www.desertislandbooks.com

The right of Edward Giles to be identified as author of this work has
been asserted under The Copyright Designs and Patents Act 1988

British Library Cataloguing-in-Publication Data
A catalogue record for this book is available from the British Library

ISBN 978-1-905328-74-1

Printed in Great Britain by the MPG Books Group, Bodmin and King's Lynn

Contents

		PAGE
	Author's Note and Dedication	6
1	Following in the Wake of Gallacher and Dean	7
2	To Everton with Grandpa Joe's approval	10
3	Finest team in which Lawton played	21
4	Surprising aversion to taking penalties	28
5	Major Buckley, Jesse Pye, Ian McPherson	33
6	Northampton the centre of League attention	39
7	Corkhill coincidence – and some light relief	45
8	Eric Houghton, the spot-kick king	53
9	Flow of Forest players to Meadow Lane	58
10	Stollery resigns; first century of goals	64
11	Goal to remember in promotion season	71
12	Disharmony mars rise to Second Division	77
13	Tragic early death of Leon Leuty	83
14	Lawton 'pupil' who became costliest player	88
15	Renewed clamour for Lawton's England recall	94
16	Jackson, Wylie, McCormack, Ken McPherson	123
17	Cup battles with Bolton amid relegation fears	129
18	Sewell and Wylie follow Houghton to Villa	134
19	Revival with George Poyser as manager	139
20	Record gate, but an FA Cup let-down	145
21	Double dismissal after a Rhyl upset	151
22	Caretaker Broome sweeps clean but rejected	157
23	Lawton back in First Division with Arsenal	164
24	Boardroom split by recall from Kettering	171
25	Relegated in Lawton's season as manager	177
26	Victims of Lincoln's great escape	183
27	'Tiny Tim' and 'Tiger' take over	189
28	Hateley and Astle, learners from Lawton	193
29	Lawton suffers crisis of confidence	200
30	The three managerial reigns of Jimmy Sirrel	205
31	Horrendous problems after third departure	211
32	The final tributes	216
	Appendices	219

AUTHOR'S NOTE

As with my previous books, in the compilation of this one I have relied heavily on the records I kept with all the enthusiasm and diligence of youth. It stemmed from the need to have facts to hand in answering readers' sports queries in my weekly feature for the *Derby Evening Telegraph*. There was then no other ready access to the wealth of information which, most notably through the internet, is available nowadays.

My researches involved a wide variety of sports, but concentrated on cricket and football. Coverage of cricket was eased by the admirable *Wisdens* that now stand as a constant, unnerving, reminder of my advancing years as they line the shelves of my study through all the seasons since the Second World War.

Association Football presented more of a problem at the outset because the published material I had to hand was restricted to the *Sunday Chronicle* (later *News of the World*) annuals before the advent in 1970 of the *Rothmans Football Yearbook* that has since been transformed into a staggering tome, latterly sponsored by Sky Sports, under the impeccable editorship of Jack Rollin (a former colleague when I was with *The Daily Telegraph*, and he *The Sunday Telegraph*) and his daughter Glenda.

It was to bolster my soccer records that I began to keep scrapbooks each season that have proved so invaluable in my preparation of histories of Derby County, Nottingham Forest, the two Bristol clubs, and now the Notts County of the Tommy Lawton era. I also kept a log of football transfers until increasing demands on my time coincided with the more comprehensive lists that became available in the *Football Yearbook*. The Football Guides published annually by the *Nottingham Evening Post* have been another valuable source of information, and Jack Rollin and Gerald Mortimer, a former Sports Editor of the *Derby Evening Telegraph*, have readily filled a couple of gaps in my records. Google and Wikipedia, those mines of information on the internet, have also been of great assistance. Other sources are referred to in the text.

EDWARD GILES

DEDICATION

To Philip and Hazel

CHAPTER ONE

Following in the Wake of Gallacher and Dean

On 15 November 1947, the thirteenth Saturday of the season, the County Ground at Northampton was the main focus of attention in the Football League. In normal circumstances, the home club's match with Notts County would have been just another of no particular interest outside the Southern Section of the Third Division. But these circumstances were far from normal. The visitors from Meadow Lane, strugglers fourth off the foot of the table, had just caused the biggest soccer sensation in years by signing Tommy Lawton, England's current centre-forward, for a record fee of £20,000.

It was nothing new for Notts County to have an international player leading their attack. There had been three others during the decade leading up to the outbreak of the Second World War in 1939, but, unlike Lawton, they had been in the twilight of their careers, not still the right side of 30 and at the peak of powers. One had been the player from whom Lawton had taken over when he had first entered the First Division with Everton, the burly, dark-haired William Ralph ('Dixie') Dean. The others were Scots: Hugh Kilpatrick Gallacher, small in stature and thin of thatch, but huge in talent – if with a tempestuous trait that made him a dynamic character of considerable controversy – and James Smith, who was less well-known outside his home country.

It was from Jimmy Smith that the 33-year-old Hughie Gallacher took over when he arrived at Meadow Lane from Derby County in September 1936. Smith, signed from Newport County, played in only the first four matches of that season, scoring just one goal, before dropping out through injury – never to be recalled. He was soon on his way back to Scotland, with Dumbarton, denied the opportunity to show Notts fans something of the form that had brought him a record 66 goals for Ayr United in the Second Division of the Scottish League in the 1927-28 season. He was capped just the once, failing to score in a drawn game with England in 1924, the first match between the two countries to be staged at Wembley.

In days when there were many fewer international matches than now, Gallacher played for Scotland twenty times, despite having to contend with strong competition that most notably came from Glasgow Celtic's

Jimmy McGrory, scorer of more than 410 goals in the Scottish League and 550 in all with the inclusion of international matches and cup-ties. Most of Gallacher's 23 goals for Scotland were scored against Northern Ireland and Wales. He put only two into England's net, at Hampden Park on his first appearance against the auld enemy in 1925, but was one of the acclaimed 'Wembley Wizards' who triumphed 5-1 in London in 1928.

At that time he was with Newcastle, an unprecedented folk hero of Tyneside. After starting out with Queen of the South, he had helped Airdrieonians to win the Scottish Cup and, for three successive seasons, finish runners-up in the Scottish First Division. With almost a hundred goals for Airdrie to his name, he cost Newcastle £6,500, then the biggest fee received by a Scottish club, when they won the race for his signature in December 1925. He scored twice on his debut in a 3-3 home draw with Everton, for whom Dean did the hat-trick, and he piled up just over 140 more for the Geordies (36 of them, a club record that still stands, as captain of their title-winning season in 1926-27, plus three more in the Cup) before his shock £10,000 transfer to Chelsea in May 1930.

By one of those freaks of the fixture list, Chelsea were Newcastle's first visitors the following season, and a record crowd packed into St James' Park, with thousands more locked out, for a Wednesday evening game that United won with a 76th-minute goal from right-winger Jackie Cape. Newcastle do not have an official attendance for this match, but it is generally given as 68,386.

Gallacher also failed to score in the drawn return game at the end of the season, but he did the hat-trick in a 4-1 win when Newcastle were next at Stamford Bridge. That was the only time he bagged three goals in a match for Chelsea, having done so thirteen times for Newcastle, including three fours. Even so, he exceeded 80 goals for the London club before his £3,000 move to Derby in November 1934.

The fact that the Rams had to pay off Gallacher's gambling debts as part of the deal was indicative of the turbulent side of his nature. As a lover of the London night life, he was reputed to have a drink problem, and had appeared in court after being involved in a fight in a cafe. His fiery temperament had also repeatedly got him into trouble with referees, incurring one suspension of two months for pushing the highly respected Bert Fogg into a bath. At Derby, however, he came up against a manager who was one of the strictest disciplinarians of the time. George Jobey was a former Newcastle player whom I later got to know as a companion on train journeys from Derby to the home matches of Notts County and Nottingham Forest while he was temporarily out of management before his final post at Mansfield.

Ironically, Gallacher was one of the big-name players who in 1941 cost Jobey his job at Derby when an FA-League inquiry into alleged illegal payments fined the club £500 and cast out members of the board along with the manager, but while he was with the Rams he scarcely put a foot wrong off the field or on it.

The dynamic little Scot (he stood 5ft 6in) repaid the trust placed in him by Jobey, whose suspension was lifted in 1945, with the high ratio of 40 goals in 55 games before his transfer to Notts County. Five of those goals, the first of them his 300th in Scottish and English League football, came in a 5-2 win at Blackburn. It was the fourth such broadside of his career, if his version of his tally in Scotland's 7-3 victory in Belfast in 1929 is included. He claimed, contrary to the record books, that one of his goals was mistakenly credited to Alex James, the then Preston, and later Arsenal, maestro with whom he had played in schools football. Gallacher's first, undisputed, five-goal feat was achieved for Airdrie against Clyde in 1923; the other in a 7-3 defeat of the Irish League in 1925.

On that second occasion, in Belfast, he defied a death threat delivered to the Scottish League's dressing room at half-time, but he was left to wonder if he had indeed been a target during those times of the Troubles when a bullet struck a nearby wall as he later walked through the city to visit friends. Shaken as he was, he could not refrain from observing that 'it seems I haven't managed to teach the Irish how to shoot straight!'

Although nearing the end of his career when he joined Notts County, Gallacher – like Lawton after him – added ten thousand to the gate when he made his debut. That was on 26 September 1936, in a 2-0 home win against Torquay United. He did not score that day, but he ended the season as the club's leading scorer with 25 goals in 32 games as Notts achieved in the Third South what he had helped Derby achieve in Division One the previous season – second place in the table. The Rams had finished eight points adrift of Sunderland; Notts were only two short of the one promotion place that went to Luton Town.

By the time he left for Grimsby Town in January 1938, Gallacher had taken his Notts goals tally to 32 in 45 League games and one FA Cup-tie, displaying much of his old sharpness with hat-tricks against Northampton and Bristol Rovers. For the Mariners, whose manager, his former Newcastle clubmate Charlie Spencer, signed him as cover for the injury-prone Welsh international Pat Glover in a successful attempt to escape relegation to the Second Division, he added three goals in a dozen appearances. Then he went into the Third North with Gateshead, for whom in 31 matches he scored eighteen more, taking him to an overall total in the region of 450. The outbreak of war in September 1939 finally brought his flamboyant career to an end.

After keeping in touch with the game by occasionally playing for veteran teams, Gallacher commented on Newcastle matches for a local newspaper until, irony of ironies, he was banned from St James' Park for being too critical. He then turned to working with mining machinery, and as a machinist in a chemical factory. It was employment of a kind that was not entirely new to him because he had been down the mines and in a munitions factory during the First World War.

Life away from football, however, continued for Gallacher in the turmoil that dated back to the swift breakdown of the Protestant-Catholic marriage into which he had entered at seventeen, and the death of a son who never had a first birthday. He resorted to heavy drinking after the fatal illness of his second wife, and it all came to a dreadful end the day before he was due to appear in court at Gateshead, accused of assaulting, ill-treating and neglecting the youngest of his three sons, fourteen-year-old Matthew. Blaming drink for his downfall, he admitted that he 'overstepped the mark' in hitting Matthew with an ornament after arriving home drunk, but nobody could have anticipated the horrifying manner in which he opted out of attending the prosecution brought by the NSPCC after Matthew had left to live with an aunt.

On 11 June 1957, Gallacher walked to the ominously named Dead Man's Crossing at Low Fell on the London to Edinburgh railway line. Eight minutes after midday, two train spotters, a boy and his sister, saw him pacing an iron footbridge as the express from York was heard approaching. As it came into view, he ran down the embankment and, out of their sight, threw himself into its path. The awful suicide of this turbulent soccer genius, at the age of 54 years and five months, spread shock-waves far wider than the confines of professional football. For all his faults, he was an outstanding personality, and will always be remembered as one of the game's truly greats.

Notts County tried four players at centre-forward in the dozen fixtures they fulfilled between Gallacher's last appearance, a defeat at Walsall on the Saturday before Christmas in 1937, and 'Dixie' Dean's debut in the loss at QPR on 12 March 1938. Dean, not long turned 31, arrived with a reputation to match Gallacher's, having amassed 377 goals in 431 League and Cup games for Everton since leaving Tranmere, at whose ground he had sold chocolates as a boy, for a bargain £3,000 thirteen years earlier. Those goals included a record 37 hat-tricks.

Fate, besides age, decreed that Dean was far from having the same impact with Notts County. In the nine first-team appearances he was able to make, he was restricted to just three goals. He went goalless through the first three of those matches, all lost, and then had to have an ankle operation. Notts were also beaten when he returned for the second match of the last pre-war season, but three days later he had his one big success with two goals in a 5-1 home win against Torquay. Two weeks after that he scored again at Meadow Lane in the 2-0 defeat of Newport County, who went on to win promotion as Third South champions, but he was injured again in the next match, lost at Northampton, and made his final exit in a scoreless home draw with Walsall on the first Saturday of November.

Early the following year Dean went into the Irish League with Sligo Rovers, for whom he scored eleven goals in as many games before, in common with Gallacher, his playing career was effectively ended by the outbreak of war. When all his matches were taken into account, including sixteen for England, in which he scored eighteen times, he had a grand total of 473 goals in 502 appearances. In one season alone, 1927-28, in which Everton were champions, he reached a record 60 in the League, completing a hat-trick on the final day with a powerful late header during a 3-3 home draw with Arsenal. That edged him ahead of the total achieved a year earlier, also on the last day, by George Camsell, who netted the winner at Swansea for Middlesbrough's Second Division table-toppers.

Everton were relegated two years later, but Dean's goals – 39 of them, plus nine more in the Cup – boosted them to immediate promotion, and they ended the season after that, 1932-33, as FA Cup winners for the second time. He scored one of their goals, with a header of course, in their 3-0 defeat of Manchester City at Wembley.

It was estimated that Dean, son of a Birkenhead railwayman, headed more goals than any other player. It was an art he perfected in hours of practice as a youth – and one that he helped to pass on to Tommy Lawton. During the short time they were together with Everton they indulged in a special training stint by leaping to head a ball suspended from a rope in the gymnasium – so wholeheartedly that, as Lawton remembered it, their foreheads were 'bruised and bloodied.'

Lawton recalled that when they first met, Dean put an arm round his shoulder and told him: 'Youngster, you've come here to take my place. Anything I can do for you, I will.' They played together, with Lawton at inside-forward, in eight League games and one Cup-tie before Dean's departure to Meadow Lane. That Cup match, at Tottenham, was especially memorable. Dean scored twice and Lawton once (a header in the opening minutes), but Everton were knocked out after being 3-2 up with only three minutes to go. Spurs' winner came in the final seconds, from a centre after the ball had bounced favourably off the back of Charlie Gee, Everton's centre-half. Lawton likened the crescendo of noise as the home crowd urged their team on to 'a miniature Hampden Roar'.

Dean's exceptional heading ability was a tribute to his courage as well as his dedication, considering that his career was threatened soon after he joined Everton when he fractured his skull and jaw in a motor-cycle accident. This meant there was a silver plate in the head that nodded so many goals. In having his future as a footballer cast into doubt, Dean had something in common with Gallacher besides an avaricious appetite for goals. The Scot had still to make his mark when he almost lost his life after being rushed to hospital with double pneumonia.

Prolific though Dean was with his headwork, he was no mean finisher with his boots. Later in life, it was in shooting that he directed his main criticism of the then current players. 'Modern centre-forwards seem afraid to shoot,' he said. 'If they kept on having a go they'd be bound to score sooner or later.' Perhaps his greatest achievement was to score 200 goals in 199 consecutive games for Everton. Lord Woolton, then the head of the John Lewis group of retail stores, and during the Second World War a Minister of Food who had a meatless pie named after him, arranged for a medal to be specially struck to mark the feat. Yet it was said that the award Dean prized most was his first medal, gained for playing for Birkenhead Boys during the 1919-20 season.

Dean disliked the 'Dixie' nickname foisted on him by fans because of his swarthy appearance and curly hair, preferring to be known among his friends as Bill. He came to accept it in later life, however, and John Keith, a prominent sports journalist with the *Daily Express*, treasured a lunch menu that Dean signed: 'To John, Best Wishes, Dixie.' That, tragically, was on the day Dean died, on 1 March 1980. Keith wrote: 'Little did I know when I suggested Dixie should be a guest of honour at the lunch, and then attend the 122nd Mersey derby, that I was merely a servant of fate for the game's most revered figure. But could there have been a more appropriate venue or setting than Goodison Park on derby day for Dixie's final curtain?'

That day's match was Everton's first against Liverpool that Dean had attended since the last of the eighteen in which he had played, on 23 January 1937. He had scored nineteen goals in those games, with two hat-tricks among the eleven he netted at Anfield. On the day of his delayed return as a spectator, however, Everton were beaten 1-2, Liverpool's decider coming from the penalty spot. Dean fatally collapsed minutes after the final whistle. His health had not been good since he had ended fifteen years as licensee of the Dublin Packet, a public house in Chester, and in 1976 he had had to have his right leg amputated.

Adept as six-footer Lawton also became with his headwork, there could be no doubt that such constant contact, on the field as well as off, contributed to the concussion to which he became prone, for the laced-up leather footballs of his time were much weightier than the bladderless plastic ones pinged about these days.

It was during May 1948, in one of the matches in which Lawton captained England, against Switzerland at Stamford Bridge, that he showed a susceptibility to being concussed that dogged him during his days with Notts County. He scored one of the four goals with which England preserved their unbeaten home record against Continental teams, after falling behind early in the second half, but he knew precious little about it. From the twentieth minute he played on in a daze, suffering the effects of an accidental blow on the back of the head in challenging for a high ball. Consequently, he was unable to attend the banquet at the Dorchester Hotel that evening, going straight to bed instead. Some confusion was also experienced by the French referee. The teams were all lined up for the start of the second half when he realised that he had left the ball behind in his dressing room.

Lawton was first concussed with Notts County in a collision with the Swansea goalkeeper near the end of the Boxing Day match, his sixth appearance for the club. Team-mates afterwards found him asleep in the dressing room, and he missed the following day's return at the Vetch Field, where a goal from Jack Marsh earned a draw. On a Thursday evening in April the following season, Lawton suffered concussion in heading the ball narrowly wide during a home defeat by Ipswich Town. He again carried on, but contributed little. The next instance occurred in the opening match of the 1948-49 season, lost at Torquay. Once more he stayed on the field and afterwards refused to see a doctor. He knew the cure – a few hours' sleep. It was said that he 'climbed so high, and hung in the air so long,' that his jaw often struck the head of a defender on his way down.

When this jinx again struck in the first minute of a home win against Sheffield United in 1951, Lawton did have to leave the field for attention. He returned half an hour later, but only for long enough to create the first of Jackie Sewell's two goals. Three more games went by before he was fit to resume. For all those mishaps and other knocks, however, Lawton was very rarely out of the Notts team during the seasons he spent at Meadow Lane before leaving for Brentford in March 1952.

CHAPTER TWO

To Everton with Grandpa Joe's approval

Tommy Lawton, who was born at Moses Gate, a suburb of Bolton, on 6 October 1919, cost Everton £6,500. This was then the biggest fee paid for a seventeen-year-old when they signed him from Burnley on the last day of December 1936.

It mattered not to the Goodison club that he was so flat-footed that he had to wear arch supports in his shoes. He was soon literally to leap into fame, though he had an off-putting 'welcome' to Liverpool when he emerged from Exchange Station on New Year's Day 1937 and asked the tram conductor if it passed Everton's ground. 'He looked at me silently for a few seconds,' Lawton recalled, 'then said: "Are you Lawton?" A trifle flattered at being recognised so quickly, I said I was. Another pause, then he said shortly, "You'll never be a good as Dean!"'

Other clubs, notably Bolton, Liverpool and Sheffield Wednesday, were frustrated when Lawton joined Burnley at the age of fifteen in May 1935 after scoring a glut of goals in schools football – 570 in three seasons, if one estimate is to be believed. Incredible as that total may seem, it was even more amazing that he was never capped as a schoolboy – not even after scoring three times in an international trial. He also did the hat-trick for Rossendale United in a Lancashire Combination match shortly before giving up his first job on leaving the Folds Road Central School in Bolton, at a tannery where golf clubs were made, to join Burnley. He was originally taken on at Turf Moor to work in the club's offices, at 50 shillings a week, as the result of a recommendation to a director from one of his former schoolmasters.

Bolton had lost their first place in the queue for Lawton because neither of the jobs with which they tried to tempt him to sign amateur forms – as an office clerk or butcher's roundsman – had been acceptable to his grandfather Jim Riley, at whose home Tommy had been taken by his mother to live after her marriage break-up. Liverpool failed because they were unable to come up with an outside job at all, Wednesday because his mother thought that Sheffield was too far away for someone so young to go there on his own. The country must have seemed a much bigger place in those days!

At Turf Moor, Lawton found time from his office duties to sharpen his shooting by driving the ball at the tin advertisements around the pitch, picking a word to aim at, and then a letter, as his accuracy improved.

Burnley were battling to avoid relegation from the Second Division when all that diligence and application was rewarded. Lawton was given his first League chance at the age of sixteen years 163 days in a home match with Doncaster on 28 March 1936. He did not score the goal that brought a 1-1 draw, but opened his account at the next opportunity with a couple in a 3-1 win at Swansea.

Three more goals in his five other games that season helped to hoist Burnley clear of the drop, and he was firmly established as a first choice when he turned professional on 9 October that year, three days after his seventeenth birthday. His pay rose to £7 a week in the season, £5 out of it. On the following afternoon, he scored in the first minute of a home match with Tottenham, completing the first of his League hat-tricks in a 3-1 victory. He was the youngest to perform that feat at that level – though subsequently challenged by Ken Chaytor, who was two months past his seventeenth birthday when he scored all three of Oldham's goals at Mansfield in January 1955.

The sleekly dark-haired Lawton (with the then familiar central part-ing) was Burnley's assistant secretary as well as their centre-forward when, sorting through the club's post one morning, he had the novel experience of taking a phone call in which his own transfer was being sought. On other end of the line was Arsenal manager George Allison who, unaware that he was speaking to the player he wanted – Lawton had identified himself as assistant to secretary Alf Boland, who had not yet arrived – asked for the message to be passed on, and said he would call again. Arsenal were to get their man, but not for another seventeen years.

Lawton answered calls from four other clubs that morning, and was to learn later that Burnley refused offers from eight altogether before agreeing to Everton's. The deal was done after two Everton directors, Will Cuff and Tom Percy, accompanied by Theo Kelly, then the club's secretary but soon to become their first manager, had turned up at Turf Moor on New Year's Eve – but not before Lawton's grandfather, then Burnley's groundsman, had also been brought into the negotiations. Joe Riley gave his approval on suggesting that he too should go to Goodison Park – ostensibly as a member of the groundstaff there, but also to keep an eye on young Tommy.

By coincidence, Lawton's last game for Burnley was against the club he had faced on his League debut, Doncaster. By another coincidence, his first game for Everton was against Burnley – in the Central League for the Reserves. His goal in a 2-0 home victory won him a bet with oppos-ing centre-half Bob Johnson. Lawton had made the understandable mis-take of first going into the visitors' dressing room, instead of Everton's, before the match, and it was there, amid the banter, that the bet was waged.

Lawton had last turned out for Burnley the previous Saturday, 28 December 1936, when Doncaster avenged their Turf Moor defeat of Christmas Day. As on his debut, Lawton did not score in either of those games, but he had a respectable total of sixteen goals in 25 Second Division appearances for Burnley. There were to be 70 more in his 95 League and Cup matches for Everton before his move to Chelsea, though they did not take into account his four in the three First Division matches of the 1939-40 season, which was abandoned when war broke out.

And there were also the 148 goals he piled up in 111 Everton appearances during the war, in which, while in the Army – originally as a lance bombardier in the Royal Engineers, then, eventually, as a Quartermaster Sergeant Major instructor with a 'Footballers' Battalion' in the Army Physical Training Corps (APTC) – he scored goals for England and as a guest with Aldershot, Chester and Tranmere. He even found time to play a couple of times for Greenock Morton while on his Scottish honeymoon. It was after his posting to Aldershot from Birkenhead, with the 8th Cheshires, that he and his fiancée, Rosaleen, decided to wed.

Lawton fitted in two games on Christmas Day 1940 – for Tranmere against Crewe in the morning, and for Everton against Liverpool at Anfield in the afternoon. Unusual, but not unique. On the same day Len Shackleton, the self-styled 'Clown Prince of Soccer' who was later with Newcastle and Sunderland, played for Bradford Park Avenue at Leeds, and for Bradford City at Huddersfield.

Overall, the number of Lawton's wartime goals exceeded 200. One source puts the number above 300, with the inclusion of his Army games. There were, of course, easy pickings in the matches of those years, with clubs having to resort at short notice to guests. As one of the many star guests at Aldershot, where Billy McCracken, the former Newcastle and Ireland full-back, was manager, Lawton scored six goals in a match against both Luton and Southampton. Four times he netted five – for Chester against the RAF, for Everton against Tranmere and, twice in the same year, for Everton at Crewe. And in the month the war in Europe ended he scored half his team's ten goals while on tour with an Army team in Italy.

It was during that tour, which also took in the Middle East and Greece, that Lawton and his colleagues had to contend with being called 'D-Day Dodgers' and 'PT Commandoes.' It was only natural that critics looked unfavourably upon fit young men who were out of the front line playing football when their own relatives and friends were fighting and dying overseas. But Lawton said his own conscience was clear. After all, he did not ask to be stationed in England, and, although that enabled him to continue playing regularly in domestic wartime competitions, he reasonably felt that he and others were playing their part by helping to keep up morale and also raise money from the numerous charity matches in which they appeared, both home and abroad.

Matt Busby was the player-manager of that Army team. In his book *My Story*, he recalled: 'Often we played matches only a few miles behind the front lines, with the noise of gunfire sometimes tending to drown the sound of the referee's whistle.'

Lawton's first footballing venture abroad as a soldier was in France, a week after he had reported for duty at Aldershot one snowy day early in January 1940. Having been posted to a Footballers' Battalion in the APTC, he was ordered to London to join the players who were to entertain troops in the British Expeditionary Force with three matches against the French Army. The party included two Everton clubmates, fellow England cap Joe Mercer and Billy Cook, an Irish international defender who had been a Cup-winner in both Scotland (Celtic, 1931) and England (Everton, 1933). Among the others were such well-known names as Matt Busby, Denis Compton and Stan Cullis.

In his autobiography *Football Is My Business*, Lawton recalled that on the train journey to Dover he was sitting with Busby when Cullis came up and persuaded them to safeguard against being seasick by paying a guinea (105p) for three pills that 'positively could not fail'. Once on board they each swallowed the pills and settled down below decks to a game of cards. Untroubled, they joked about escaping the queasiness they expected some of the other players to suffer. An hour and a half later, believing they were they were about to dock, they went back upstairs to have a look at France. 'We could see shaded lights of a blacked-out harbour,' said Lawton. 'Calais, I exclaimed gaily. "No," said a voice from the darkness. "Dover. We are still in harbour." When we did move from our berth Matt, Stan and I dead-heated for the ship's side. I tell you, I've been ill going from Liverpool to New Brighton on the ferry!'

And Lawton's upset stomach was not all. In staying on deck throughout the chilly trip, he caught a heavy cold, and, although still able to play, he gave what he conceded were some of his worst displays in the games in Paris, Lille and Rheims. He rated the match in the French capital as the best of the three, watched by a crowd of about 35,000, but admitted that it would have been lost but for an inspired display by Reg Allen, a QPR goalkeeper later with Manchester United. And even then it took a late clearance off the line by Mercer to ensure a draw.

Lawton's susceptibility to sea-travel was again put to the test, and this time more severely, when he was chosen to play for the Army in Ireland during the 1941-42 season. The first part of the crossing, from Stranraer to Larne, passed uneventfully enough, but he and his companions had more than seasickness to worry about when an explosion made them fear they had been torpedoed. Fortunately, when they hurried up on deck they found that the blacked-out ship was still intact. Their alarm had been caused by a member of the crew who had been shooting at a floating mine. 'There were a few bumping hearts for a while after that scare,' said Lawton.

Unhappy as he was as a sailor, Lawton admitted to being even more of 'a bundle of nerves' when he made his first flights to play in Belgium in late March 1945. It turned out, however, to be 'a wonderful ride, no trouble at all', though on boarding the aircraft, a Dakota, he had the unnerving experience of being told to 'put your Mae West [inflatable life jacket] on tight, otherwise it'll strangle you when you come down in the drink!'

In one match on that trip, Lawton scored four goals in an 8-1 win over Diables Rouge, and thereby won a bet for a watching Liverpudlian soldier in the crowd. Lawton had already completed his hat-trick when his attention was caught by this gesticulating compatriot as a corner was about to be taken. 'He beckoned me over,' recalled Lawton, 'and said "Hey, make it four. I've got 200 francs on you to score more than three."' Lawton was only too pleased to oblige. The kick taken by Brentford's Leslie Smith was perfectly placed for a typical scoring header.

On other wartime footballing excursions, the mode of transport left much to be desired, even on land. When next in Belgium, Lawton and the men he captained went from Brussels to Bruges in a dilapidated motor coach with wooden seats abandoned by the retreating Germans. It broke down three times after the driver twice lost his way, and the journey had to be completed in cars belonging to the RAF. On another occasion, an Army lorry was used, into which, as Lawton described it, the players were 'packed like sardines'.

Inferior as the opposition was in a good number of Lawton's wartime matches, it was more formidable when another of his eight four-goal feats and three of his fifteen 'normal' hat-tricks were registered against Scotland, one during an Army international. Furthermore, he had already shown his ability to compete at the highest level by heading the First Division scoring list in both his full peacetime seasons with Everton. In 1937-38 he led with 28 goals in 39 games; in 1938-39, when Everton were champions, he was joint top with Middlesbrough's Mickey Fenton. Both scored 34 times in the League – Fenton in 33 matches, Lawton in 38 – but the Boro sharpshooter was outscored by Lawton in that season's FA Cup by four goals to one, in five ties to four. Middlesbrough needed three games to get past Bolton before going out to Sunderland. Everton, half of whose eight goals against Doncaster in the second round were scored by Lawton, reached the quarter-finals before losing to Wolves, who were surprisingly beaten by Portsmouth at Wembley.

In that last full pre-war season Lawton scored seven of his goals against Middlesbrough – three in a 4-0 win at Goodison Park, four in a 4-4 draw at Ayresome Park, where Fenton had to be content with just one.

With the war in Europe drawing to its conclusion after six traumatic years, there was much conjecture in the sports pages about Lawton's decision to seek a change of club in the autumn of 1945. He certainly had no disagreement with Everton, where he had enjoyed so much success and made so many friends. It was officially put down to 'domestic reasons', the breakdown of his marriage masked by a statement that his wife had been medically advised to move to the south of England for health reasons. There was also the fact that Lawton, in his own words, was 'bang out of form owing to the mental strain', and felt that a fresh start would also be to his own advantage. He had been dropped from the England side and, as he also said, 'that worried me more than somewhat.'

At the time, Lawton was stationed in the Army at Chester, so it was to a hotel in that city that Chelsea's manager, Billy Birrell, and vice-chairman, Jack Budd, travelled on 7 November 1945 to attend the formality of his signing. It was a major coup in the London club's preparation for the resumption of League soccer. Others taken to Stamford Bridge during that period included Danny Winter, a Welsh wartime international full-back from Bolton Wanderers; John Harris, a centre-half from Wolves who had represented Scotland when caps were not awarded and captained Chelsea as a guest in two wartime Wembley cup finals; Len Goulden, an England forward from West Ham; and Tommy Walker, a Hearts forward, hailed as one of the game's gentlemen, who had also been a wartime guest.

With Lawton the costliest, the total outlay of £30,000 made Chelsea the first of the big spenders as football returned to its peacetime pattern. Yet nine post-war seasons went by before the Bridge was at long last the home of the champions – with a team in which Harris, of those five, was the only survivor.

Fifteenth was Chelsea's final position in the one full First Division season Lawton spent with them. He ended it as their top scorer with 26 goals (including a hat-trick at Huddersfield), plus four in the FA Cup. The most remarkable of the 34 League games in which he played was an Anfield thriller of eleven goals in which he went without even one. Liverpool led 6-0. Chelsea hit back four times, only for the prospect of an astounding revival to be snuffed out as the shocked home side regrouped and completed the scoring three minutes from time.

Another game typical of the unpredictable Chelsea 'Pensioners' of those days saw Stoke 5-2 winners at Stamford Bridge after two goals from Lawton had put the outplayed home side into an unlikely lead. There was also a match in which Chelsea scored four goals, one of them by Lawton, away from home, yet still lost. Wolves hit them for six. During the war Lawton had taken part in what he recalled as 'perhaps the most exciting game in which I played during that period'. With half an hour to go, his Aldershot side led Arsenal 3-0, only for the Gunners to score six times in a row and pull off a 7-4 victory.

In the 1946-47 FA Cup, Chelsea needed two replays, in which Lawton scored three of their four goals to knock out Arsenal in the third round. Then they were taken to another replay as Raich Carter snatched a last-gasp equaliser for holders Derby at Stamford Bridge, and were beaten by an extra-time goal at the snow-covered Baseball Ground. In that second meeting with the Rams, Lawton and company were unable to break down a defence in which the not over-big Frank Broome, another fellow inter-national forward, who was to play with Lawton for both Notts and Brentford, kept goal from the fourth minute in which Alec Grant dislo-cated his left elbow in a heavy fall on the frozen surface.

With the inclusion of his 21 Chelsea goals in the transitional season of 1945-46, Lawton increased his club tally to 56 in 80 games before the November day in 1947 when Billy Birrell called his unsettled centre-for-ward to his office, handed him a list of the clubs seeking his transfer and told him: 'Cross out the ones you don't fancy.' That was when he first knew that Notts County were among them.

CHAPTER THREE

Finest team in which Lawton played

Notts County's top-scoring peacetime centre-forward before Tommy Lawton was Tom Keetley, one of eight Derby brothers who all played professionally in the Football League (there were three others who did not, plus a sister). In 110 games from the first day of the 1929-30 season, when he did the hat-trick in a 3-1 home win over Bristol City, until the penultimate match of 1932-33, in which he scored once, against four by visiting Bradford Park Avenue, he netted 98 times.

That total comprised 94 League goals, the four others in the Cup. If, however, matches outside those two competitions are taken into account, the top-scoring distinction passes to Jimmy Cantrell, another Derbyshire man (born Chesterfield) whose overall haul was boosted to 143 with the inclusion of 78 as a guest during the Great War of 1914-18. That is six more than the club's official record, set by Les Bradd in almost 450 games over ten years from 1967. Cantrell's League and Cup total for Notts County was a much more modest 65 in 136 matches before his transfer to Tottenham in October 1912.

It was shortly after the 1914-18 War that Tom Keetley left the Victoria Ironworks in Derby to join Bradford Park Avenue. In 1923 he moved to Doncaster Rovers, re-elected to the Northern Section of the Third Division, and he was joined there by three of his brothers, Frank (the only one also to play for Derby County), Harold and Joe, before his transfer to Notts County. All four were signed for Rovers by Dick Ray, a former full-back who had helped Manchester City to the Second Division title in 1899. Ray promptly snapped up a fifth brother after leaving to manage Leeds United during the summer of 1927. This was Charlie, the youngest, who scored eighteen goals in only sixteen Second Division games in Leeds' promotion season of 1927-28, after feasting on seven for the Reserves in a Central League match against Bolton.

Tom Keetley amassed 180 goals in his six seasons with Doncaster, setting a club record of 40 in 1928-29 that lasted until Clarrie Jordan netted 42 for the Third North champions of 1946-47. There is, however, another Doncaster record still credited to Keetley. On 16 February 1929, he scored six goals against Ashington, the Northumberland club among the original members of the Northern Section in 1921 but voted out of the League after finishing bottom eight years later. On 16 January 1932, Frank also scored six, for Lincoln against Halifax. It remains the only instance of two brothers each achieving a double hat-trick in a League game. Tom was quite a hat-trick specialist. He broke a Notts record with ten – three in consecutive away matches against Plymouth, Manchester United and Chesterfield in the October and November of 1931. Early the following season, following relegation, which Notts ended eight points clear as Southern Section champions, his four-goal flourish at home to Fulham set him on the way to another club League record of 39 (plus two in the Cup). From Meadow Lane he went to Lincoln, for whom Frank also played, and then retired with over 300 goals to his name.

Jimmy Cantrell was a dainty, artistic centre-forward, in marked contrast to the battering-ram type so prevalent in his day. He entered League football as an inside-forward with Aston Villa in 1904 and scored about two dozen goals in 50-odd games before his departure to Notts County, along with right-winger Rowland Harper in 1908. Harper was unable to establish himself, but Cantrell's successful switch to the head of the attack soon afterwards made him the club's leading scorer for three successive seasons, and it was no coincidence that the team tumbled out of the First Division in the wake of his exit to Spurs.

Notts might well have stayed up if Cantrell's replacement, Jack Peart, had arrived a little earlier from Newcastle. Peart, who, as a player-manager, later negotiated his own transfer from Ebbw Vale to Port Vale, was the club's leading marksman of 1912-13, despite playing only eleven games, scoring seven times in their new low total of 28. He again headed the list, with 28 goals in 30 appearances, in the promotion-winning side of the following season, and boasted the high ratio of 52 in 84 by the time he left for Birmingham after guesting for Leeds City and Rochdale during the war. As manager, Peart was more of an administrator, but the Fulham team that reached the First Division for the first time in 1949, the year after his death in office, was the one he had built.

Wartime work in an ordnance factory took Jimmy Cantrell back to Nottingham and his high-scoring return to Notts County as a guest. Afterwards reunited with Spurs, he contributed eighteen goals (there was also a hat-trick against Bristol Rovers in the Cup) to their promotion as Second Division champions in the first post-war season of 1919-20, and in 1921 he was in the team that carried off the Cup by beating Wolves with an individual goal by left-winger Jimmy Dimmock on a Stamford Bridge quagmire. Cantrell's first-team opportunities dwindled after that, but he left for Sutton United in the autumn of 1923 with the creditable total of 84 goals in his 174 games for Tottenham.

Unlike Tommy Lawton, neither Cantrell nor Keetley played for England. It was not altogether surprising that a cap eluded Keetley because, for all his prolific scoring, he operated in the lower divisions. Cantrell, however, was distinctly unlucky to be overlooked. Several times he was on the brink of selection as a first reserve, but fortune never favoured his undoubted skill in that respect.

Lawton already had nineteen full caps when he joined Notts County, and on the Wednesday after his Third Division debut at Northampton (more about that later) he gained the first of the four he would add while with the Meadow Lane club. He was the seventeenth to play for England while with Notts, but the first since Bill Ashurst won the last of his five caps in 1925. Horace Cope, whose full-back partnership with Ashurst operated an efficient offside trap, was selected to play against Ireland in Belfast later that year, but he had to drop out through injury and was not called on again. Soon afterwards he moved to Arsenal.

The opponents in Lawton's first England match as a Notts County player were Sweden, at Highbury, on 19 November 1947. England won 4-2, but it was Stan Mortensen's match, not Lawton's. The Blackpool marksman scored three goals. Lawton had to be content with one from a penalty – his first spot-kick for England since his international debut in a defeat by Wales by the same score in Cardiff on 22 October 1938, only sixteen days after his nineteenth birthday. As he afterwards admitted, that had been 'quite an ordeal' for one so young on such an important occasion, but it had at least enabled him to find the net in a display he had otherwise felt was 'particularly disappointing'. The man who kept him quiet was Tommy Jones, the centre-half who played behind him for Everton.

Lawton put himself firmly in line for that first cap by scoring four of the Football League's eight goals against the Irish League at Windsor Park, Belfast, the previous month. The teams were level at 2-2 in blustery conditions with half an hour to go, but play was interrupted when a downpour caused spectators on the uncovered terracing to swarm across the pitch to seek shelter under the covered stand. The hold-up lasted only a few minutes, after which the Irish were unable to cope with another deluge as their visitors scored six more times.

Lawton's fears of being dropped after failing to do himself justice on his Ninian Park debut were swiftly dispelled. Four days later he was retained as England gained a 3-0 win against FIFA at Arsenal's ground, in a match to mark the Football Association's 75th anniversary. Again he scored – as he would in the following month's victories over Norway, by 4-0 at Newcastle, and Ireland, by 7-0 at Old Trafford. He reminisced on the FIFA team's visit as 'a wonderful occasion' not only for the match but also for the banquet that followed at the Holborn Restaurant. The flags

of 24 nations were unfurled, and the distinguished company was enter-
tained by the singing of Webster Booth and Gracie Fields, two of the
most acclaimed performers of the time.

The Irish were undone at Manchester United's ground by the wizardry
of Stanley Matthews and the finishing power of his partner Willie Hall,
the curly-haired Tottenham and former Notts County forward who
scored five of the seven goals. Such a spree was quite an eye-opener, for
Hall was not normally noted as a plunderer of goals. He netted only eight
in 35 first-team games for Notts, and just 29 in 225 League and Cup
appearances for Spurs.

Not yet 21 when he left Meadow Lane for Tottenham in December
1932, Hall brought Notts an extra £500 as part of the deal when he won
the first of his ten caps in a 4-1 victory over France at White Hart Lane
a year later, six months after helping Tottenham back to the First
Division. He was out injured for much of the 1934-35 season in which
they were relegated, but afterwards continued to play regularly until 1943.
His playing career was ended by thrombosis in his right ankle, an afflic-
tion that also caused him to give up the management of Clapton (now
Leyton) Orient and Chingford Town, and compelled the amputation of
both legs.

On 18 September 1946, a match serving as an international trial was
played at Nottingham Forest in aid of Hall's benefit fund. The crowd
would have been much bigger than 18,700 (receipts £1,935) but for the
driving rain that Wednesday afternoon. The England selectors' delibera-
tions were also affected, for several players, including Lawton, withdrew
through injury. An FA representative side and a Combined XI shared
four goals. Lawton's replacement for the FA, Albert Stubbins, of
Liverpool and formerly Newcastle, was among the scorers. Three Forest
players were in the Combined XI – Bob McCall, and two who were later
with Notts County, Bill Baxter and Tom Johnston.

The period from mid-October to mid-November 1938 was busy for
the young Tommy Lawton. In addition to playing four times for England,
he was in the Football League team that beat the Scottish League 3-1 and
also registered the first of his Everton hat-tricks in the 4-0 win over
Middlesbrough. After that he had to wait five more months for his next
international appearance – and what a memorable one it was. On 15 April
1939, England met Scotland at Hampden Park, where they had not triumphed for twelve years – not since 'Dixie' Dean, Lawton's predecessor
on Merseyside, scored both their goals in a 2-1 win.

Willie Hall was also in the side that broke the hoodoo in dramatic
fashion. England fell behind in the first half, and it was not until twenty

minutes from time that they equalised through 'Pat' Beasley, the Huddersfield and former Arsenal winger who was winning his only cap. With three minutes left that was how the scores still stood – but the 1927 result was then repeated as Lawton rose to meet a centre from Matthews. Up into the top corner of the net the ball sped, inches beyond the out-stretched fingers of goalkeeper Dawson. 'I'm glad I scored that goal,' Lawton said afterwards with modest understatement. 'It made up for the one I missed earlier.' His captain, Eddie Hapgood, was more demonstra-tive. The Arsenal left-back jumped up and down, arms outstretched, as if doing a war dance. After all his years in the game, this was the win he declared he had longed for.

Lawton's remaining three pre-war appearances for England were all abroad. He kept up his goal-a-game record in a 2-2 draw with Italy in Milan, but failed to score in a 1-2 defeat by Yugoslavia in Belgrade and a 2-0 win against Romania in Bucharest. The lead he gained in Italy with another header laid on by Matthews was wiped out before half-time, and the home side went ahead with a goal the German referee allowed, despite protests that centre-forward Piola had punched the ball into the net – and struck George Male, the Arsenal right-back, in the eye in his follow through. Justice was done when Willie Hall equalised, from an opening also made by Matthews.

Normal service was resumed as Lawton scored in each of his first five wartime games for England. Four of these were against Scotland, with two wins apiece. England suffered defeat in Glasgow in April 1942, even when Lawton scored three of their four goals. It was the first of his inter-national hat-tricks, though he had recorded one in an Army game against the Scots in Sheffield two weeks earlier. At Hampden, Scotland outscored England with five goals, three of them from burly 'Jock' Dodds, who that season had nine hat-tricks among his 65 goals for Blackpool alone – including seven goals in a 15-3 demolition of Tranmere.

Victory in that nine-goal thriller was the last Scotland gained against England during the war, however. The result was goalless when the coun-tries met at Wembley six months later, Lawton's full-blooded drive com-ing back off the crossbar, but England were winners of the seven other matches – four of them by big margins – before Scotland broke the sequence in one of the Victory internationals arranged to celebrate the end of the war in Europe. Mind you, that overdue success was a close run thing. Not until the last 22 seconds, according to one account, did Jimmy Delaney, newly signed by Manchester United from Celtic, side-flick the only goal at Hampden on 13 April 1946. It was one of those rare days when Lawton found himself blotted out – by Frank Brennan, then of

Airdrieonians, but soon to become a bulwark at the heart of Newcastle's defence.

Lawton was seen at his potent best the next time he faced Scotland after the scoreless draw of 1942 at Wembley, scoring half the goals in the record 8-0 win at Maine Road on 16 October 1943. After back-heeling the pass from which Jimmy Hagan began the blitz in the fifteenth minute, Lawton did the hat-trick inside ten minutes, even finding the net with an acrobatic effort while sitting with his back to goal. Raich Carter made it 5-0 before missing a penalty early in the second half. After Hagan and Lawton had both scored again, Stan Matthews brought the house down by weaving his way through to apply the finishing touch a quarter of an hour before the end. This was the England team that Lawton not surprisingly rated the finest in which he ever played: Swift (Manchester City); Scott (Arsenal), Hardwick (Middlesbrough); Britton (Everton), Cullis (Wolves capt), Mercer (Everton); Matthews (Stoke), Carter (Sunderland), Lawton (Everton), Hagan (Sheffield United), Compton, D (Arsenal).

It was the first time Lawton had led the England attack for a year – and even he had not expected to be recalled. Only the month before, the man keeping him out, Don Welsh, of Charlton, had been the hat-trick hero of an 8-3 eclipse of Wales at Wembley. Lawton's exclusion had stemmed from two defeats by Wales, first 0-1 in Cardiff, where Lawton's luck was out with another shot that hit the bar and a late header brilliantly saved, then 1-2 at Wolverhampton, where the experiment of fielding three centre-forwards (Lawton between Ronnie Rooke, then of Fulham, and the Spurs amateur 'Jackie' Gibbons) misfired. Lawton gave England an early lead, but Wales won with two goals from Horace Cumner, an Arsenal winger who later joined Notts County. Only a few weeks before, Cumner had been in hospital with burns to the hands and face suffered when a hydrogen cylinder had exploded during his wartime service as a Royal Marine.

After his four goals against Scotland, Lawton was back in England's team to stay for their remaining nine wartime internationals. Some of his previous absences had been due to Army commitments, with the attack then mostly led by Welsh or Dennis Westcott, of Wolves – both of whom would stay uncapped The two others to play in that position for England during the war also gained selection in peacetime. One of these was Lawton's future clubmate Frank Broome, then of Aston Villa; the other Leslie Compton, who had twice been an England trialist before the war, despite being mainly a reserve full-back with Arsenal.

Broome was chosen at No 9 and on both wings in the course of his seven appearances on the last two pre-war Continental tours. Compton, whose brother, Test cricketer Denis, played on England's left wing during the war and also in a Victory international, led the attack in the first match England played after hostilities began. It was drawn 1-1 with Wales in Cardiff, on 11 November 1939. West Ham's Len Goulden was England's scorer, but Les Compton was readily among the goals as his club's centre-forward in the first two seasons of the war. In one match with Clapton Orient he scored ten times. He was Arsenal's centre-half when he won the first of his two caps in that position as the oldest to make his full debut for England at the age of 38 against Wales at Roker Park, Sunderland, in 1950.

Broome's international debut coincided with the team's distasteful experience, to avoid a diplomatic incident, of giving the raised-arm Nazi salute during the German national anthem in Berlin on 14 May 1938. There was bedlam in the England dressing room when an FA official gave that instruction. Eddie Hapgood, the England captain, made it clear that they were totally opposed, but they reluctantly climbed down when informed that this was a direct order from Sir Neville Henderson, the British Ambassador in Germany, with the endorsement of Stanley Rous, the FA secretary.

The political situation between Britain and Germany was considered so sensitive that it needed 'only a spark to set Europe alight'. The German crowd had reacted with hostility when the English representatives (including the English amateur football team) had given only the 'eyes right' in the march-past before the Olympic Games in the same stadium two years before. Adolf Hitler was present on that former occasion – but not when Broome and company played there. The dictator had the mortification of witnessing the perfect riposte made to the intense Nazi propaganda against the coloured American athletes when one of them, Jesse Owens, set a world record by winning four Olympic gold medals, but he was spared seeing his countrymen well beaten, 6-3. The scorers included Broome, who had Lawton among his team-mates when he won the last three of his England caps on the Continental tour a year later.

CHAPTER FOUR

Surprising aversion to taking penalties

Nineteen of the 24 goals Tommy Lawton scored for England in eighteen wartime internationals made him the scourge of the Scots. Four of the others went into the Welsh net, one into France's.

Having already scored seven in five wartime games against Scotland, Lawton followed up his four-goal romp in Manchester by scoring in each of England's three further victories against the auld enemy in 1944, netting one in a 6-2 win at Wembley, two in a 3-2 victory in Glasgow, and three in another 6-2 triumph back in London. He also nicked the winner in an Army international at Hampden Park, after Scotland had taken the lead. And then, in the last wartime match between the countries, he scored twice in the record 6-1 win in Glasgow in 1945.

The game with France, 2-2 at Wembley on 26 May 1945, was the first in which Lawton captained England – the first centre-forward to do so since the famous amateur Vivian Woodward, who also skippered the British team that won the Olympic titles of 1908 and 1912. In *Football is my Business*, Lawton recalled that 'there was quite a touch of drama in the handing over of the leadership by my great friend Joe Mercer.' He added: 'Little more than 24 hours before the match, Stanley Rous, the FA secretary, called Joe aside and said: "In view of Lawton's great season, the selection committee would like him to lead the side against France, and they think it best if you would ask Lawton yourself." Joe told me of this conversation, and I appreciated the nice gesture in handing over the honour.'

Lawton scored only once in the five Victory internationals in which he subsequently took part, when Switzerland were beaten 4-1 at Stamford Bridge, but he was back on target in England's 7-2 defeat of Northern Ireland in the first post-war international match at Windsor Park, Belfast in September 1946. And although he obtained only one of those goals (Wilf Mannion, of Middlesbrough, led the way with a hat-trick), he did not take long to get into top gear with four goals against Holland, who were beaten 8-2 at Huddersfield's ground, and, most eye-catching of all, four more in the 10-0 'wonder display' against Portugal in Lisbon.

England never looked back against the Irish after going ahead through Raich Carter in the second minute, but the match was in danger because many in the 57,000 crowd swarmed over the barriers onto the running track at the railway end shortly before the scheduled kick-off time. Over the loudspeakers, the England players were instructed not to take the field until those invaders were back on the banking, but order was restored for the start to be delayed for only ten minutes. That was after the national anthem – for which a dozen or so spectators who had climbed onto the roof of the stand solemnly stood to attention.

Lawton beat three men to provide the pass for one of Mannion's goals. The other scorers included Preston's Tom Finney, making the first of what were to be 76 full international appearances in the absence of the injured Matthews.

Six of England's eight goals against the Dutch were scored in the 25 minutes before half-time. The first of them was one of Lawton's best. The move began with goalkeeper Frank Swift and was carried on by left-winger Bobby Langton, from whom the ball went to Lawton via Carter. Faced by three defenders, Lawton pivoted to the left, feinted as if to change feet, and then smashed the ball inside an upright as the goalkeeper went the wrong way. At that night's banquet at Harrogate, which both teams attended, the president of the Netherlands FA, Karl Lotsky, declared: 'After 30 years of football both on the Continent and in England, I today saw a forward line such as I have never seen before.' This was that line: Finney, Carter, Lawton, Mannion, Langton. And the defeat might have been still heavier, for skipper George Hardwick, the Middlesbrough full-back, missed with a penalty that could have brought a seventh goal in that dazzling first-half spell.

For all the Dutch praise, only Lawton and Mannion retained their forward places in Lisbon. In the intervening three matches, England drew with Scotland at Wembley and accounted for France at Highbury, but then slumped to a shock defeat by Switzerland. Stanley Matthews, who had returned against Scotland but missed the game with France, was retained after being involved in the Zurich upset, but Carter and Langton were replaced by Stan Mortensen, Matthews' club partner at Blackpool, and the recalled Tom Finney. Carter had scored against both Scotland and France, but he was then in his 34th year and had reached the end of his international road.

Mortensen, on the other hand, was just starting out as an England international, though he had made his debut against his own country during the war. In September 1943, he was England's reserve at Wembley when Wales lost their left-half, Ivor Powell, through injury, and it was agreed that Mortensen take his place. That was the match in which Don Welsh scored three of England's eight goals in Lawton's absence.

Mortensen was a four-goal man in his first game for England, who steamrollered to their astonishing triumph despite having thirteen men to beat in the Portuguese capital. Regardless of the visitors' protests, the home country changed their goalkeeper and right-back after going four down in the first half-hour. They also changed the ball. After much argument, it had been agreed to use the larger and heavier British type of ball, but after Lawton's first goal it was booted into the crowd and 'lost'. The replacement was of the Continental type, smaller and lighter. Not that it made any difference to the balance of play.

It was another crushing defeat that could have been even heavier, for two goals were controversially disallowed for offside by the French referee. There was also an unpleasant sequel. An inquiry into the Portuguese players' behaviour resulted in the suspension of the captain for one year, the substitute goalkeeper for six months, and ten others for two months. A fortnight earlier, Lawton had touched another peak by scoring twice in Great Britain's 6-1 defeat of the Rest of Europe in front of 134,000 at Hampden. He and Stanley Matthews, transferred to Blackpool from Stoke the same evening of 10 May 1947, were the only survivors from the team fielded in the corresponding match of 1938. The composition of the two sides makes an interesting comparison: the choice for Highbury was all-English; in Glasgow it comprised five Englishmen, three Scots, two Welshmen, and one from Northern Ireland. These were the line-ups:

1938 (26 October): Woodley (Chelsea); Sproston (Tottenham), Hapgood (Arsenal, capt), Willingham (Huddersfield), Cullis (Wolves), Copping (Arsenal); Matthews (Stoke), Hall (Tottenham), Lawton (Everton), Goulden (West Ham), Boyes (Everton).

1947 (10 May): Swift (Manchester C); Hardwick (Middlesbrough), Hughes (Birmingham); Macaulay (Brentford), Vernon (WBA), Burgess (Tottenham); Matthews (Stoke), Mannion (Middlesbrough), Lawton (Chelsea), Steel (Morton), Liddell (Liverpool).

Reporting on Britain's Hampden victory in the *Daily Mail*, Roy Peskett gave 'full marks' to Lawton, saying that had had 'come right back to his best form, which we thought had been lost with a struggling Chelsea side'. But Lawton was not entrusted with the penalty the visitors conceded. That gave Mannion one of his two goals. The other scorers for Britain were Steel, spectacularly, and Carlo Parola, the Italian centre-half, who put the ball into his own net. Gunnar Nordahl, of Sweden, replied. It was Steel's electrifying display in that match which had English clubs hot on his trail, leading to his transfer to Derby for the then record fee – all of £15,500.

For someone who obtained goals so readily in open play, it was remarkable that Lawton did not relish taking penalties, even though,

besides the one he scored at the beginning of his England career, he converted one for his first goal on his League debut for Everton as Dean's
deputy. On that occasion he was in a team beaten 2-7 at Wolves, but a
fortnight later, on his senior Goodison debut at inside-right alongside
Dean, he scored again, in open play, when Everton themselves ran up
seven goals, against Leeds.

Lawton failed with his first penalty for Notts County, firing over the
bar during the home match with Ipswich in which he was later concussed.
The Suffolk club won with a penalty of their own. It was a very different
story when Ipswich next visited Meadow Lane, in September 1948. Notts
County won 9-2 that time, Lawton scoring four without recourse to
penalties and making three of the others. Consequently, a close watch
was kept on him in the return at Portman Road the following Wednesday.
Although often made to pass hurriedly, he still managed to score, with a
typical header from a free-kick, but Ipswich won 3-2.

Not until 22 October 1949 did Lawton take another penalty for Notts
County. He was persuaded to put aside his aversion after Jackie Sewell
and Tom Johnston, a left-winger from Nottingham Forest, had both
failed from the spot on the opening day of that season, when Southend
were still beaten 2-0. Lawton, for all his reluctance, was again seen as the
best man for the job. He had to wait a dozen games before having that
renewed faith in him put to the test. He rose to it with the conversion that
sparked a revival from two goals down away to Brighton. Sir Stanley
Rous, the newly knighted FA secretary, was among those who saw
Lawton also score with a free-kick from nearly 30 yards. Johnston
snatched the winner in the last minute.

Lawton popped in another penalty in the next game, salvaging a home
point against Walsall, also in the last minute, and on his next appearance
at Meadow Lane a fortnight later he scored twice more from the spot in
a hat-trick that accounted for Swindon. One of his two goals in a 7-0
crushing of Newport the following February also came from a penalty.
Far from having his spot-kick confidence restored by those successes,
however, he again relinquished the responsibility at the earliest opportunity – and when called upon to accept it he blasted the ball wide. That
happened in another evening home match, early in the 1951-52 season
that was to be his last with the club. Even so, Notts won handsomely,
Lawton heading one of their four goals against Hull, and creating another, in his first confrontation with his former England colleague Neil
Franklin since the centre-half had been with Stoke six seasons before.

Full-back Billy Cook was Everton's regular penalty-taker while
Lawton was with the Goodison club, and Len Goulden was the man who

shouldered that responsibility during Lawton's time at Stamford Bridge. For England, Raich Carter was a penalty-taker while Lawton was also in the attack, but Carter's failure from the spot during the 8-0 wartime swamping of Scotland in Manchester led to the role being entrusted in pre-match preparations to Leslie Smith, the Brentford outside-left who was later with Aston Villa. Smith had a deceptive swerving approach to the ball when taking a penalty, and one such effort enabled him to avoid being the only England forward not to score in the 6-1 win over the Scots in April 1945.

In his *Daily Express* report of England's biggest victory in Glasgow, Tommy Muirhead, the former Rangers player, said that Lawton was 'the finest centre-forward in the game, and must be classed with all the giants of the past – he has everything.' In the *News Chronicle*, Arthur Shrive wrote: 'Lawton again displayed his powers of leadership. He is undoubtedly the finest centre-forward of modern times.'

Lawton was 'spot on' with one of his four goals the win against the Diables Rouge, to which reference has already been made, but while on another Army tour, to Italy, he had an extra reason for not wanting to take a penalty when asked to do so by Mercer, his Everton clubmate who captained the side. It was awarded against a team selected from Army units stationed between Bari and Gibraltar, but Lawton declined because it would have meant having to face Frank Swift. 'At home, yes, he said, 'but not against Frank, my mate, out here.'

Although the Manchester City goalkeeper was among the tourists rested for that game, he came on as a substitute for the opposition when Bert Hoyle, who excelled for Bristol Rovers in the early post-war years before injuries in a car crash ended his career, had to go off with an injured hand. With his height, long reach and large hands, Swift was a difficult man to beat, but he was unable to prevent Sheffield Wednesday's Duggie Hunt completing a hat-trick from the spot. Undoubtedly, however, he was under some handicap, for he was still wearing his Army boots and khaki shorts, and a jersey taken from Hoyle that was several sizes too small.

CHAPTER FIVE

Major Buckley, Jesse Pye, Ian McPherson

Notts County's first big expenditure in their preparations for the resumption of post-war League football was not for a player but for a manager. At the beginning of March 1944 they lured to Meadow Lane one of the game's most colourful and publicity minded characters by agreeing to pay him an exceptionally high wage for the time, said to be £4,000 a year.

From Molineux came Major Frank Buckley, who in the last pre-war season of 1938-39 had steered Wolves to the brink of the first League and Cup double of the twentieth century. Tall and imposing, raised in the Urmston district of Manchester, Buckley served with the Army during the Boer War, but it was not until he joined the 17th Middlesex Regiment, known as the Footballers' Battalion, in the Great War that he was commissioned. Given command of the serving professional players, he was promoted in 1916 to the rank he retained for the rest of his life. From having seven clubs in a dozen seasons as a formidable centre-half, beginning with Aston Villa in 1903 and including one England call-up in 1914 while with Derby, he was to notch seven more in 33 as a manager, ending at Walsall in 1955 – nine years before his death at the age of 82.

For three years in the early 1920s, Buckley was out of football, working as a commercial traveller after resigning from his first managerial post at Norwich. A crisis at the then Southern League club also caused the resignation of six directors and the departure of several players. Blackpool brought him back, but it was with Wolves, whom he joined in 1927, that he achieved most success as a manager. In 1932 they won promotion as Second Division champions, and in the last two pre-war seasons they were runners-up in Division One, besides reaching the 1939 FA Cup final. Their 1-4 defeat by Portsmouth at Wembley was one of the biggest upsets, but three years later they carried off the League War Cup, beating Sunderland over two legs. Frank Broome was then the Wanderers' guest right-winger, and he scored one of the goals in the 4-1 home win after a 2-2 draw on Wearside.

The major regularly made newspaper headlines. At Blackpool, his strict management provoked fans into forming the Seasiders' first Supporters' Club. At Molineux, when Wolves were not doing well, the crowd stormed the pitch, uprooted the goal-posts, and, in the words of skipper Stan Cullis, 'more or less demanded the major's head on a charger.' There was also the notorious 'monkey gland' treatment for players, which turned out to be nothing more than injections to protect against the common cold, and their sessions with a psychologist.

Buckley also attracted attention with his pursuance of a youth policy. At Wolves he carried this to the extremes of putting Cameron Buchanan into the first team at the age of fourteen years and six weeks in 1942, pitching two sixteen-year-old wingers, Alan Steen and Jimmy Mullen, into First Division action in 1939, and making Cullis captain of the Reserves at eighteen and the League side at twenty. It was evident from the age of eleven, when he skippered his school team, that Cullis had leadership qualities, and he became the youngest to captain the senior England side at 22. Later, while with Leeds United, Buckley signed John Charles on the player's sixteenth birthday and introduced him to League action within three months. Charles went on to become the then youngest Welsh international at eighteen years and 71 days.

The major's stay with Notts County lasted for only two years, during which he had little chance to build a settled team. In his first full season, the last wartime one of 1944-45, he called upon no fewer than a hundred players, almost half of them guests, and many of the others made just fleeting appearances. The numbers were reduced to 70-odd in the following transitional season, with guests, being phased out in preparation for the resumption of League football, down to around twenty.

In May 1946, Buckley was tempted away to Hull, who also had a new ground, Boothferry Park, new colours of amber and blue, a re-formed board of directors and, with just one exception, a brand new team. Only the turnstiles and goalkeeper Billy Bly remained from their pre-war home at Anlaby Road. Buckley turned up with the avowed intention of building a team fit for the First Division, but Hull were still in the Third Division's North section when he left – after just under two years. And he almost departed before that, for he was on the verge of going earlier to Leeds, following a rift with the board during the autumn of 1947. He was responsible for an excessive turnover of youngsters recruited, and his constant team changes, with more than 40 players used during the first post-war League season, caused unrest as Hull sank towards the middle of the table instead of rising towards the top.

Buckley's resignation, in March 1948, came shortly after the transfer from Derby of Tommy Lawton's old pal Raich Carter, who was promoted to player-manager and immediately achieved the promotion that had eluded Buckley.

Despite leaving Notts County so soon, Buckley had time to introduce several players who quickly become the envy of other clubs. One of them, Jackie Sewell, subject of a later chapter, was the player to whom he referred on departure as 'I've left a legacy'. He might have added that Sewell's introduction came about only accidentally. The scout sent to watch a full-back at Whitehaven had his attention diverted to the more impressive form of Bestwood Colliery's sixteen-year-old inside-right.

Unlike Sewell, three others who attracted attention while Buckley was the manager left Meadow Lane before the resumption of League football in 1946. They were Cyril Hatton, Ian McPherson and Jesse Pye – all then in their mid-twenties.

Hatton, an inside-forward whose fair hair was almost white, had been with the club for eight years by the time of Buckley's appointment. He had turned professional at seventeen in December 1936 after playing for Notts Corinthians and Grantham Co-op in the Notts Thursday League, and two months later had scored a last-minute equaliser on his League debut at Northampton. His first-team appearances exceeded 80 before the outbreak of war, in which he served with the Royal Signals in France, North Africa, Italy and Germany. In March 1946, Buckley transferred him to QPR in part-exchange for goalkeeper Harry Brown, but he continued to live in his home town of Grantham, where he and his brother-in-law had a newsagent's shop, and to train at Meadow Lane. He stayed with QPR until the summer of 1953, then moving to Chesterfield, and he was afterwards player-manager of Grantham in the Midland League.

Arsenal manager George Allison planned to snap up both McPherson and Pye, but only half succeeded. He signed McPherson, who, as a Squadron Leader in the RAF during the war, had been awarded a DFC and bar while piloting Mosquitoes, but Pye eluded him.

McPherson, a winger whose form fluctuated between the brilliant and the mundane, made 30 of 160-plus appearances for Arsenal in their title-winning season of 1947-48, but lost his place during their run to an FA Cup final win against Liverpool in 1950, and was back with Notts County by the time the Gunners again reached Wembley in 1952 (when they lost to Newcastle).

Pye was transferred to Wolves for £12,000, and, ironically, did the hat-trick against Arsenal in a 6-1 victory when he made his debut for them at the end of August in 1946, on the day the League resumed for the first time since September 1939. There was a coincidence about McPherson's signing for Arsenal. It was the first important deal conducted by Allison since he had broken the transfer record to take £14,000 Bryn Jones from Wolves in 1938. Buckley was the manager with whom he dealt in both cases.

The crinkly-haired Yorkshire-born Pye, who was an amateur with Sheffield United before wartime service in the Royal Engineers, came to

Frank Buckley's notice as he developed his game in the company of more experienced players in Army football. In one match in North Africa he scored seven goals, three of them penalties. He was to be with Notts County for an even shorter time than Buckley, less than a year, but within five months of joining them he played for England in the Victory international against Belgium at Wembley on 19 January 1946.

At that time, Pye was Notts' leading scorer with fifteen goals, including a hat-trick against Southend, in the transitional and contradictorily named Third South (North) League. His ability shone through despite being in a team that finished sixth out of eleven, and failed to progress in the Third South (North) Cup qualifying competition when finishing bottom. Neither could interest be sustained in the resumed FA Cup, in which, for that season only, all rounds up to the semi-finals were decided over two legs. Notts went out to Northampton, the club against which they had gained their biggest win, 7-1 (just one goal for Pye), in the truncated league. In too many other games Notts were on the receiving end of big scores, conceding seven goals in their first meeting with Southend and also at Watford, six at QPR and in another visit to Watford, and five at Norwich.

Pye was not an original choice for the match with Belgium, but, as one of the reserves along with Birmingham's Frank Mitchell, he was brought in at inside-right, between Matthews and Lawton, in the reshuffle caused by the withdrawal through injury of Frank Soo, the Leicester and former Stoke right-half.

Billy Wright, soon to be joined by Pye at Wolves and, like him, making his international debut (though no caps were then awarded), dropped back from inside-left to fill the vacancy. Charlton's Bert Brown crossed over from inside-right to partner Jimmy Mullen on the left flank of the attack. Whereas Wright, one of Notts County's guest players during the war, went on to become the first to win a hundred England caps, Pye managed just one, against the Republic of Ireland at Goodison on 21 September 1949. And even then he was not a wholly acceptable selection among critics who had their own favourites, despite being the successful centre-forward of a club then at the top of the First Division (Wolves were pipped for that season's title by Portsmouth on goal average), and one who a few months before had scored two of the goals that had beaten Leicester City in the FA Cup final.

Against Belgium, Pye emerged with credit from a match that began in brilliant sunshine but was played throughout the second half in the eerie gloom of a sudden fog. The linesmen were equipped with luminous flags that had been used for the landing and taking-off of aircraft on an RAF strip in Burma during the jungle campaign, and at intervals a light-hearted spectator gave blasts on what sounded like a foghorn.

One national newspaperman, Roy Peskett in the *Daily Mail*, mildly criticised Pye for being inclined to over-feed Matthews, who recovered from a chill to make a then record 44th appearance for England. That, however, was understandable of a newcomer – especially as the winger was again at his bewildering best. It was from one Matthews cross that Lawton headed the ball down for Pye to score the second goal of the match, after Brown had given England a twelfth-minute lead. Lawton, who soon afterwards was on the opposite side to Pye at Wembley in an Army Physical Training Corps XI that faced an FA team (he scored one of their goals in a 5-3 win), might well have had another of his hat-tricks against the Belgians. One of his shots was spectacularly saved, another almost seriously harmed a photographer at the side of the goal, and a third, a blistering effort from thirty yards, struck a post.

Pye did not receive such a good press when he gained his full cap, but he was not alone. England's preparations for the following year's World Cup in Brazil were dealt the demoralising blow of an unexpected 0-2 defeat by the Republic of Ireland. Bert Mozley, the Derby right-back who was making his international debut on his 23rd birthday, conceded the penalty from which Con Martin, the Aston Villa centre-half, opened the scoring, and Peter Farrell, an Everton wing-half playing at inside-forward, completed it. Frank Butler, one of the leading sports journalists of the time, lamented: 'Oh for a Matthews, or a Stan Mortensen, or a Tommy Lawton to have pulled this match round.'

Lawton's claims for an international recall were strongly touted that season as he spearheaded Notts County's surge to promotion, but he had made what was to be the last of his 23 full England appearances almost exactly a year earlier, in an abysmal scoreless draw with the amateurs of Denmark in Copenhagen. Such an abrupt casting-out had looked unlikely after his 22nd peacetime England goal had helped towards a 4-0 win against Italy in Turin on 16 May 1948, yet all was irretrievably undone in the Denmark debacle only four months later. Britain's amateurs, seven of them English, had lost to almost the same Danish side (just the one change) during that year's Olympic Games, but they had at least scored three goals. Now here the pick of England's professionals could not muster even one, though Lawton was controversially denied when he ran past two defenders and hooked the ball into the net off a post in the twentieth minute. The Dutch referee ruled that before the ball reached Lawton another England player was guilty of pushing as the goalkeeper punched out a shot from Jimmy Hagan.

Stanley Matthews was the only forward to retain his place for the next match that October, won by 6-2 in Belfast. Out with Lawton went the inside-forwards Hagan and Len Shackleton, and left-winger Bobby Langton, who by then had left Blackburn for Bolton. Hagan, a real force for England in wartime, was discarded with Lawton for good. There were few further opportunities for Shackleton, who, like Hagan, made his full debut against the Danes, and Langton. For Lawton, the challenges had become too great, not only from Mortensen, who scored three of the goals at Windsor Park, but also Jackie Milburn (Newcastle) and Jack Rowley (Manchester United).

Although Jesse Pye, a stutterer in speech but fluent in football, did not get back in the senior national team either, he also played for the Football League, and three times for England 'B', before leaving Molineux with six hat-tricks in his impressive Wolves total of almost 100 goals in over 200 games. Luton succeeded where Brentford, Huddersfield, Middlesbrough and Sheffield Wednesday had failed when they made him, at £10,000, 'the season's best buy' of 1952-53. After almost helping the Hatters into the First Division – they finished third behind promoted Sheffield United and Huddersfield – he completed his League career with Derby before moving in 1957 to a Wisbech Town team managed by Oscar Hold, also a forward who had played for Notts County.

Late that year, Pye was one of nine ex-League players in the Wisbech side that reached the second round of the FA Cup for the first time in the club's history, scoring the winner against Colchester United. The others included three more who had been with Notts County, right-back Tommy Deans, left-half Henry Adamson, and right-winger 'Tot' Leverton. The run ended at Reading, but only by 1-2. Johnny Downie, who had been in the First Division with Manchester United, was Wisbech's scorer that day.

In March 1960, Pye was appointed player-manager of the Cambridgeshire club after Hold had resigned in an attempt to ease their financial problems. Towards the end of 1966 Pye himself resigned, also rejecting an offer to join the board. He was in his 64th year when he died in Blackpool in February 1984.

CHAPTER SIX

Northampton the centre of League attention

Bill Dickson, then a little-known former Glenavon half-back, was valued at £3,000 in joining Chelsea from Notts County when Tommy Lawton made his shock move in the opposite direction. Dickson played in fewer than two dozen League games for the Magpies – as Notts County have been nicknamed since changing their colours from chocolate and blue to black and white when becoming a limited company in 1890 – but he took part in just over a hundred more for the Stamford Bridge club, and while with them he also made the first nine of his dozen appearances for Northern Ireland.

During that period, Dickson fully justified the assessment of him by Chelsea's manager, the former Arsenal and England centre-forward Ted Drake, as 'a natural footballer who can play anywhere' by occupying seven different positions in one season. That versatility ranged from keeping goal to leading the attack, though it was in a reserve game that he remained unbeaten while goalkeeper Harry Medhurst was off the field for a quarter of an hour receiving treatment for an injury.

Dickson had just one first-team opportunity with Chelsea in the season he and Lawton swapped clubs, and only five more in the two seasons after that. For the next three, however, he was outstanding as a regular choice, swiftly back in action after breaking his nose in an FA Cup semi-final replay against Arsenal. It was only through his own obstinacy that he then no longer figured in Drake's team rebuilding that was to carry off the League championship in the club's Golden Jubilee year of 1955. He refused to re-sign when refused permission to go on the Irish FA's tour of Canada in 1953. In the autumn of that year he was transferred to Arsenal for £15,000, after declining a move to Preston. Among his new clubmates at Highbury was none other than Lawton, who had been brought back into the First Division by the Gunners a fortnight before (more about that in its proper turn).

Injuries and illness dogged Dickson's three-year stay with Arsenal. The 1954-55 season was particularly unfortunate. He dislocated a shoulder, needed knee surgery, suffered from appendicitis, and slipped a disc. No wonder he was described as 'one of the unluckiest players Arsenal have had with regard to injuries'. His contract was not renewed in the summer of 1956, and he was back home at Lurgan, near Belfast, when brought back into English football, along with fellow Irishman Sammy Chapman, by Mansfield player-manager Charlie Mitten. Chapman had been signed at fifteen by Manchester United, the club with which Mitten had made his name, but had been released without getting into the first team. He was not to be confused with another player of the same name who was later a Nottingham Forest centre-half and captain – though 'Sammy' was a nickname for that Chapman, who also played for Notts County. He was christened Robert.

Dickson again dislocated a shoulder in his first game for Mansfield, and more disc trouble soon brought his League career to a close. He became Arsenal's scout in Northern Ireland on his return there, and went back into the joinery trade he had left to concentrate on football.

Lawton's forsaking of the First Division for the outposts of the Third South, which he came to regard as 'a terrible mistake', stemmed from his refusal to go on Chelsea's tour of Sweden in the May.. Having spent the previous close-season coaching in Switzerland at the Football Association's request, he claimed that he felt jaded after nearly eighteen months without a break. He was also in the process of settling down at his new home in London, and was having problems in his marriage. It was in the hope of improving his domestic situation by seeking a change of scene in the South that had taken him from Everton to Chelsea. But that hope had proved a forlorn one. As he put it, 'I realised I should have transferred my wife and stayed at Goodison Park by myself.'

Chelsea's threat to stop his wages and report him to the FA widened the breach, and his relationship with the club's management became so strained that he asked for a transfer only a few matches into the 1947-48 season. He was left out of the first two, and although he scored the only goal of a home game with Derby when he was reinstated, he earned no praise from the late Frank Nicklin, an old friend and colleague of mine who reported on the Rams' matches for the *Derby Evening Telegraph* in those days, and was later Sports Editor of *The Sun*. In Nicklin's opinion, 'the mighty Lawton's stock went down several per cent by his half-speed, half-hearted display. He played like a spoiled child.'

On the first Saturday of October, Lawton scored twice against Aston Villa in what proved to be his last home appearance in Chelsea's first team. A week later, he was on Merseyside in a 0-3 defeat by Liverpool, and on the Saturday after that he netted one of England's goals in their victory by the same score against Wales in Cardiff. He was not, however, to appear in Chelsea's League line-up again. On having his request for a change of club granted, he was relegated to the second team. A crowd of almost 23,000, roughly double the usual size for a home reserve game, saw him score again in a 2-2 Football Combination draw with Arsenal at Highbury, while the First Division match between the clubs finished goalless in front of 67,000 at the Bridge.

That game with the 'stiffs' was Lawton's last in Chelsea colours. The following Wednesday he was also on the mark against Northern Ireland, watched by a crowd of 68,000 at his old Goodison stamping ground. England came from behind to lead with goals from Wilf Mannion and Lawton in the last eight minutes, only for Peter Doherty to knock himself out in snatching a dramatic 2-2 draw 40 seconds from the finish, plunging forward to meet a ball floating across the goalmouth. Doherty, then of Huddersfield and later to have an advisory connection with Notts County, was still receiving treatment on the pitch when the final whistle blew.

Lawton spent the next Saturday as a spectator at the Second Division match in which Fulham defeated Cardiff at Craven Cottage, and it was during the following week that he made his startling decision to drop into Division Three. Notts County's offer of no fewer than fourteen houses from which he and his wife could choose led to the Health Minister, Aneurin Bevan, being asked in Parliament if he would requisition them because there were more than 10,000 names on the Nottingham housing committee's waiting list.

Arsenal would have been Lawton's preferred choice of club, and they would also have been keen to have him, but they were just about the last one Chelsea were prepared to let him join. To play for Arsenal was 'an honour', as he himself termed it, for which he would have to wait almost six more years. The list of clubs Chelsea gave Lawton to select from included several other members of the First Division. Prominent among them, after Portsmouth and Sunderland had dropped out of contention, were Derby, who had already tried seven players at centre-forward that season.

Derby fans had the brief mouth-watering prospect of Lawton leading their club's front line between two of the best inside-forwards of the time – Raich Carter, of England, and Billy Steel, of Scotland – but the bid from the Baseball Ground foundered on the inability to agree to the part-exchange Chelsea wanted. With Derby reported to have offered £17,000 for Lawton, a deal was still hanging fire. Their admission of a £50,000 overdraft scarcely strengthened their hand so soon after they had raised the British transfer record to sign Steel from Morton for £15,500. Even so, although lean years for the Rams were not far ahead, with a demeaning descent into the Third Division North, they once again broke the record to get £24,5000 Johnny Morris from Manchester United within eighteen months of failing to land Lawton.

So, with Derby out of the hunt, it was to the other County over at Meadow Lane that England's reigning centre-forward so unexpectedly headed while still the right side of 30. But Notts were not the only Third Division club to want Lawton. So did Crystal Palace, whose chairman, Percy Harper, yearned to make them 'the Arsenal of South London', and newly relegated Swansea, who offered Roy Paul, a coming Welsh international, in part-exchange. Millwall, fast heading out of the Second Division for the Third's Southern Section, were also said to be interested, but that was hardly likely to be taken seriously, considering that they had a war-damaged ground without adequate seating and no money to spare for such an expensive luxury.

Some observers took a dim view of lowly clubs aspiring to acquire one of the game's high and mighty. 'The rush of Third Division clubs to make offers for Lawton does not amuse me,' declared one critic not averse to exaggeration. 'A cat can look at a king, but let us keep some sanity.' The cat, however, was out of the bag, and, in many eyes, sanity out of the window, for within days Lawton plumped for a club among those he had been least expected to join.

He chose Notts County partly because they guaranteed him the security of a £2,000-a-year job outside football selling typewriters, making him much better paid than the majority of First Division players in those days of the maximum wage. The main reason he gave, however, was that he wished to keep a promise he had made to a friend. When Arthur Stollery was dismissed as Chelsea's masseur after a disagreement with the chairman, he confided in Lawton that he wanted to become a manager. Lawton gave his word that, if Stollery succeeded, he would consider signing for him, should he be seeking a new club. Stollery, who had been a physical training instructor in the RAF during the 1939-45 War, was manager of Notts County when Lawton signed.

The deal went through on 13 November 1947, paving the way for the hullaballoo of the big man's Third Division debut at Northampton, with spectators crammed close to the touchlines in a crowd of 18,300, double the number at the last match played there. Cameramen jostled for vantage points as extra police strove to maintain some semblance of order.

A great roar greeted the teams as they came out, but it was as nothing compared with the one the visiting supporters let loose as Lawton opened the scoring with a trademark header inside five minutes. Jack Marsh, who had been switched to inside-left to make room for the costly newcomer, also scored in the opening half, and Notts went on to gain their first away victory of the season, by 2-1, under the handicap of an injury to centre-half Billy Baxter, their captain until Lawton's arrival.

It was typical of the battling Baxter that he insisted on completing the match out on the wing, but he was so dazed when he staggered off at the final whistle that he needed to be told who had won. In fact, he was close to being given a different answer, for the home side were unlucky not to pick up both points. Bob Dennison, their centre-half and captain, who turned to management with Northampton on retiring from playing that summer, came out of the game with considerable credit. Unruffled by Lawton's reputation, and the extreme publicity that had inevitably been aroused ('I didn't lose any sleep'), he did his job so well that Notts' new centre-forward was overshadowed in the last half-hour by his opposite number. This was Archie Garrett, who left for Birmingham City later that month but rejoined Northampton towards the end of the following year after having his progress at St Andrew's retarded by a broken collar bone. Garrett, scorer of the Town's goal, hit the crossbar and forced goalkeeper Harry Brown to four excellent saves.

Dennison's parents, nine brothers and sisters were born in Scotland, but his own birthplace was Ambleside, in Northumberland. It was with Newcastle, as an inside-forward, that he started out, and he also played for Nottingham Forest and Fulham before beginning his association with Northampton as a guest during the Second World War. His stay there was extended as manager until the spring of 1954, when, having declined a chance to join Southampton two years earlier, he was released from a contract that had three years still to run to take charge at Middlesbrough – a post originally offered to Alec Stock, then of Leyton Orient, after the resignation of Walter Rowley through ill-health.

Nine years later, having been awarded £3,200 damages after suing Boro for unfair dismissal, Dennison took over at Hereford and guided them to the Southern League championship. After that he was chief scout with Coventry, a club he also served as assistant and caretaker manager. He was 84 when he died in June 1996. As a player he did himself proud against Lawton. As a manager he excelled him, for, as we shall see in due course, Tommy's time at the helm was fraught with problems he was unable to overcome.

Until everything turned sour for Lawton at Meadow Lane, however, Notts County and their fans were flattered and delighted to have in their ranks a player who arrived as England's reigning centre-forward. They also had the country's most popular footballer, and the third most popular sportsman, of 1947 according to a poll conducted by the *Sporting Record*. It was scarcely a surprise when a majority of that publication's readers awarded top place to Denis Compton, the Middlesex and England cricketer who that year broke records for first-class runs and centuries scored in one season. More than 88,000 votes were cast, and 22,827 of them, almost 25 per cent, went to Compton. Reg Harris, the world's amateur sprint cycling champion, was the runner-up with 14,177. Then came Lawton with 7,350.

The others in the leading dozen also make interesting reading, representing the pick of Britain's sporting talent of that early post-war period as seen by a section of the public: 4, Jack Parker (speedway); 5, Peter Kane (boxer); 6, Stanley Matthews (soccer); 7, Gordon Richards (jockey); 8, Bill Kitchen (speedway); 9, Bill Edrich (cricketer); 10, Bruce Woodcock (boxer); 11, Frank Swift (soccer); 12, Freddie Mills (boxer).

CHAPTER SEVEN

Corkhill coincidence
– and some light relief

While Tommy Lawton was leading Notts County to their fortunate victory at Northampton, the club he had left were making light of their loss by beating Stoke, if by a flattering 4-1 margin, at Stamford Bridge. Ken Armstrong, temporarily converted from the wing-half position in which in 1955 was to help Chelsea to the League title and England to a 7-2 trouncing of the Scots at Wembley, led their attack with such verve that he did the hat-trick against Neil Franklin, a centre-half who was far from being one of those come-and-go internationals.

Winner of nearly 30 caps, Franklin remained an automatic England selection until, like Charlie Mitten, he was ill-advisedly lured away to the much-vaunted riches that South American football had to offer at Bogota in 1950. He was never again in the England running after returning to play in the Second Division for Hull, and his career later petered out with Crewe and Stockport.

Armstrong, a Yorkshireman signed from Army football, ended the 1947-48 season as Chelsea's leading scorer with thirteen goals, which was creditable enough considering that he played the last third of it at wing-half following the arrival of Hugh Billington, an experienced centre-for-ward, from Luton. As Billington was in his thirties, a more regular filler of the slot vacated by Lawton was found by moving Roy Bentley from inside-right – a switch that also led to his being one of Lawton's successors as leader of the England line. Armstrong, meanwhile, was on his way to being a regular Chelsea wing-half for ten seasons, holding for a time the club's record for League appearances (362).

The match in which Armstrong last played for Chelsea before emigrating to New Zealand was the first in which seventeen-year-old Jimmy Greaves was seen in their senior side. It was Armstrong's testimonial, against Leicester's Second Division champions in May 1957. Armstrong spent the rest of his life in New Zealand, where he played in and coached the national football team, rising to become Director of Coaching to the NZFA. He was also player-coach to the amateur club Eastern Union at Gisborne, the North Island town where he worked as an insurance sales-man. After his death aged 60 in 1984, his ashes were brought back to England and scattered on the Stamford Bridge pitch.

Another link with Tommy Lawton's entry into the Third Division was the fact that it was not the first time England's reigning centre-forward had played for Notts County. He made his one appearance for the club as a wartime guest from Everton at home to Forest on 24 April 1943 – and one of his team-mates was also in the side at Northampton. William Grant Corkhill, born in Belfast but brought up in Retford, was at right-back in the 2-1 win (Lawton did not score), and at left-half against Bob Dennison and his men.

First signed from Marine, near Liverpool, in 1931, Bill Corkhill left for Cardiff in 1938, but, after guesting for Notts and Mansfield during the war, he rejoined the Meadow Lane ranks in time of the Football League's resumption in 1946 and stayed until 1951. His versatility as a defender stretched to keeping goal when railway disruptions during the bitter winter of the first post-war season prevented Harry Brown travelling from London in time for a match at Walsall.

Corkhill's long playing career, after which he went to Scunthorpe as coach and trainer, then into management in succession to former Welsh international Leslie Jones, made him the second oldest to turn out for County. He was younger, in his 42nd year, by only a few months, than goalkeeper Albert Iremonger, who was born on 15 June 1884 and played the last of his record 564 League games for Notts in May 1926. Corkhill, born on 23 April 1910, made his 288th and final senior appearance on 12 September 1951, at a time when he was the reserve team's coach.

Coincidentally, Barnsley were the opponents in Corkhill's first and final League games for Notts County. He also had the unusual experience of scoring two FA Cup goals that were fifteen years apart – in a defeat away to Tranmere in January 1933 and in a win at Birmingham in January 1948.

With the inclusion of wartime fixtures, Corkhill played over 350 times in the Notts first team. Scunthorpe finished third in the Third Division North in the middle two of the four seasons he spent there in the mid-1950s. He then had another season as manager of Bradford Park Avenue. After that, he was the Nottinghamshire FA's senior coach, and for the last thirteen years before his death in 1978 he ran a public house back in Nottingham.

Of all the players who were with Notts County in their prime, Albert Iremonger was by far the biggest personality before Lawton came along. With the addition of nearly 40 FA Cup-ties and appearances during the 1914-18 War, he was not far off 700 in his 21 years with the club. Through six seasons, from February 1907 to October 1912, he did not miss a match – a sequence of 222 that ended only when suspended by the club. He had addressed the referee in over-ripe terms when a game at Tottenham was abandoned because of fog with Notts two goals ahead (in his absence they won the rearranged fixture by three).

Iremonger was a long, lean, gangling beanpole, of whom somebody once said: 'His head sticks up above the crossbar. His arms reach up to heaven.' At a height variously given from 6ft 3in to 6ft 6in, he was said to be the League's tallest player of his time. That advantage, plus his abnormal reach, enabled him to exasperate opponents with amazing saves, but he had one big weakness – his temperament. Excitable and eccentric, he was liable to get up to some extraordinary antics if anything, or anybody, upset him. It was not uncommon for him to sit on the ball in midfield to protest against a decision. He was also known to chase the referee right back to the centre spot to argue about a goal awarded against him.

That once happened at a time when sprinter Harry Hutchins was a household name. The tormented official, threatening marching orders all round after being jostled by enraged Notts players, whirled on the gawky giant leading the pack and snarled: 'And you, Iremonger, I give you ten seconds to get back in your goal.' To which Albert the Alp replied: 'Who do you think I am, Harry Hutchins?' On another occasion, late in his career at West Ham, he so antagonised a woman supporter that she ran onto the field and assaulted him with her umbrella.

Consistently efficient as he was, Albert Iremonger never played for England, having to be content with selection for the Football League XI. His brother Jim, also a six-footer but not of the same volatile behaviour, was capped twice – at full-back, though he, too, was an excellent goalkeeper. Indeed, it was in goal that Jim made the last dozen of his 300 League and Cup appearances for Nottingham Forest. In April 1909 he was provided with the quietest afternoon of his career when Forest gained their record 12-0 victory in a home First Division game against Leicester Fosse.

Both brothers were born in Yorkshire, at Norton, a town opposite Malton across the River Derwent, but were brought up in Nottingham. They also both played cricket for Nottinghamshire – Albert much less often than Jim, who, in the words of *Wisden*, was 'one of the finest batsmen ever to play for the county.' Jim, who was later Nottinghamshire's coach (and also Notts County's), toured Australia with the MCC in 1911-12, but without getting into the Test team.

It was entirely inappropriate that Albert Iremonger's final season with Notts County should end in the club's relegation from the First Division, to which they were not to return for 55 years. But he at least had the satisfaction of bowing out in victory, especially as it was gained, by 4-2 at

Meadow Lane, against Huddersfield, champions for a third successive year. After completing his playing career with Lincoln City, Iremonger travelled thousands of miles in the Notts cause to watch players, and in 1952, six years before his death in his mid-70s, the board elected him as the club's first honorary vice-president in recognition of his long service. He also had a road named after him, next to the Meadow Lane ground, to which Notts moved from Trent Bridge in 1910.

A postman had to be detailed to deliver nearly 200 'good luck' messages to Tommy Lawton before his first home game, the week after he and Corkhill had been brought together again at Northampton. It fell to Bristol Rovers to have the unenviable task of being the visitors, and they were beaten 4-2 in a match that demonstrated Lawton's value to Notts County, not only for his goals, of which he scored two under the eyes of two England selectors, but also as a crowd-puller. The gate of 31,500 showed an increase of 10,000 on that at Meadow Lane's previous League match, lost to Aldershot. Due to Cup calls, over a month then went by before the next Third Division home fixture, and then, on Boxing Day, with many locked out, the attendance of 45,116 broke the record of 45,019 set for an FA Cup-tie with holders Aston Villa in 1921. As we shall be coming to, it was raised still further while Lawton was a Magpie.

Villa, who had beaten Huddersfield with an extra-time goal in the final at Stamford Bridge the previous April, were held 0-0 in that 1921 tie, but they won the replay. The result at Christmas-time in 1947 was very different. Swansea, who were to finish two points above Notts in fifth place, were swept aside 5-1, Lawton again scoring twice. That took him to eleven goals since his signing, in an unbeaten run of six League and Cup games during which he also helped his inside-forwards, the Jacks Sewell and Marsh, to another eleven between them.

In the intervening Cup-ties, Lawton bagged three goals (as did Sewell) in a 9-1 first-round romp against the amateurs of Horsham, and three more in a 4-1 replay victory against another non-League side, Stockton. The day's biggest Cup crowd of nearly 25,000 saw Horsham overrun after taking a shock lead within two minutes through Ron Smallwood, a 29-year-old butcher's assistant who had been a cook in the Army. Two goals from Marsh and one by Tony Freeman, a teenage winger from Melton Mowbray who was later with Boston United, were the other scorers as Notts' superior stamina told. Horsham, whose 1,500 following included half their local councillors, also took away the match ball, autographed by the Notts players, and overall benefited by about £700, for spending on improvements at their ground, as their share of the gate receipts.

After that crushing win, Notts were expected also to make short work at home to Stockton of the North-Eastern League in the second round – especially as they were given an extra week's respite because Brighton, their scheduled League opponents the previous Saturday, were involved in a first-round replay (which they won) after being held to a draw by another side from outside the Football League, Trowbridge Town.

Although the ban on midweek football during the 1946-47 season had been removed, the national emergency of those early post-war years still existed. The FA Consultative Committee therefore decreed that 'in order to meet the wishes of the Government, fixture secretaries of Saturday competitions should avoid midweek matches except at the beginning and end of the 1947-48 season when an evening kick-off time can be fixed, and on national and local holidays.' To ease these restrictions, the League season started a week earlier than usual, on the third Saturday of August, but it was not to be extended beyond the first Saturday of May 'unless exceptional circumstances arise'. Fortunately, they did not. There was no repetition if the extreme weather conditions that had caused the previous season to stretch into mid-June.

So, with midweek replays avoided, Notts County benefited from having no match for a fortnight, but what an upset Stockton so nearly caused. The score was 1-1 after extra time, both goals coming in the first half. Lawton kept quiet by 23-year-old Bill Thompson, a £5-a-week electrician at Horden Colliery whom Notts, among half-a-dozen other clubs, had been trying to sign. Sewell was the scorer of the goal that misguidedly raised home hopes in a gate of over 30,000. The nippy inside-right was convinced he should have had a second. He said the ball went into the net off his face; the referee ruled he had handled.

Notts were reported to have made the biggest-ever offer to a non-League club for Thompson, but they were not alone in dropping out of the chase. The big centre-half was going nowhere at that time, also to the disappointment of Aston Villa, Bury, Charlton, Chelsea, Sunderland and Wolves. He had given up playing football at the age of fourteen, but had restarted after completing his National Service in the RAF a year before facing Lawton, and had since been in consistently formidable form.

After that match at Meadow Lane, one newspaper put up the headline: COLLIERY ELECTRICIAN PUT LAWTON'S LIGHT OUT. After the replay, switched to Middlesbrough's ground, the same paper received a telegram reading: LIGHT STILL BURNING BRIGHTLY – LAWTON. A crowd of more than 34,000 saw his hat-trick. The other scorer for Notts, who led 3-1 at half-time, was Horace Cumner, the Welsh international left-winger from Arsenal who was later with Watford, Scunthorpe and Bradford City before leaving the Football League to become Swanage's player-coach. At Scunthorpe, Cumner was reunited not only with Leslie Jones, the club's first manager in the League and a former Arsenal colleague, but also with Wally Boyes, who moved to the Lincolnshire club from Notts County the month before him, and then with Bill Corkhill. Jones and Cumner both hailed from Aberdare. Boyes had been one of Lawton's team-mates with Everton before the war.

Although the winner of three caps, Cumner played only a dozen League games for Arsenal before exceeding 50 appearances for Notts. He scored the Gunners' deciding goal against Wolves on ending a three-year wait for his debut in the last pre-war season, after being loaned out to Margate and Hull. A match that must have been even more memorable for him in their colours was the fog-shrouded farce in which Moscow Dynamo ghosted to a 4-3 victory in November 1945 at White Hart Lane. Not for almost another year was Highbury to be fit for football again after being an ARP base during the war. Arsenal's use of Tottenham's ground was a reversal of what happened in the previous world conflict, when Spurs had played 'home' matches at Highbury because their ground had then been requisitioned by the Ministry of Munitions for the manufacture of gas masks.

Because a number of Arsenal's players were still serving overseas, Cumner was one of only five belonging to the club in a line-up against Dynamo that was made up with guests. Although it was also true that the visitors were not exclusively from Moscow, this prompted the Soviet radio and newspaper commentators to insist that the Arsenal side should be seen as 'one of the representative English teams', disregarding the fact that it included just two members of the contemporary national side (Laurie Scott, the Arsenal right-back, and right-winger Stanley Matthews, then with Stoke), and also a couple of Welshmen.

Cumner's compatriot was Wyn Griffiths, a young Cardiff City amateur goalkeeper who had to be replaced during the interval, with Arsenal 3-2 ahead, after being concussed in a collision. Harry Brown, who was to leave QPR for Notts County a few months later, was called from the crowd by loudspeaker to deputise. Conditions became so bad as a real London pea-souper enveloped the ground that the match would surely have been abandoned, or not even started, if it had been a League or Cup encounter.

Early the following April, Griffiths was transferred to Derby, making his debut in a transitional League South match at Villa Park. The Rams would have been beaten by more than four goals but for the daring saves he made, yet he never played for them again. His spectacular display cost him his career, for he suffered a spinal injury that forced him into an early retirement.

The first match of the Dynamo tour, drawn 3-3 as an estimated record 85,000 packed into Stamford Bridge on a Tuesday afternoon the week before the Arsenal game, was also the first in which Tommy Lawton played for Chelsea after his £11,500 move from Everton. Nothing, in fact, could dissuade the men from Moscow that he had been signed specifically to turn out against them. He marked the occasion with a magnificent goal after Chelsea's 2-0 lead had been wiped out, but Moscow's final equaliser was conceded with only five minutes to go – from a palpably offside position.

On the intervening Saturday, Dynamo thrashed Cardiff City, then a Third Division club, by 10-1 before a 40,000 crowd at Ninian Park. The tour was rounded off at Ibrox, where a midweek crowd of 90,000 saw a 2-2 draw with Rangers. With the four games having been seen by more than a quarter of a million people, the Football Association planned to arrange a fifth for a representative side to meet Dynamo at Villa Park. They even selected a team, including Lawton, and had 70,000 tickets printed, but the Soviet stars were recalled home before it could be played.

Crowds at Meadow Lane, though obviously on a more modest scale, continued to be boosted during the Lawton era which supporters hailed as 'magical.' Besides spearheading Notts County's promotion to the Second Division, he had a huge influence on increasing the club's average home gate from 7,500 to 37,500.

County reached the fourth round of the FA Cup in both the first two seasons Lawton spent with them. In 1947-48, they again hit the headlines with a 2-0 third-round away victory over a Birmingham City side heading for the Second Division championship. Mrs Lawton, watching her husband play for the first time since his move to Meadow Lane, was among the 53,000 who saw the plans made in midweek training work to perfection. In the first half, Lawton deceived the home defence by dropping deep behind his inside-forwards. After the interval, those tactics having succeeded with goals from Corkhill and Marsh, Lawton resumed his normal role while Sewell and Marsh fell back to help their defence.

Sewell added a hat-trick in a home League game against Reading to the one he had notched in the first-round Cup-tie with Horsham, but another week later a goal fifteen minutes from time by Swindon's Welsh international Billy Lucas ended Notts' hopes of further progress in the knock-out competition. For those of a superstitious disposition, that outcome could be attributed to the fact that five minutes before the kick-off Swindon's manager, Louis Page, donned the famous spats sent to him by

Jack Tinn, who had worn them when the Portsmouth team he had managed had shocked Wolves to win the FA Cup in the last pre-war final, 1939.

A more realistic influence, however, was the plan Page operated to subdue Lawton. This put faith in centre-half Ithell, who had the sole responsibility for dealing with the Notts skipper – a task he carried out so efficiently that Lawton had only one shot at goal. Instead of going to Ithell's aid, wing-halves Kaye and Painter were delegated to keep a close watch on Sewell and Marsh, thus snuffing out the few of those renowned head-flicked passes by Lawton that managed to reach his inside men.

Page, who in 1926, in his first match as Burnley's centre-forward, had scored a double hat-trick against Birmingham, afterwards paid two tributes. No, not to his players, even though his plan had been such a success. He picked out for particular praise the air of Clevedon, where the Swindon players had trained, and Lawton himself. 'Tommy went into our dressing room before changing after the game,' he said, 'and was full of praise for my lads, particularly singling out our centre-forward, Maurice Owen. It was a grand gesture.'

CHAPTER EIGHT

Eric Houghton, the spot-kick king

Although Notts County were down in the Division Three depths when Tommy Lawton so unexpectedly threw in his lot with them, they could at least point to the distinction of being the Football League's oldest club.

But they are not the oldest of all, for Sheffield FC, amateur members of the Yorkshire League, started out several years earlier. The Wednesday came into existence in 1866, Sheffield United in 1889, but Sheffield FC rightly consider themselves the founders of organised football throughout the world. For many years, Notts County's foundation year was given as 1862, and their centenary was duly celebrated in 1962. Since then, however, researches by Keith Warsop have shown that little more than practice matches were initially played, and it was not until December 1864 that the club, then known as Notts FC, was put on a firm footing.

A seasoned fellow international was already on Notts County's books when Lawton joined the club. William Eric Houghton's stay of nearly seven years at Meadow Lane, first as a player, then manager, divided his nineteen years as a player with Aston Villa and the five of his return to Villa Park as manager. In all, he served Villa across more than 50 years, also as a director and finally as a vice-president.

Born at Billingborough, a village nine miles north of Bourne in Lincolnshire, Eric Houghton played for Donnington Grammar School, Boston Town and Billingborough before first joining Aston Villa as an amateur in August 1927, on the recommendation of an uncle, Cecil Harris, a former Villa player. He gave up his job in a bakery to become a full-time professional a year later.

A forceful, no-frills winger, noted for the extreme power of his penalties and free-kicks, Houghton gave an early indication of his fierce finishing when he scored 88 goals in one of his seasons as a schoolboy. With the inclusion of almost a hundred plundered during the Second World War (though none in his three games as a Notts County guest), there were 278 more in his senior first-team career. Of that impressive tally, 170 were scored in the Football League, ten in the FA Cup, five for England. And 72 of them were penalties, from 79 attempts. He compiled the quickest century of goals by a winger in the game's history.

Houghton's most successful season as a scorer was that of 1930-31, in which his 30 goals, seven of them from penalties, would normally have made him Villa's top marksman. But that season was far from being a normal one. Centre-forward 'Pongo' Waring netted a club record 49, plus another in the Cup, and although Villa piled up their biggest total of 128 they still finished second to Arsenal. Later that year, Houghton gave fans something else special to remember him by. One of his two goals in a victory over Derby was among the most spectacular ever seen at Villa Park. It came from one of his blockbuster free-kicks, delivered from 40 yards.

The first of Houghton's rare spot-kick failures came, ironically, on his League debut at home to Leeds United, who won 4-3 on the first Saturday of 1930. He was also called upon to take a penalty in his last appearance for the club, in the Central League against Huddersfield Reserves on Boxing Day in 1946 – the day before his transfer to Notts County. On that occasion he converted, with his last kick of the match.

Houghton, who also played county cricket for Warwickshire and Lincolnshire, had only 30 League games behind him when he won the first of his seven England caps, netting one of the five goals Ireland conceded in Sheffield on 20 October 1930. In the following year, he also scored as Belgium were beaten 4-1 in Brussels, and twice more against the Irish in a 6-2 victory in Belfast, but keen competition for the outside-left position – notably from Manchester City's Eric Brook – kept him out after he had scored again in England's 4-3 win over Austria at Chelsea's ground on 7 December 1932.

It also counted against Houghton's chances of an England recall that for two seasons in the 1930s he played in the Second Division. In 1935-36, Aston Villa were relegated for the first time in their history – as also were Blackburn Rovers, fellow founder members of the Football League in 1888. Villa spent £35,000, a massive outlay for those days, on seven new players in their unsuccessful efforts to avoid the drop, but Houghton remained a regular choice amid that influx, and he was a key member of the side that climbed back as champions in 1938.

So was Frank Broome, who was signed by Houghton later for Notts County from Derby in exchange for goalkeeper Harry Brown. Broome, an astute Villa capture from his home club Berkhamstead Town, was the top scorer in that promotion team with twenty goals from outside-right or centre-forward – and six more in a Cup run to the semi-finals. Houghton contributed a dozen, with another couple in the Cup. Both players also helped Villa win the League North Cup in 1944. Houghton missed the first leg of the final, which Blackpool won 2-1, but he was back for the return home leg in which Broome scored twice in a 4-2 victory that clinched the trophy. Both were also in the team that drew 1-1 with Charlton, the South Cup winners, in a challenge match at Stamford Bridge, Houghton scoring.

The last four of Houghton's 392 League and Cup appearances for Aston Villa were made in the opening weeks of the 1946-47 season. That made him, with Broome, one of the few to play for the club before, during, and after the Second World War. Notts County were only four places off the bottom of the Third Division's Southern Section when Houghton joined them, but in their next match – in which he was unable to make his debut because of injury – they ended Cardiff's winning sequence of nine League matches (six of them away from home). Donald Flanagan, a new centre-forward from Dundalk, gave Notts a 35th-minute lead against the leaders and coming champions, and it was not until twenty minutes from time that Bryn Allen salvaged a point for the visitors with a goal that looked suspiciously offside. Cardiff might have won if Stan Richards had not missed an open goal, but they had been fortunate not to have gone two goals behind when Cumner hit a post.

Flanagan had also scored in a 2-1 win at Bournemouth the previous week, yet those were the only two first-team games he played for Notts County. He went back to Ireland to join Shelbourne. It was indicative of the unsettled state of the Notts team in those early post-war days that he was the eighth player to lead the attack that season, even though it was only half over – and there were changes in that position for both the next two games, in which Houghton played the first of his five FA Cup-ties for the club and the first of his 55 League matches.

A week after Cardiff's visit, the centre-forward choice fell on Gordon Jayes, an amateur from Leicester who was later with Nuneaton Borough, for a third-round Cup-tie in which Houghton had an unhappy introduction into the side dumped out of the competition at Luton. All but one of the Hatters' six goals that January afternoon were scored by Hugh Billington, a veteran who had helped the Bedfordshire club to the Third South title ten years before, but still had life in the First Division with Chelsea ahead of him. On the Saturday after that exit at the hands of the club who had themselves been hit for six in the previous year's third round, the choice at the head of the Notts front line fell on another of Flanagan's successors. John Hubbard was a Yorkshireman from Wath-upon-Dearne who had first played for the club in the last wartime season of 1944-45. He failed to score in a 2-2 draw at Norwich, and soon afterwards was on his way out to Scarborough.

The number of centre-forwards used by County in post-war League football rose to twelve over 58 games before Tommy Lawton took over. The first of them was Fred Whittaker, the last Jack Marsh. Whittaker, who also played lacrosse, was the first player Arthur Stollery signed after succeeding Frank Buckley as manager during the 1946 close season.

Stollery had to fly off to Canada to get him, following up a tip-off his predecessor had received. It was a long way to go for just two goals and ten games, for that was all Whittaker had to show before going back to British Columbia. And three of those games were not at centre-forward. Whittaker was at left-back in a 1-4 defeat at QPR and, even more remarkably, in goal as an emergency deputy for Harry Brown on two other occasions. He was beaten only once when Notts drew with Bristol City at Ashton Gate, and, in his final appearance, kept a clean sheet as the weather-hit 1946-47 season ended for Notts County on 29 May with a home win over Reading. It was also rather surprising that one of his goals came from the penalty spot, in a victory over Brighton, for sure-shot Houghton was by then also in the team.

Back in Canada, Whittaker rejoined Vancouver North Shore United, for whom he had been a prolific scorer, and he led them to their national championship in 1949. He also played for, and coached, the British Columbia All-Stars, and in 2002 he was inducted into Canadian football's Hall of Fame.

Jack Marsh, who served in the Sudan with the RAF during the war, made his League debut a few weeks before Lawton's arrival, after being taken on from a junior club in his home town of Mansfield. After being switched to inside-left to accommodate the England leader, he also played a couple of times on the right wing, totalling nearly 50 appearances, before moving to Coventry in the autumn of 1948. He was later with Leicester and Chesterfield.

Eric Houghton's new clubmates at Meadow Lane also included two coming internationals, besides Jackie Sewell. They were Eddie Gannon, a stylish wing-half signed from Shelbourne the previous summer, and Bill Dickson, who was to be the makeweight in the Lawton deal. Gannon, who was an attacking type but a maker of goals for others rather than a ready scorer himself, played the first of his fourteen games for the Republic of Ireland while still with County, in defeat by Switzerland at Dalymount Park in his home city of Dublin on 5 December 1948. His next cap, in a defeat by Belgium at the same ground the following April, was gained the month after his £15,000 move to Sheffield Wednesday. He was in the Owls' promotion-winning teams of 1950 and, with Sewell, 1952, but touched his peak during the season of 1953-54 in which he excelled in the run to the last four of the FA Cup.

In September 1954, Gannon closed his home in Sheffield and took his family back to Dublin, where he had a part-time job. From then until he rejoined Shelbourne as player-manager and coach the following April, he flew back each weekend to play for Wednesday, altogether adding 219

games for the Owls (just four goals) to the 118 (two goals) he had played
for Notts County. While back with Shelbourne, whose manager, the former Arsenal and England forward David Jack, had resigned to take a post
at the Air Ministry, he became an international with three clubs by taking
part in a 3-1 win against Norway in Oslo, but in a 1-2 defeat by West
Germany in Hamburg. He also captained the League of Ireland part-
timers who were beaten 1-5 by the Football League at Everton.

Among Eric Houghton's new colleagues in Nottingham there were
also the only two players who had been with the Magpies before the war
– Bill Fallon and Bill Corkhill, who were both back for a second spell at
Meadow Lane.

Fallon, a lively winger originally signed from the Dublin club Dolphin
in 1933, won five Republic of Ireland caps (three against Hungary, the
others against Switzerland and France) before his transfer to Sheffield
Wednesday in March 1938, and four more in 1938-39 against Switzerland,
Poland, Hungary and Germany. He was in his mid-30s when he rejoined
Notts County in the summer of 1946, and, although it was therefore only
a curtailed comeback, he was close to 150 League and Cup appearances
for the club in all when he left again, for Exeter. With the addition of the
first-team matches he played for Wednesday, he was not far short of 200,
with some 40 goals to his credit. His younger brother Peter was given trials at Meadow Lane during the first post-war season, but was released to
Exeter on a free transfer.

Corkhill was to be joined on more than 300 appearances for Notts
County by Aubrey Southwell, a doughty full-back who was among the
club's captains. Indeed, Southwell's games went into a fourth century if
others played after his switch from Forest in 1944 are taken into account
– during the war and in the transitional season that followed it. When
Houghton arrived, Southwell was just getting into his stride in a sequence
of League and Cup appearances that reached 120 before injury caused
him to miss three games towards the end of the 1948-49 season.

It was in a scoreless home game against Forest, for whom he never
played in the first team, that Southwell made his Notts debut at right-half
on the last day of September in 1944. Not until late February in 1957, in
a 2-2 home draw with Sheffield United, did he finally bow out. After that
he returned to Lincolnshire (like Cyril Hatton, he hailed from Grantham)
for a final season with Boston. He died in February 2005, in his 84th year.

CHAPTER NINE

Flow of Forest Players to Meadow Lane

While Arthur Stollery was manager, Aubrey Southwell was followed from Forest to the other side of the River Trent at Meadow Lane by Bill Baxter, Colin Lyman and Tom Johnston.

Lyman, a versatile Northampton-born forward who had five clubs before the war, six as a guest during it, and was with half-dozen afterwards, did not stay long. This was scarcely surprising for such a roamer, but Baxter and Johnston between them totalled more than 400 appearances before moving on. Notts were among the clubs for whom Lyman had guested, but only briefly, and he left for Nuneaton Borough after being the Magpies' own player in 21 League games. Afterwards he returned to the Nottingham area as player-manager of Long Eaton Town, but it was in Cambridgeshire that he died in 1986, two months after his 72nd birthday.

Bill Baxter, a Nottingham man, was newly into his 30th year when he joined Notts in October 1946, but he still had time to add just over 150 first-team games to the similar number (with the inclusion of those in wartime) he had played for Forest before he left for Grantham. Notts were also one of the clubs for whom he guested during he war – just the once, in a defeat away to Grimsby in 1940. Corkhill and Hatton were also in the team that day.

The other clubs for which Baxter played in wartime included Derby and Leicester, and thereby hung the tale of one of the oddities of those makeshift footballing years. Baxter played at left-half for Leicester against a Derby side in which Tom Johnston was at outside-left, and less than two months later they were in the same positions, also at the Baseball Ground but on opposite sides, in another match between those clubs. Johnston was in the winning team on the first occasion, Baxter on the second. And that was not all. One week later, Baxter was up against his Forest clubmate yet again, for Derby at Leicester. Derby won that match too, but Baxter had to leave the field in the second half for attention to an eye injury suffered in a collision – with Johnston.

Baxter made his League debut for Forest at left-half in their scoreless Second Division draw at Burnley on 11 September 1937. It was against Forest, at the City Ground, that he made his final first-team appearance for Notts County in his more usual position of centre-half on 10 October 1953. It was a sad farewell. He was recalled, with Johnston, after

Notts had plunged to the bottom of the table the previous Saturday in losing by three goals at Lincoln with a team into which two newcomers had been introduced hours before – Billy Coole, on the right wing, from Mansfield, and 'Tot' Leverton, at centre-forward, from Forest.

With Southwell already in the side, besides Leverton, the number of former Forest players in the County line-up on the afternoon Baxter and Johnston returned against their old club was increased to five with the inclusion of Jack Edwards at inside-left. Edwards, a skilful, ball-playing Mancunian, had cost Southampton £10,000 from Forest in the summer of 1949. Three years later he had gone into the Southern League with Kidderminster after being transfer-listed by the Hampshire club, along with another inside-forward, George Curtis, a £9,000 signing from Arsenal. Edwards was on Notts' doorstep – still training in Nottingham – and he was snapped up from Southampton in exchange for Alec Simpson, a former Wolves player who comes back into this account shortly.

All five Forest 'exiles' were as powerless as their six team-mates, however, as their old club cruised to a 5-0 victory. One of those goals was a penalty, another an own-goal conceded by Johnston, whose adaptability was exploited at right-half to the exclusion of Tony Allen, yet another ex-Forester. During his career, Johnston occupied all five positions in the forward line of the then accepted 2-3-5 team formation, and towards the end he also frequently played at left-half. He even kept goal for Forest in a Second Division match at Luton, in an emergency that arose when Larry Platts, later with Chesterfield and Burton, missed his train from Brighton, where he was stationed in the Forces.

Johnston, a Scot from Chirnside, a Berwickshire village near Duns in the Borders, was signed by Forest after impressing their manager, Billy Walker, when he played against them at the age of seventeen during the war while on a month's trial with Peterborough from the Edinburgh club St Bernard's. After also having trials with Leicester and Northampton, he scored almost 50 goals in over 100 games for Forest before League football got under way again, top-scoring with 26 goals in missing only one of their 42 League South matches in the transitional season of 1945-46.

In the first two post-war Division Two seasons, Johnston, who was once a reserve for Scotland, increased his overall first-team totals for Forest to 171 games and 72 goals before his £8,000 transfer to Notts County five days before the start of the 1948-49 campaign. With Notts, he notched 92 goals in 285 appearances, the last of them away to Grimsby shortly before Christmas 1956. Having qualified as an FA coach, he obtained his first post in that role in Finland before succeeding Duggie

Davidson, who had moved to Portsmouth, as Birmingham City's coach in August 1957.

A year later, Johnston had a short stint as player-manager of the Derbyshire club Heanor Town in the Central Alliance before entering management in the Football League – first with Rotherham, then Grimsby. He guided Rotherham to safety from relegation and to the first League Cup final, in which they lost in extra-time to Aston Villa on aggregate. Rotherham's escape from the drop into Division Three was to Grimsby's cost, and although the Mariners had just been promoted when Johnston joined them in 1962, he was unable to keep them up. They just survived in his first season at Blundell Park, but down they went again at the end of the following one.

Johnston's next job was with Huddersfield, a club with which he was to have three spells. In the first, from October 1964 to May 1968, he took them within two points of a return to the First Division, and to the brink of another League Cup final, but resigned in the wake of an upheaval that caused eight players to be transfer-listed. In the second, from January 1975 to April 1977, he was in turn general manager and team manager as Huddersfield spent it mainly in the Fourth Division, to which they were relegated for the first time. In the third, which began in September 1977, he earned a year's extension of his contract the following January in recognition of improved results, but resigned near the end of August in 1978 without seeing it through.

'The trouble with Huddersfield,' he said, 'is that they expect you to win every match. The pressure and aggravation became just too much, and I decided it was better to go.' When he made that final exit the tooth-less Terriers had taken only one point from their first three games of the new season, and had already been knocked out of the League Cup.

During all his years as a manager, spread over some twenty seasons, Johnston built up a reputation for improving the financial position of each of his clubs. But his quietly spoken, pipe-smoking image belied the fact that he was a strict disciplinarian, and the disharmony that marred his time at Huddersfield also blighted, to an even greater extent, his reign of six years with York, after his first departure from Leeds Road. He worked wonders in taking York from the foot of the Fourth Division to promotion to the Second for the first time, yet incurred the wrath of his players to such a degree that they sought to force his resignation, or dismissal. Signs of unrest at Bootham Crescent first became public during the 1972-73 season, when five members of the team, including skipper Barry Swallow, asked for a transfer. Only one, Laurie Calloway, was allowed to leave at that time, for Shrewsbury, but matters came to a head when, threatened by relegation from the Third Division, the players were left seething by the departure of popular trainer Billy Horner, 'for business reasons'. The players' union, the PFA, was consulted, and Swallow presented a list of grievances to Johnston, chairman Eric Magson and another director at a two-hour meeting. All four afterwards refused to state the reason for the dispute, but one player was quoted as saying: 'It's fair to say that we are in revolt against Mr Johnston's authority.'

But Johnston, who was on a five-year contract, had no intention of resigning. 'I have done nothing wrong,' he declared. Nor were the board prepared to dismiss him. York had been struggling since he had guided them out of the Fourth Division in 1971, in the fourth promotion position in a table headed by Notts County, but they avoided relegation after that crisis meeting and in the following season of 1973-74 their fortunes were transformed as they rose into Division Two. And that was where Johnston left them for his first return to Huddersfield.

His departure was of his own choosing, and on a high note. He rejoined Huddersfield as their general manager within days of York providing one of the big surprises of the FA Cup's third round on 4 January 1975, holding Arsenal to a 1-1 draw at Highbury. Johnston stayed on until after the replay the following Tuesday evening, and it was only after extra time that York succumbed to a Brian Kidd hat-trick. Huddersfield were Johnston's last club. When he died in December 1994 he was only a few days from his 76th birthday.

Alan Brown was another martinet of a manager who was a player with Notts County during the Tommy Lawton era. His transfer from Burnley on 5 October 1948 for £12,500 was initially hailed as a master-stroke, to match in defence the one that had brought Lawton into the attack, but it was a lot of money to spend on a 34-year-old, especially in those days of austerity in the early post-war years. Indeed, it was the first five-figure fee paid for a player of that age, and the high expectations were quickly dispelled. Brown, who had been another of Notts County's wartime guests, played in only thirteen League games and two FA Cup-ties, after which Bill Baxter was reinstated as the club's first choice centre-half.

The reason why Brown's arrival was greeted with such enthusiasm was that he had been the strong man of Burnley's 'Iron Curtain' defence throughout the first two post-war seasons, captaining the team with an arresting efficiency that befitted a former policeman, after his transfer from Huddersfield. In the first of those seasons, when he did not miss a match, Burnley won promotion, conceding a club record low of 29 goals in their 42 Second Division fixtures, and reached an FA Cup final in which they lost to an extra-time Charlton goal scored by left-winger Chris

Duffy. And in the following 1947-48 season, with injury a rare cause of Brown's absence, Burnley had a defensive record second only to Arsenal's champions, letting in 43 goals to the Gunners' 32.

Why then, were Burnley then so ready to let Brown go? His age may have had something to do with it, although the player they first called upon to take his place was even older. The aforementioned Bob Johnson, given a free transfer by Blackburn and discarded by Blackpool after a month's trial before joining Burnley from Bishop Auckland in 1934, was almost 37 and in his fifteenth year at Turf Moor. He stayed for only a couple of matches, leaving to become Nelson's player-manager, but another veteran, 35-year-old Arthur Woodruff, was then briefly switched from full-back to centre-half before Tommy Cummings, not long turned 21, came in to make the position his own for not far off 500 games.

The main reason why Burnley were prepared to part with Brown was that they wanted the money for a cash-plus-exchange deal they hoped to complete for Wilf Mannion, the England forward who was refusing to re-sign for Middlesbrough. In the event, Mannion changed his mind and stayed with Boro for six more years, then moving to Hull on Christmas Eve in 1954. As for Brown, he asked Notts County for a transfer after only ten weeks in the Third Division.

Brown, who had captained a Football League XI and once been an England reserve, made his request after being dropped from a home match in which County defeated Torquay 5-0 on 18 December 1948. Charles Barnes, the club's chairman, stated: 'Some days ago Brown told me he was not settling down in Nottingham. I was rather surprised because, before we signed him, both the player and his wife saw the house they were to live in and seemed happy about it.' Brown soon made it clear that the house had nothing to do with it. 'I've not settled down to my best form,' he said. 'I have my own ideas of defensive policy, but I've been unable to use them. I am not complaining about being dropped, but after watching the game with Torquay I am convinced that for my own good I should get back into Second or First Division football.'

There was to be no other opening for Brown as a player, however. He got back into the Notts side for a few more games when Baxter was out injured the following April, but, with no suitable offers forthcoming, he decided to retire from playing and moved back to Burnley to open a restaurant. His return to the game in 1951, as a member of the Sheffield Wednesday coaching staff, was made with the encouragement of Stanley Rous, the FA secretary. It was his second comeback, for before the war he had left Huddersfield because of his limited opportunities and had spent 2½ years as a policeman before rejoining them.

The managerial career in which Brown continued to instil the values of integrity and hard work he prized so highly began in 1954 at Burnley, where he kept his old club in the top half of the First Division for three seasons before his appointment at Sunderland in his native North-East. He took over at Roker Park in the midst of a series of scandals over illegal payments and with the team at the foot of the First Division. Relegation was unavoidable, Sunderland's first since entering the League in 1890, but Brown guided them back in 1964. Then, however, he sprang a surprise by resigning, tempted back to Hillsborough. Wednesday's directors saw him as just the man to restore order and respect in the wake of a another scandal, this time match-fixing, and he not only swiftly obliged but also piloted the club to their first FA Cup final for over thirty years. It was one of Wembley's best, but Wednesday were beaten by Everton after going two goals ahead.

Two years later, in February 1968, Brown went back to Sunderland. Again, however, he was unable to avert relegation, and after two failed attempts to pull off promotion he had his contract terminated 'by mutual consent' on 1 November 1972, as Sunderland sagged to fourteenth in the Second Division table. He subsequently coached in Norway and at Plymouth before retiring – forced out as Argyle's chief coach in February 1976, with the club fifth from the bottom of Division Two, only eight months after signing a three-year contract.

Argyle manager Tony Waiters said: 'We have parted with Alan Brown because he and I had reached a point of no return. It was simply a case of one man's ideas and methods not dovetailing with another's. The situation had been building up until we got to the stage where it had to be sorted out. There was no possible compromise.' Another example of Brown's unrelenting attitude.

Brown's last years were dogged by ill health, and he died in Barnstaple, Devon, on 8 March 1996, aged 81. For a man of such character and leadership, his second Christian name of Winston was entirely appropriate.

CHAPTER TEN

Stollery resigns; first century of goals

Notts County were comfortably in the top half of the Third Division's Southern Section, but trailing leaders Swansea by ten points, largely because of a disappointing away record, when Arthur Stollery resigned as manager in February 1949 because of ill health.

Wilf Fisher, the club's secretary, was put in charge of team affairs as caretaker until the end of that season while the directors looked around for a successor. The search ended on their own doorstep. On 25 May, the job went to Eric Houghton. With Billy Walker, Houghton's former inside partner in the Aston Villa attack, installed over at Forest, there was an ex-Villa and England forward as manager at both Nottingham grounds. Houghton's appointment came eighteen days after his recall at outside-left as Tom Johnston's deputy for what was to be his final League appearance in a defeat at Southend. He had been on the right wing in all but one of his 30 other first-team games that season. That one exception was at inside-left.

In the season that ended with the loss at Roots Hall, County scored a century of goals for the first time – the only club in the four divisions to get into three figures – yet they finished eleventh. The most surprising thing about their total of 102 (surpassing the 97 of the 1930-31 Third South promotion win) was that Tommy Lawton was outscored not only by Sewell, but also by Johnston, even though that was the season in which he three times notched four goals in a match. He scored in just eight of his 33 other League games, but added three in the Cup for a total of 23. Johnston, who missed only that final fixture, ended two behind Sewell with 24 in the League, but in the Cup scored twice to Sewell's once. Johnston did the hat-trick in successive games, won by 5-1 against Crystal Palace at Selhurst Park and 4-0 at home to Watford.

That big victory over Palace, who had to seek re-election, was a rare departure from the bleak away form that was Notts' undoing in their quest for promotion. They lost as many times on their travels as they won at home (fifteen) and picked up only ten points, from four wins and two draws, on their other visits. After being pepped up by special training at Torquay, they gained another away win in the Cup, after extra-time in the third round at Plymouth. Sewell's goal left Argyle still seeking their first victory in the competition since 1936-37. Plymouth's plan to mark Lawton out of the game worked until they conceded that late decider. He foiled those keeping a close watch on him by moving to the edge of the penalty area when Notts forced a corner. They followed him there, leaving Sewell free to head home at the far post.

The Notts attack, to which Lawton returned after missing the previous week's defeat at Bristol Rovers because of a head wound suffered in a car accident, was weakened by an injury to Yorkshireman Oscar Hold, a former Aldershot inside-forward who had been signed from Norwich for £6,000 three months before. Hold, who finished the game limping, missed the following Saturday's 11-1 drubbing of Newport, but was back in time for the fourth-round tie in which Notts were knocked out by a second-half goal by Scottish international Billy Liddell, when they met First Division Liverpool in front of 60,000 at Anfield.

Before the next season, Hold moved from the League to Chelmsford, but he soon returned with Everton. He was later with QPR, and then had Jesse Pye in his team while player-manager of Wisbech after spells in that role with March Town and Gainsborough Trinity. Hold, who afterwards managed Cambridge City and Doncaster Rovers, also coached abroad, taking Fenerbahce to the Turkish League championship, and the National Sporting Club of Saudi Arabia to that country's first national title. For Notts County, this man of so many clubs scored only nine of his career total of 40 goals and fewer than two dozen of about 100 first-team appearances. He was just eight days from his 87th birthday when he died at Sunderland in October 2005.

Other newcomers to the Notts County team during the 1948-49 season included Roy Smith, a prematurely bald goalkeeper, and full-back Bart Purvis, both of whom made their debut in the 5-0 home win against Torquay on the Saturday before Christmas. Smith, signed from Sheffield Wednesday, went straight into the side and performed so efficiently that Harry Brown never did get back before his transfer to Derby the following October.

Smith was unlucky with Wednesday, whom he joined from Selby Town in 1936. He was just establishing himself in their first team, after having been kept out by Derek Goodfellow, when war was declared. He resumed as first choice for much of the first post-war season, at the end of which Goodfellow moved to Middlesbrough. Smith, however, lost his place through injury, and then found his way back barred by Dave McIntosh, a Scot who would exceed 300 club appearances despite twice breaking an arm within a year. With Notts, Smith achieved what he had missed with Wednesday. He completed a century of games.

Purvis, whose first name was Bartholomew, took over as Southwell's partner from Bert Howe, who until then had been first choice since his arrival from Leicester in the summer of 1947, for all but one of Notts' remaining 22 matches of the season. The one Purvis missed, at Swindon in late April, was unfortunately the last for the recalled Howe, who broke a leg in trying to prevent the first of the Wiltshire club's three goals. The Gateshead-born Purvis, formerly of Plymouth and next headed for Carlisle, was also displaced after the first two games of the ensuing season of 1949-50 in which Notts at last clinched the promotion for which they had been looking to Lawton to lead them.

Into the left-back berth, then, competently stepped the lean and rangy Norman Rigby, who had made his debut in a wartime match Notts lost 5-8 at Lincoln, but had been mainly overlooked since his return from Army service in India. Indeed, the Worksop-born Rigby, originally a centre-half with Newark, would surely no longer have been on County's books when he was finally given a decent run in the side but for the intervention of Eric Houghton. One of the new manager's first tasks was to persuade the directors to take Rigby off the transfer list onto which they had placed him.

That faith was rewarded as this hard tackler belatedly developed into one of the most dependable defenders in the division, absent only four times as Notts surged to the Third South title. And although he was unable to ward off competition for a first-team place in the higher section, he proceeded to give Peterborough excellent service, as player, trainer and manager, over sixteen years. On leaving Notts in 1951, after only just falling short of 50 League and Cup games, he helped Peterborough to five successive Midland League titles and two good FA Cup runs, then led them to the Fourth Division championship in their first Football League season of 1960-61. Released a year later, he was with Boston before rejoining Peterborough as assistant trainer in 1964. Two years after that, he was promoted to first-team trainer, then appointed manager in October 1967 after the resignation of Gordon Clark, who left to become Arsenal's chief scout.

Peterborough were back in Division Four when Rigby again left them, demoted for financial irregularities after finishing ninth in Division Three in 1967-68. Rigby resigned in January 1969, and six months later he joined March Town in the Eastern Counties League. He was back at Newark when he died in August 2001, aged 77.

For much of Notts County's promotion season of 1949-50, Rigby was partnered at full-back by a doughty Scot who totted up nearly 250 League and Cup appearances before preceding him to Boston in 1955. The international caps for which Tommy Deans was tipped never materialised, but he proved a real bargain for Notts at £6,500 from Clyde in

October 1949. In four consecutive seasons he was out of the team only five times, and in two of them he was an ever-present.

Other prominent newcomers to the side that finished eight points clear of runners-up Northampton were Frank Broome. Billy Evans and Alec Simpson.

Broome, whose fifteen goals in twenty games as a wartime Notts guest included a hat-trick against Walsall, went into the side at outside-right on signing from Derby in exchange for Harry Brown. He replaced Fred Evans, a former Portsmouth winger who was later with Crystal Palace and Rochdale, but he also filled in on the opposite wing and at centre-forward in the occasional absences of Johnston and Lawton.

Billy Evans, for whom Eric Houghton returned to his old club, had only limited first-team chances with Aston Villa. He was, however, just one match shy of being ever-present in the promotion side with Roy Smith and Henry Adamson, a wing-half from the Scottish junior club Jeanfield Swifts who had been at Meadow Lane since August 1946. Billy Evans exceeded 100 appearances, but scored only fourteen goals, before going to Gillingham. He was afterwards with Grimsby, latterly as reserve trainer, but was only 38 when he died in July 1960. He had been in poor health for about a year.

Simpson, a £7,500 buy from Wolves, began at centre-half, but after Baxter's return to that position from injury he also played at right-half and in both right-sided positions of the forward line. For most of the season, the right-half alongside Baxter and Adamson – behind an attack that at its strongest comprised Broome, Sewell, Lawton, Evans (W) and Johnston – was Harry Chapman, like Broome and Billy Evans a former Villa player.

In each of the past two seasons Notts had been beaten on the opening afternoon, but in 1949-50 they got off to a winning start, at home to Southend, despite the penalty misses by Sewell and Johnston to which reference has already been made. Sewell atoned by doubling the first-half lead gained by Fred Evans, watched by a crowd of 33,500. This was not only the biggest of the day in the Third Division, but also bigger than all but two of the eleven games in the Second, and three in the First.

Defensive doubts returned as three goals, scored by Lawton, Billy Evans and Sewell, could not even earn a draw at Norwich in midweek, but that was the only defeat Notts suffered in twenty matches, two of them Cup-ties, before Southend reversed the result of their opening-day visit to Meadow Lane on the Saturday before Christmas. Even so, the leadership was held by Bournemouth, Torquay and Nottingham Forest before Notts rose to the top for the first time. And Southend,

Northampton and Reading also briefly set the pace before Lawton and his men forged in front to stay.

A first away win was comfortably gained with two goals from Lawton and one from Johnston against Bristol Rovers, and the 3-4 defeat at Norwich was emphatically avenged, 5-0, the following Thursday. At Eastville, there were howls of protest when the referee blew for half-time after 35 minutes. He corrected himself on checking with a linesman, and afterwards explained: 'I was carrying three watches, one on either wrist, plus a new stop watch I used to record the time. It is marked with a red line across the 45-minute mark, and when consulting it to add a couple of minutes for stoppages I found the minute hand indicated that play had been going on for 47 minutes. I am sending it back for readjustment.'

At home to Norwich, in front of a 35,000 crowd, Fred Evans opened the scoring after two minutes, and his namesake doubled the lead near the half-hour. Johnston drove in a third from Sewell's cross, Lawton added the fourth with a typical header, and Fred Evans rounded things off in the closing minutes with a tame shot the goalkeeper should have cleared.

Two more goals by Lawton next accounted for Bournemouth on the first Saturday of September and wrested first place from Forest, whose relegation had put both Nottingham clubs in the same division for the first time since Notts' own descent from the Second Division in 1935. Forest, beaten at Millwall after leading through Leverton, slipped to third place behind Southend, whose home win against Leyton Orient the following Tuesday gave them the lead they retained on goal-average when Notts could only draw at home to Exeter, a club that had been clobbered by nine goals on their last visit.

In fact, Notts were lucky to escape defeat by Exeter. A Johnston free-kick and Lawton header put them two up, but the lead was halved by half-time and Geoff Stone, a former Beeston Boys' Club player deputising at centre-half for the injured Baxter, afterwards had the misfortune to make the mistakes that presented Exeter with two more goals. Not until nine minutes from time did Johnston equalise from a pass by Lawton, who lacked support in a side showing five changes. In the absence of Sewell with gastric influenza, Fred Evans was partnered by the Yorkshire-born Wally Boyes, who had scored seventeen goals in one match in Sheffield schools football. With Johnston dropping back into the half-back line, Bob Crookes filled the left-wing position that Boyes had occupied with both WBA and Everton – and in three games for England.

Boyes, who overcame the handicap of having one leg shorter than the other in helping Albion to the FA Cup and Everton to the League title, was soon on his way out to Scunthorpe at the age of 37, but Crookes, a

Retford schoolmaster newly signed as a full-time professional after first playing for the club as a part-timer, approached 200 games and 50 goals before leaving for Worksop Town. Crookes would have departed earlier, in September 1952, if Notts had accepted an offer from Derby that involved an exchange for Johnny Morris, the costly former England forward who went to Leicester instead. Like Crookes, Boyes had a Retford connection. He joined the Town club as player-manager before managing Hyde United and was finally with Swansea as trainer until his retirement for health reasons three months before his death in a Sheffield hospital in September 1960. He was only 47.

The match with Exeter was another of those in which Lawton was concussed, but he was passed fit for the visit to Crystal Palace, and, although Billy Evans and Johnston did the scoring, he gave an outstanding display in a 2-1 win that hoisted Notts back to the head of the table. Unfortunately for him, no England selector was there to see it. Attention was drawn instead to three of the other candidates for a centre-forward cap who were also in action in London – Roy Bentley (Chelsea) and Jack Rowley (Manchester United) at Stamford Bridge, and Jackie Milburn (Newcastle) at Charlton.

All three scored, yet England's next match eleven days later was the one in which Jesse Pye had his one-off call-up against the Republic of Ireland. And Lawton's hopes of an international recall finally faded away as Stan Mortensen (Blackpool), Jack Lee (Derby) and Nat Lofthouse (Bolton) all subsequently led the England front line, as well as Milburn, Rowley and Bentley. Yet as late as 1950 the majority of the players in the England senior and 'B' teams which went on tour that summer voted Lawton as still the country's best centre-forward.

Southend's defeat at Bournemouth that enabled Notts to regain the leadership also let Forest into second place after a home victory over Swindon. But Forest were just one of five clubs only one point behind, and during the following week, when Notts had no match, Northampton won narrowly at the City Ground to take their turn at the top. For the Cobblers, however, it was not long to last. In their next game they conceded six goals at Swindon, and Notts were restored to pride of place with a goal by the returning Sewell at home to Watford. The closest challengers were now Reading, even though they could only pick up a point at Port Vale, and four days later they became the seventh leaders of a season that was still in September by beating Millwall. But again Notts were without a midweek fixture, so, with just one point fewer, they had two games in hand – and the scene was therefore perfectly set for their trip that Saturday to, of all places, Reading.

Full advantage was taken with a second consecutive 1-0 victory, Billy Evans this time the scorer. The regained lead was also precarious, with four clubs only a point worse off, and Forest recovering on the fringe of that group after a few slip-ups. Notts were not to be caught again, though, and their goal-figures of 22-8 at that stage gave them an average second only to that of Tottenham's Second Division leaders (21-7) in the whole League. After another week it was further improved by a 7-1 win over Leyton Orient, with more than 36,000 packed into Meadow Lane. Lawton, again in great form, Sewell and Billy Evans each scored twice, the other goal coming from Johnston. With 29 goals from ten games, Notts overtook Gateshead, who failed to score in a Northern Section defeat at Lincoln, as the season's highest scorers in the League.

Following a draw at Newport in which Tommy Deans made his debut, the home gate was boosted to nearly 38,000 for a match in which Aubrey Southwell added his first goal in his 136th post-war appearance to two by Sewell and one by Lawton in a 4-1 win over Bristol City. Southwell had previously scored once in his 66 wartime games, in a home defeat by Leicester, and he was to stray from his defensive duties in that respect only once more. That was in a win against Swansea in 1953, also at Meadow Lane.

CHAPTER ELEVEN

Goal to remember in promotion season

Although there was to be no international recall for Tommy Lawton, he was at last regaining the England selectors' attention as Notts County took an unbreakable grip on the Third South leadership in the autumn of 1949.

After being watched by Sir Stanley Rous in the 3-2 win over Brighton in which, as mentioned earlier, he temporarily overcame his aversion to taking penalties, he was under the eyes of Arthur Drewry, the chairman of the selection committee no less, when he scored his late equaliser from the spot against Walsall the following Saturday. That match, Frank Broome's first as a Notts player, attracted 42,676 to the Lane, and, as we shall be coming to shortly, it was still not the ground's biggest crowd of the season.

Despite only just scrambling a draw with Walsall, although Lawton hit both bar and post and had two headers spectacularly saved by Jack Lewis, a goalkeeper who stood only 5ft 8in, Notts extended their lead to four points, thanks to the defeat of second-placed Northampton at Reading. A week later, County's first victory at Millwall for seventeen years was restricted to 3-1 by the brilliance of another goalkeeper, nineteen-year-old Malcolm Finlayson, a late replacement for Irish international Ted Hinton.

What a stormy game that was – and not only because it was played on a pitch made slippery by heavy rain and completed in semi-darkness. Roy Smith was the main butt of abuse that flowed from the saturated terraces after Millwall's right-winger, Jack Johnson, had been carried off to hospital with concussion following a collision with the Notts goalkeeper in the second half. One critic commented: 'If the Millwall crowd used the energy to cheer on their side which they waste in shrieking invective at the opposition, then, perhaps, Millwall would rise up the table.'

His words obviously had no effect. Millwall failed to escape from last place, but were saved from having to seek re-election by an extension from 22 to 24 clubs with the admission of Colchester and Gillingham. Nor did it make any difference to the crowd's attitude on the day of County's visit when Jimmy Constantine, a Millwall forward who had also been in a collision with Smith, waited at the end to walk off with an arm around the goalkeeper's shoulder. It was Constantine who opened the scoring, but Lawton equalised within a minute. Sewell put Notts ahead before half-time with a fierce close-range drive, and he netted again a quarter of an hour from the end.

A Lawton hat-trick, with the aid of two penalties, put paid to Swindon in front of another bumper Meadow Lane crowd of 37,000 and widened the gap at the top to five points. Notts, clad in an Aston Villa strip to avoid a colour clash, then failed to score for the first time that season in a draw before a then record Torquay gate of a 13,824, but they were out of luck when a Lawton 'goal' was discounted because Billy Evans handled the ball as it flashed past him into the net.

Nottingham Forest moved back to second place that day, and were at home to their neighbours in their next home match – with a win for County. That was the match in which Lawton scored with a header that is still talked about in Nottingham, even by those who were not in the all-ticket crowd of 37,903 on that Saturday afternoon of 3 December 1949. It was without doubt the most memorable headed goal I have ever seen, and one I never expect to see bettered.

It came in the 28th minute, from a corner kick on the right forced by Sewell and taken by Broome. 'I never hit a header as hard before,' Lawton said afterwards. 'Everything went exactly right. I just got clear and my jump was carrying me forward as I met the ball full on my forehead.' And what a gigantic leap it was, just outside the penalty area as the ball swung out towards him beyond the reach of the flummoxed defenders. Goalkeeper Harry Walker, beaten by sheer speed, had not the slightest chance of saving a projectile that threatened either to burst the top corner of his net or rip it from its moorings.

Both sides scored in the second half of a game that was a credit to the Third Division. Lawton's determined burst down the right and baffling dribble made the second Notts goal for Broome; the long-striding Tommy Capel, a recent costly signing from Birmingham, obtained a late consolation. 'All season,' wrote Roy Peskett in the *Daily Mail*, 'I have been a lone voice in praise of Lawton, emphasising his speed, tactical brilliance and shooting ability. On Saturday, a number of distinguished visitors saw him for the first time this season, and they agreed with me wholeheartedly that he is still as dangerous and talented a centre-forward as we have in Britain.'

But it made not the slightest difference. There was still no England recall for the Notts captain. The fact that he was in the Third Division could surely have been the only real reason why he was never brought back by the international selectors, although Notts were as good as back in the Second by the time England's next game, a World Cup qualifier against Scotland in Glasgow, came round in April.

National attention may also have been diverted away from Lawton, however, by the fact that Notts County's next League game after Forest was the one in which Southend ended their undefeated run with two second-half goals. And although they then enjoyed a happy Christmas, beating Bristol Rovers and completing a double over Ipswich without conceding a goal, they then had their lead cut to one point as they struck their worst patch of the season in losing at Bournemouth, at home to Crystal Palace, and away to Watford.

That slump also included a third-round FA Cup exit at the hands of Lawton's old club Burnley, a top-six First Division side. A Johnston goal kept the score to 1-1 by the interval, but only Burnley scored in the second half, three more times. There had been another crowd of more than 40,000 for the match with Ipswich on Boxing Day, and 44,000 flocked in for Burnley's visit.

Other examples of Lawton and company's pulling power had been given in their previous Cup-ties that season. The attendance at the 4-0 home win over non-League Tilbury, though under 30,000, was the biggest of the first round. Not much more than half that number saw Forest beat Bristol City across the river on the same day. In the second round, Rochdale's ground record was increased to over 24,000 for the match in which Notts had to come from behind to win with a late goal by Lawton. That, however, was not one of the big man's best efforts. The ball, from a Sewell centre, went slowly into the net off his head and shoulder.

It was around this time that Eric Houghton engaged Fred Tunstall, like himself a former England outside-left, as scout and supervisor of the junior players at Meadow Lane. But Tunstall, scorer of Sheffield United's winning goal in the 1925 FA Cup final against Cardiff, stayed for less than a year before becoming trainer with Boston United, a club he later managed. In March 1951, though just turned 50, he gave a good account of himself in a one-off comeback as a player when Boston turned up with only nine men for a Midland League match at Peterborough. Tunstall and a director made up the numbers.

After the four successive defeats in League and Cup, Notts got back to their winning ways in the League against lowly Aldershot, and on the first Saturday of February, at full strength for the first time since early December, over 36,000 saw them land another double at Reading's expense. All their forwards except Billy Evans scored in a 4-0 victory, with Broome outstanding. February was a good month for the Magpies. After having an extra week's respite because their scheduled opponents, Northampton, were at Derby instead (in the Cup), they won 4-1 away to

Leyton Orient and gained their biggest success of the season, by 7-0, at home to their 'bunnies' from Newport.

The fire brigade had to deal with an outbreak under the stand during the game at Orient's ground, but it was Notts who were 'on fire' against Newport, racing four goals ahead in the first half-hour. Harry Fearnley, the Welsh club's goalkeeper, was injured in his attempts to cope with that barrage. Full-back Doug Hayward took over for the second half, in which Sewell's completion of a hat-trick took him to third place in the Third South scoring list – five behind Lawton's 23 and two behind Forest's Wally Ardron.

In my reports for the *Derby Evening Telegraph* on matches at Meadow Lane and the City Ground, it was my good fortune to see two of the most prolific scorers of those days, Lawton and Ardron, so regularly in action. But from their fifteen goals of February, and their biggest win, Notts went to being denied any in losing 0-4 at Ashton Gate, as Bristol City inflicted one of their biggest defeats of the season. Five goals were later conceded at Northampton, though one for Notts on that occasion, by Broome, made the margin the same. Sewell was injured during the game in Bristol, and his deputies, Chapman and Simpson, both scored in his absence from the next three matches. After a 4-2 home victory against Brighton in which Chapman was on the mark, Simpson snatched a late equaliser at Walsall, where Notts made a remarkable recovery from being three down ten minutes from time, then nicked both goals in the defeat of Millwall.

Sewell returned on the right wing at Swindon, where an equaliser for the injury-hit home side cost Notts their first away win over the Wiltshire club for fourteen years, after Simpson had once more been their scorer. After that, Sewell missed three more games. In the first, Simpson was again among the goals in a 3-1 Good Friday home win against Port Vale, a mid-table side fresh from dimming the promotion hopes of Torquay. The Devon club's failure at Vale Park was sandwiched between their defeat at Bristol Rovers and the loss of their unbeaten home record to Southend in the lead up to Easter. Another setback for Torquay on Good Friday, at Brighton, was therefore their fourth in succession. Despite that, they clung onto the runners-up spot they had held since Notts' January defeat at Watford, where Simpson, deputising for Baxter at centre-half, had also scored – but into his own net.

After the matches on Good Friday, however, the gap between Notts, who had two games in hand, and Torquay had widened to seven points, with Forest two points further away in third place. And where were Torquay the next day? At Meadow Lane, of course. It was another of the ground's big attractions, and nearly 44,000 saw Torquay gain a first-half lead that it took one of Lawton's specials to wipe out. The hard-earned point left Notts needing just three more from their remaining six games to make sure of promotion – only for them to falter again with defeats at Port Vale and Aldershot. On an Easter Monday of high winds and heavy rain, with snow in some parts (an uncomfortably sharp contrast to the sunshine of Good Friday), another Lawton goal was the lone counter to the three conceded at Vale Park. Against Aldershot, second from the foot of the table, Notts looked anything but a promotion side in failing to score at all while having their defence breached twice.

Consolation for those setbacks came with the knowledge that Torquay, down to third, and Nottingham Forest, fourth, were now out of the reckoning, and that Southend, who moved up to second by beating Forest at the City Ground, had only an outside chance – five points behind Notts, both with four games to play. Once more, the fixture list served up a match fit for the occasion. Where better than at home to their Forest neighbours for Notts to clinch the rise for which they had been yearning? And that is precisely how things worked out. The Meadow Lane attendance record was boosted to 46,000 for a pulsating encounter won with second-half goals from, most appropriately, Sewell and Lawton.

Notts' team that memorable afternoon was also the one that had won at the City Ground, but Forest were without Geoff Thomas and Jack Hutchinson at full-back, and Horace Gager and Jack Burkitt in the half-back line. This was how they lined up:

County: Smith; Deans, Rigby; Chapman, Baxter, Adamson; Broome, Sewell, Lawton, Evans (W), Johnston.

Forest: Walker; Whare, McCall; Anderson, Rawson, Morley; Scott, Love, Ardron, Capel, Kaile.

On the same day, 22 April, Doncaster Rovers became champions of the Third Division's Northern Section.

Northampton, who had dislodged Southend from second place by narrowly defeating them in Essex, were County's visitors on the following Thursday evening, when two more Lawton goals rounded off the Lane season in championship style, but with the crowd reduced to under 32,000. Lawton, as well as Sewell, missed the return game two days later in which Northampton gained their emphatic 5-1 revenge, and also the final 2-2 draw at Exeter on the following Saturday. These were the final top-of-the-table positions, with Notts' points total the lowest for a club promoted from the Southern Section of the Third Division since Newport's 55 in the last pre-war season:

1949-50	P	W	D	L	F	A	Pts
1 Notts Co	42	25	8	9	95	50	58
2 Northampton	42	20	11	11	72	50	51
3 Southend	42	19	13	10	66	48	51
4 Nott'm For	42	20	9	13	67	39	49
5 Torquay	42	19	10	13	66	63	48

In the lowest-scoring season since the offside rule was altered in 1925-26, Notts County were again the leading scorers in the whole League, if with seven goals fewer than in the previous season. Gateshead, runners-up in the Third North, were second to Notts' 95 with 87. Lawton's share of 31, plus two in the Cup, headed the Third South individual list, but the League's overall top marksman was Grimsby's Tommy Briggs. He scored 36 in the Second Division (despite which the Mariners could finish only 11th), four in the Cup, and another for England 'B'.

The transformation at Notts County, for which Lawton was largely responsible, was so marked that the only surprise was that the climb out of the Third Division did not come sooner. The title seemed firmly in sight when the team he had found struggling with only three wins from sixteen games improved to end his first season sixth from the top of the table. Yet Notts slipped to eleventh in 1948-49, when the gap between themselves and the promoted side widened from the previous season's fifteen points behind QPR to nineteen adrift of Swansea, before the long-awaited rise was achieved in 1950.

Nearly two dozen players were called upon during the promotion season, but nine of them were called upon only rarely – five just the once. Harry Adamson and Roy Smith were ever-presents, with Billy Evans one game short of joining them. The other regular members of the side were Chapman (39 appearances), Johnston and Lawton (both 37), Rigby (36), Baxter (33), Sewell (32), Deans (29) and Broome (24).

CHAPTER TWELVE

Disharmony mars rise to Second Division

Promotion brought Notts County not peace and prosperity but disharmony and decline. Life at Meadow Lane was never the same again for
Tommy Lawton. He described it as 'a shocking contrast to the idolisation
and admiration I had received earlier, and one I could no longer tolerate.'
Not only did his marriage end in divorce around that time. He also had
to contend with growing unrest in the dressing room. This was how he
saw it, as expressed in his book *When The Cheering Stopped*:

'Some of the players got swollen-headed because they were now in
the Second Division, and started telling me how to play the game.
Naturally, this caused ructions. I was a man who had to speak his mind.
It was my influence as much as anything which had won the championship, and I resented the implications which were being made.'

The situation was not helped because there were also allegations that
Lawton wanted to be the manager. He revealed that the board had sounded him out about becoming player-manager following the departure of
Arthur Stollery, whom he rated as 'a great masseur', but considered 'too
kind a man to be a good manager'. Lawton claimed that after his refusal
of the post the directors had turned to Eric Houghton at his suggestion,
and he further maintained that Houghton had accepted only after visiting him at his home and being assured that he could depend on his support. Even so, Lawton conceded that he had had 'many arguments on
policy' with Stollery, despite the fact that they were good friends, and had
taken on some of his responsibilities by conducting tactical talks in the
dressing room in addition to having 'quite a lot to do with the coaching'.

In such circumstances it was perhaps only to be expected that some
suspicion of Lawton's intentions should remain, especially as he did not
endear himself to several members of the playing staff by making it clear
that he did not consider them to be up to Division Two standard. There
were also allegations that he received preferential treatment from the
directors, though he did not exactly encourage full backing from that
direction either by saying he 'just couldn't see eye to eye' with some of
them. And, on top of all that, Lawton's marital affairs were in what he
called 'purgatory'. He tried to push them into the background by concentrating on his football, but eventually, the gossip around Nottingham
led him to hire a private detective to seek the legal evidence for the
divorce he obtained.

Without Lawton, who was unfit, County got off to a miserable start to the 1950-51 season by going without a goal through losing each of their first three matches. In his absence, the forward line was led first by Alec Simpson at home to Coventry, by Fred Evans away to QPR, then by Frank Broome at Cardiff. A team otherwise little changed from the full-strength promoted line-up dismayed the expectant majority in a crowd of 41,000 by conceding a goal in each half to Coventry. That was on the mid-August day when the League's aggregate attendance of 1,189,401 set a record for a Saturday with the inclusion of more than 30,000 at the two additional Third Division games involving the four newly elected clubs in the North and South sections.

One goal decided the match with QPR in which John Paxton, a full-back from Wolves, made the first of only two first-team appearances, and there was much confusion about that solitary score. In the scramble that ensued from the last of three corners taken in rapid succession by Rangers' outside-right Billy Waugh, it was first credited to Bert Addinall, then to Cyril Hatton against his old club. Afterwards, Henry Adamson admitted the ball had gone into his own net off his head.

As on the opening day, a goal either side of half-time was conceded in the defeat at Cardiff, where Sewell, replaced by Bob Crookes, was also absent through injury, and the adaptable Simpson continued in the centre-half berth he had taken over from Baxter at Shepherd's Bush.

So it was into a team at the bottom of the table, and still minus Sewell, that Lawton reappeared in the return Thursday evening match with QPR. He did not score, but a first point was picked up and last place handed over to Swansea. Billy Evans and Crookes netted for Notts, and George Wardle, a former Exeter and Cardiff winger, for QPR, before Addinall put the visitors 3-2 ahead with his second goal with ten minutes to go, but Broome, back on the right wing, equalised a minute later.

Meanwhile, fortunes were flourishing across the Trent, where Forest were building on four opening wins on their way to following their neighbours as champions of the Third South. Tommy Capel, a key member of that Forest team, was a friend from schooldays of Peter Robinson, who now established himself as Notts' right-half in Division Two after playing in a couple of games during the run-in to promotion. Both Manchester-born, Capel and Robinson had played together for Manchester Boys, and had signed amateur forms for Manchester City on the same day. Two years later, shortly after turning professional, they had also enlisted on the same day – Capel in the Royal Marines, Robinson in the Army – and in 1946 they had been demobilised yet again on the same day. They had left Manchester City together for Chesterfield on 23

October 1947, in an exchange deal that had taken winger Billy ('Legs') Linacre from Saltergate to Maine Road.

The pair's path had finally divided in the summer of 1949 with the move Capel briefly made to Birmingham before joining Forest. Now, through Robinson's transfer from Chesterfield after a spell out of the League with Buxton, here they were back together in the same city, but on opposite sides of the river.

After getting back into the team for the visit of Birmingham, Robinson was to hold his place for the rest of the club's first season back in the Second Division, and for much of the next, before leaving for King's Lynn. Birmingham turned up at Meadow Lane as Second Division leaders, but they were lucky to win by an only goal against a side that played the better football and hit the crossbar three times.

Having failed with a £15,000 offer to Cardiff for inside-forward Doug Blair, Notts followed a draw at Leicester with a 4-1 win at Grimsby in which the returning Sewell scored twice and Gordon Bradley replaced Roy Smith in goal seven months after arriving from Leicester. Sewell could not have failed to impress the watching Arthur Drewry, but the intention of the chairman of the England selectors to have another look at Lawton as a spearhead happened to coincide with a change of forward tactics, whereby the Notts captain stayed deep to direct attacks in which Broome and Johnston were the visitors' other scorers.

Gordon Bradley had been the goalkeeper twice beaten by Jesse Pye in the 1949 FA Cup final, but he had been in that Leicester side at Wembley only because Ian McGraw broke a finger in a battle with Grimsby after the shock semi-final win over Portsmouth, the First Division leaders and coming champions. The FA granted applications for consolation medals to be struck not only for McGraw but also for his clubmate Don Revie, unable to play at Wembley because of a serious loss of blood after breaking his nose, and Larry Kelly, the Wolves full-back who also missed the final through injury.

Bradley, a professional lawn tennis player, began his senior soccer career with his home club Scunthorpe in their Midland League days. He joined Leicester in 1942, and played almost 70 League games before his move to Notts in search of regular first-team football. He would make more than 200 further appearances in League and Cup up to 1958, when he left for Cambridge United.

The next newcomer to the Notts team after Bradley in September 1950 had also played in an FA Cup final, but on the winning side – for Derby against Charlton four years before, when the trophy had first been at stake after the war. In common with Lawton and Broome, however,

Leon Harry Leuty, a polished and resourceful centre-half, had previously played for Notts in wartime, his dozen games during that period having included the one against Forest in which Lawton had guested.

Leuty was born at the quaintly named Meole Brace, a village near Shrewsbury, on 23 October 1920, but he moved with his family to Derby when only two or three years old and first played football there as a schoolboy – in goal. That, though, was for just the one match, in which he let in eight. He was next an inside-forward before settling down in defence, where he became a regular member of the Derby Boys team.

Successful as he was in that sphere, Leuty had no hankering after a career in football when the time came for leaving school. 'I wanted something that would stand me in better stead of the future,' he told me, 'so I turned to engineering. I became a fully fledged toolmaker during the nine years or so I spent with Rolls-Royce, and it was not until after I had completed my apprenticeship that I began to think seriously about full-time football.' And then, as he put it, his career was nearly over before it had even started. Bolton and Chesterfield both turned him down after trials, and, although he was then signed as an amateur by Derby, he had to have a cartilage operation when he damaged his right knee in an 'A' team match shortly before war broke out.

Soon after he had made his comeback in the Rolls-Royce team, Leuty was offered a trial by Frank Womack, a former Birmingham full-back who was then manager of Notts County, having guided Grimsby into the First Division, and to an FA Cup semi-final, during the 1930s. But again Leuty's luck was out. He fell awkwardly in the loose earth that filled a crater caused by a German bomb, and, as he put it, 'bang went another cartilage.' Considerable damage was done to the Meadow Lane pitch and the north end of the main stand during an air raid in May 1941, preventing the club from playing any matches in the following season. The one after that, 1942-43, was well advanced by the time Leuty had fully recovered from his second operation, but Womack did not forget him. In being given a regular place with Notts over the season's last three months, Leuty came to consider that he owed more to Womack, the first to recognise that centre-half was his best position, than to anybody else for getting under way up the football ladder.

Lee (as Leuty was known in the abbreviated form of his first name) would have been brought into the Notts team a month earlier, but had been unable to travel to Lincoln because he was on the night shift at Rolls-Royce. Jack Nicholas, the long-serving full-back who was then acting as Derby's team manager, got to hear of this, so he called round at Leuty's home, got him out of bed, and persuaded him to help out the

Rams instead. That was how Leuty came to make his first-team debut for Derby, still as an amateur, in their then record 10-0 home win against Mansfield on 9 January 1943. Five of the goals were scored by Dave McCulloch, a pre-war Scottish international, but he was out of the first-team reckoning by the time Leuty helped Derby, captained by Nicholas, to win the FA Cup for the first time.

Leuty also played in Derby's return game with Mansfield, drawn without McCulloch the following Saturday, before answering Womack's renewed call. A few weeks later, he was in the Notts team that knocked Derby out of a wartime League Cup in the first round, by 5-3 on aggregate over two legs. Bill Corkhill was also in the side that won 3-1 at Meadow Lane, helped by a goal from Stoke's George Antonio, later a Derby player, and then drew 2-2 at the Baseball Ground.

The only defeat Notts suffered in the dozen games Leuty played for them that season was inflicted by Sheffield United at Bramall Lane, where Colin Collindridge, guesting against the club he was soon to join, made the only reply, from the penalty spot, to the four goals conceded. Notts had to wait only a week for 2-1 revenge. There was one other defeat for the Magpies during that period, their heaviest of the season in their penultimate match, but Leuty missed it to play again for Derby. In his absence from the Notts defence, the man he would have been marking, Welsh international George Lowrie, scored four of Coventry's seven goals. Leuty, too, was on the losing side that day. Crewe Alexandra won 3-1 at the Baseball Ground.

If Womack, who subsequently managed Oldham, had stayed at Meadow Lane, Leuty might well have remained there too – and thus saved Notts the £25,000 fee, then the record for a defender, that they had to shell out in September 1950 to get him from Bradford Park Avenue, the club to which he had moved from Derby for £20,000 the previous March. Those quick deals temporarily made him the costliest player in the game, ahead of Bobby Brennan, Trevor Ford and Leslie Johnston, the three other players on whom more than £40,000 had then been spent in total. And of the two dozen biggest transfer fees up to that time, the only two not involving forwards were those paid for this handsome, debonair central defender who had been hailed as 'probably the best of the wartime football finds'. Peter Doherty, the famous Irish international who was among Leuty's team-mates at Derby, described him as 'the coolest centre-half I knew'. Tommy Lawton once named him as the most difficult centre-half he had faced.

To have such high praise heaped on a player who never turned out for his country in a full international was highly unusual, but Leuty must surely have been capped if his peak years had not coincided with those in which Neil Franklin was England's automatic centre-half. Ironically, the Stoke pivot was one of his best friends in football. They also shared an interest outside the game as their local representative for a London firm of wine and spirits merchants. Derby allowed Leuty that job in the autumn of 1949, to placate him after refusing the first of his transfer requests; Franklin took up his around the same time after re-signing for the Potters on the settlement of a dispute with the club's directors.

Leuty, four times an England reserve, had become a forgotten man as far as his country was concerned by the time Franklin ended his international career in making his ill-starred venture into South American soccer, but he had already played for England in a match for which caps were not awarded, and had also captained the national 'B' team and Football League XI, besides appearing for the FA. The first of Leuty's representative honours was gained in an FA team that defeated a Combined Services side 5-2 in Dusseldorf. This was shortly after he had paid his first visit to the Continent on a tour Derby made to entertain the troops in the autumn of 1945. Jesse Pye was also in that FA XI.

The 'capless' England game in which Leuty took part was against Scotland at Maine Road on 24 August 1946, in aid of the Bolton Disaster Distress Fund. This followed the death of 33 spectators, with five hundred injured, in the crush when barriers broke at an FA Cup-tie between Bolton and Stoke the previous March. Tommy Lawton was also to have played in the Fund match, but had to withdraw through groin trouble suffered during Chelsea's summer tour of Switzerland. The result was a 2-2 draw, Willie Thornton, the Rangers centre-forward, equalising with his second goal five minutes from the end. England's goals were scored by Charlton's Don Welsh, one of them from a penalty.

In the month after that match, Leuty was at centre-half in the Combined XI which drew with an FA XI at Nottingham Forest's ground in the unofficial international trial that was also a charity game in aid of Willie Hall's benefit fund.

'Neil Franklin expressed some surprise that I did not jump from being his shadow to becoming his successor when he went to Bogota,' said Leuty, 'but, irrespective of anything else, my prospects no doubt suffered because I was then outside the First Division. It was no new experience for me to be a runner-up for international honours. I also just failed to make the grade during my schooldays in the mid-1930s. I played in a North v South trial, and for England against The Rest, but the nearest I could get to the England Boys team was to be selected as reserve against Ireland and Scotland.'

CHAPTER THIRTEEN

Tragic early death of Leon Leuty

On being reclaimed by Derby after his spell with Notts County, Leon Leuty became a fixture in the Rams' team from the beginning of the 1943-44 season, and on its last day made his professional debut. It was not an auspicious entry into the paid ranks, for he put the ball into his own net for the only goal of a game at Leicester

Leuty would total almost 300 appearances for Derby, 158 of them in League and Cup, before his unexpected move to a Bradford side struggling in the Second Division, in preference to staying in the First with Sunderland. He explained: 'Fred Emery, then manager of Bradford, was so persevering – even after I had given him a "No" – that I finally decided to take the plunge with him and his lads to try to help them out. To begin with, I fancied we might do it, but two successive defeats virtually put paid to our hopes, and down we went.'

Leuty had become dissatisfied at Derby mainly because he had been expected to keep playing when not fully fit, troubled by strained stomach muscles. It was, however, when he was not chosen even though reporting fit that he repeated his request for a transfer. Difficulties had also arisen over a benefit. Derby had been prepared to pay him the maximum £750, but the League had refused to sanction more than £600 because they had no record of his having been with the club before the war. The amateur forms he had signed had been lost or mislaid.

Although Notts were in a similar plight to Bradford's when he joined them, Leuty welcomed the chance to go back to the East Midlands, especially as he had not relished life in the rigorous outposts of the Third Division North. 'I had been well treated by Bradford, who, I must say, were very decent about letting me leave so quickly,' he said, 'but I wanted to get back on home ground.'

He took over from Simpson, who switched to inside-left, for the visit of Preston on 23 September 1950. Although Notts had picked up only one point from the season's first four games at Meadow Lane, Preston had lost each of their previous four away matches. There were therefore some hopes of a home victory, but they were not to be realised. Notts, urged on by another 44,000-plus crowd, dominated for the first half-hour, but lacked punch. One of Preston's three goals, to which Simpson made the only response, was scored by left-winger Angus Morrison, who had been with Leuty at Derby.

Leuty remained a first choice for the rest of that season, and also for the following four, apart from being dropped on just one occasion. That was for the visit to Forest in the autumn of 1953 to which reference has already been made – the match in which Bill Baxter, as Leuty's replacement, made his farewell appearance. Leuty was promptly restored after the heavy defeat suffered in his absence, and it was through injury that he missed only fifteen other matches in totalling 188 League appearances, and a dozen in the Cup, before his death at the early age of 35 on 19 December 1955.

Constant battering around the kidney area in his aerial tussles with rampaging opposing forwards took their dreadful toll. Leuty was admitted to hospital for observation and treatment in September that year, and, although he returned to his Beeston home in October, he was readmitted the week before his death. Until then, having bought a car, he was able to undertake a few scouting duties for the club.

Notts finished in the bottom half of the Second Division for all but the last of the full seasons Leuty spent with them, but he still managed to attract revived interest from the England selectors. This was especially so after he had been among the players whose names were considered for the FA tour of Australia in which Broome and Sewell took part, but the closest he came to an international recall after joining Notts County was to play for the England XI that defeated Young England 2-1 at Highbury in April 1954. Tommy Lawton headed the winner in a match that raised more than £8,000 for charity. The teams were:

England XI: Bartram (Charlton); Mozley (Derby), Smith, L (Arsenal); Johnston (Blackpool), Leuty (Notts Co), Cockburn (Manchester United); Matthews (Blackpool), Mannion (Middlesbrough), Lawton (Arsenal), Shackleton (Sunderland), Langton (Blackburn).

Young England: Sims (Wolves); Sillett (Chelsea), Byrne (Manchester United); Adamson (Burnley), Smith, T (Birmingham), Edwards (Manchester United); Hooper (West Ham), Quixall (Sheffield Wednesday), Hines (Leicester), Viollet (Manchester United), Pilkington (Burnley).

An England selector had another look at Leuty when Notts conceded six goals at Luton. This was after Notts had dropped only one point in their first five games of the 1951-52 season. Leuty was below his best that September afternoon. He had not been getting enough sleep while his son Stephen, then six months old, was cutting his teeth, and two of those goals were scored by the man he was marking, George Stobbart, a former Newcastle centre-forward. Two of the others came from Jack Taylor, who was to make Notts County his next club.

Dominant as Leuty usually was, there were two other 'hits for six' he had to endure. Two months after that hammering by the Hatters, Derek Dooley scored five against him for Sheffield Wednesday at Hillsborough (Sewell got the other goal against his former club), and on the opening day of the 1953-54 season Welsh international John Charles bagged four of Leeds' six at Elland Road. Dooley equalled the record individual scoring feat against Notts in their then 63 years of League football. Five had previously been put into their net by Fred Morris of WBA in 1919, and 'Artillery Billy' Hartill, of Wolves, in 1929.

Roy Smith, the former Owl who was in goal for the Magpies before again losing his place to Gordon Bradley, instilled false confidence with his reply when team-mates asked about Dooley, then still little known after only five first-team games. 'Oh, that big useless bugger,' Smith said. 'Don't worry about him, he'll never score.' For the first half that prediction looked spot on. Leuty hardly allowed Dooley a kick.

But what a transformation after the interval. Wednesday were then playing towards the Kop, and Dooley fancied that. 'It was like a magnet to me,' he recalled. 'It was an awful day, and the heavy going suited me because I was a bit quick. With Albert Quixall and Jackie Sewell alongside, I managed to score five times in 32 minutes. Three times I ran onto through balls. One was a header, and I chested the other in. I even got a sixth, but that was disallowed for offside. I remember Smith coming up to me afterwards and putting his hand on my shoulder. It meant a lot did that.' It was the first time a Wednesday player had scored so many goals in a League match since Duggie Hunt's six against Norwich in 1938.

In complete contrast to today, there was no big car for Dooley to ride home in as hero of the hour. After the match he queued in the rain for his No 2 bus. As he said himself, 'Five goals in the second half, and you got the bus home!' He also remembered an old fellow climbing aboard wet through and telling the conductor: 'I was just going to leave the match when this young Dooley scored, so I thought I'd stop and see if he got another. When he did, I said, blow me, maybe he'll get three. And so it went on. I just stood there and got ruddy soaked!'

That was the season in which Dooley's 46 goals propelled Wednesday to promotion. Leuty was himself tried at centre-forward – just the once – after Notts had gone through four games without a goal. Lacking support because his inside-forwards lay too far back in an exaggerated 'W' formation, he did not score in the 2-3 defeat at Everton in September 1953, but hit the bar with a header for Johnston to net from the rebound. The four goals Leuty did score for Notts all came in his first season with the club, while playing in his usual centre-half position. Two of them were penalties – the winner in the League at home to Chesterfield, the other in a Cup-tie that Southampton won 4-3, also at Meadow Lane.

For Derby, Leuty had scored once in wartime and once in the League, but had been denied a perfectly good goal in the Cup. A substitute referee, called in at short notice when the original official went down with influenza, failed to notice that a Bury defender was standing on the goal-line as Leuty headed the ball in, so he blew for offside. On having a linesman confirm his mistake, he opted for a bounce-up because he felt that the Bury defenders had relaxed on hearing the whistle. Fortunately for him and for Derby, who were a goal behind at the time, the Rams recovered to force a replay they won emphatically.

Rare as straying from defence was for Leon Leuty the footballer, when it came to cricket he was ever eager to go on the attack. One Sunday afternoon in 1949, I was among the onlookers when he smote fourteen sixes in scoring 138 runs in 47 minutes for the Derby County cricket team in a match at Breedon-on-the-Hill in Leicestershire. He reached his hundred in 37 minutes. Set 230 to win, the Rams lost lost their opening pair in the first over, both run out without scoring, but they reached their target with a few balls to spare.

Leuty was Notts' captain until he was taken ill. Tommy Lawton, having become increasingly disillusioned with life at the Lane, expressed a wish to be relieved of the post, and it was at his suggestion that Leuty led the team out for the first time for a home game with Leeds on 10 November 1951. As the change had not been announced beforehand, it was quite a surprise for the fans, giving rise to much speculation that remained rife until Lawton's departure the following March. Leuty won the toss, but Leeds recovered from a half-time deficit to win 2-1.

There were then some 150 games ahead for Leuty before he became ill over the summer of 1955. He played in Notts' first two games of the new season, lost by three goals at Middlesbrough and drawn 2-2 at home to Barnsley, but it was obvious that he was far from well, and he had treatment at home before going into hospital for the first time. What was to be his final appearance, for Barnsley's visit on the Thursday evening of 25 August 1955, was also Gordon Bradley's 100th in succession.

After his first discharge from hospital, Leuty returned to Meadow Lane to watch the match in which Notts defeated Plymouth Argyle 3-0 on 5 November. On the following Monday he also revisited the Baseball Ground for the last time to attend the game in which Derby played an All-Stars XI in aid of the wife and two children of his former Rams colleague 'Chick' Musson, who had died from leukaemia the previous April – also tragically young, five months short of his 35th birthday.

Leuty had been one of the pall-bearers at Musson's funeral, but his own health had since deteriorated alarmingly. Suffering from anaemia, in addition to his kidney trouble, he was soon back in hospital for a blood transfusion. On his return home a few days later he declared himself much improved, but his condition quickly worsened again, and he went back into hospital for the last time after being examined by the club's doctor. He died six weeks after returning to Derby for the match at which he had joined those paying tribute to the memory of his friend and former team-mate. As there had been for Musson, there was an overflowing attendance for his funeral service, held at Christ Church, Chilwell.

A match was also arranged, between Notts County and Wolves, for the fund opened in support of Lee's wife Wendy and their two sons, but it had to be postponed from early February in 1956 until later in the season. Burst pipes after a sudden thaw caused flooding in the Meadow Lane dressing rooms and damaged ceilings. The receipts from the rearranged game produced a £1,750 cheque for Mrs Leuty, shortly after she received £500 from a testimonial fund started by the Notts County Supporters' Club. She was also given the benefit money for which her husband had qualified shortly before his death, and there were also donations from the players of a number of other League clubs.

Oswald Jackson, then Derby County's president, described Leuty as 'a man of wonderful character, a footballer of outstanding ability. He was always a genuine fellow, and a player who did a tremendous lot for Derby County, and, in more recent seasons, for Notts County.' George Poyser, Notts' manager at the time, said: 'I shall never have a greater clubman. Leon's death is a great loss to football.' Among the many other tributes, one from Peter Doherty stood out: 'He was a grand fellow, one of my dearest pals. As a centre-half he was in the top class. Had the old Derby team stayed together, I am certain he would have gained the honours he certainly deserved.'

CHAPTER FOURTEEN

Lawton 'pupil' who became costliest player

If there was one Notts County player who most benefited from being in the same team as Tommy Lawton, then that man was surely Jackie Sewell. This quick-moving Cumbrian was the Mapgies' leading scorer in the season before the great man arrived, but he really blossomed out alongside him. He became the costliest player in the game, at £34,500, when he left for Sheffield Wednesday on 15 March 1951, the day before the annual deadline for unrestricted transfers – and only four days after a suggestion that transfer fees be restricted to £15,000 had been put forward at a Football League meeting in London. 'I owe a lot to Tommy Lawton,' said Sewell, then not quite two months past his 24th birthday.

The deal, which valued Sewell at about £500 an inch, also deprived Notts County of their president, George Cottee, and another director, J H Levey. Both resigned shortly before Christmas that year because, as they explained in a joint statement, they were 'in disagreement with the policy of the board and part of the minority who strongly opposed the transfer of Jack Sewell as we felt it was not in the best interests of the club.' The other members of the board, from which H S Hobson had recently also resigned, said the decision had been made 'to strengthen the club's resources for future team building,' adding that 'the offer was of such magnitude as to demand full consideration of the club's interests'.

But fans, too, were quick to express their displeasure. One branch of the Supporters' Club, at Southwell, even threatened a boycott. Yet the deal almost certainly would never have been done if Wednesday had not first failed to sign either Jimmy Hagan or Jesse Pye. Hagan refused to cross the city from Sheffield United after a fee of £32,000 had been agreed; Pye declined to leave Wolves after the clubs had also come to terms. Only then did the Owls' manager, Eric Taylor, turn to Sewell.

Notts County had signed Sewell as a part-time professional on his seventeenth birthday, 24 January 1944, and he made his first-team debut in a League North match at Doncaster the following October. He played twenty other matches that season, scoring six goals, but opportunities to show his undoubted potential became rarer in the transitional one of 1945-46 that followed, and it was not until the Football League got under way again that he really began to make his mark. Until then his appearances were restricted by his work at the Bestwood Colliery coalface as one of the conscripted Bevin Boys. These were named after Ernest

Bevin, then the Minister of Labour and National Service who, late in 1943, introduced a bill whereby youths due to be called up for National Service could be employed down the mines instead of going into the armed forces. They were urgently needed to help cope with the acute coal shortage.

Sewell's 21 goals in the first post-war Third South season of 1946-47 trebled the output of the club's next highest scorer, Gordon Jayes. Had he been given better support, County could have ended closer to Cardiff's champions instead of being 26 points behind in mid-table. Alongside Lawton the next season, Sewell himself provided the support as Notts climbed from fourth off the foot of the table to sixth from the top. Lawton scored eighteen goals in the nineteen League games he played after his transfer from Chelsea. Sewell netted only one fewer, but from 41 matches. To those totals, Lawton added six in the Cup, Sewell four.

In 1948-49, when Notts slipped back to mid-table, Sewell was the club's only ever-present, and in the League he outscored Lawton, who was absent six times, by 26 goals to twenty. Twice they both netted four times in a home match – in a 9-0 romp against Exeter, who conceded six in twelve second-half minutes, and a hammering of Newport that could have been even greater than 11-1 because Lawton hit a post from 35 yards and Doug Pimbley, a versatile player from Birmingham, had a goal controversially disallowed. Newport must have come to dread their visits to Meadow Lane. They conceded 33 goals in five consecutive League matches there, ranging from that double-figure eclipse to a 1-8 beating on the last day of September in 1961. A record of its kind.

That 1948-49 season was the one in which Lawton also scored four goals in the 9-2 defeat of Ipswich. By the end of it he and Sewell, not yet 22, had already plundered 87 goals between them since coming together – a combined tally that finally reached 160 in the 116 games they shared. Notts County's promotion in 1949-50 was followed by the season in which Sewell made his disrupting exit to Sheffield. His rapid development earned him a tour of Canada with an FA party in 1950, and he made another, in company with Frank Broome, to Australia in 1951, shortly after going to Hillsborough. From getting just seven goals in Canada, he advanced to being the tourists' top scorer in Australia with 34 – six out of seventeen in the second 'test' in Sydney and all seven in the defeat of Victoria in front of a record crowd of almost 30,000. One of the goalkeepers he and Broome came up against Down Under was a motor engineer by the name of Norman Conquest – not at all apt as it turned out. He let in six goals.

Sewell, who replaced Stoke's injured Frank Bowyer in the Canadian Touring XI that lost 2-4 to a World Cup XI at Stamford Bridge in the Charity Shield match of 1950, went on to overtake Tom Keetley as Notts County's all-time leading goalscorer. He completed a century of goals in a 3-2 defeat of Grimsby at Meadow Lane on 13 January 1951, and left the club with a total of 104 (97 in the League, seven in the FA Cup). In 166 games, Tommy Lawton went on to reach 103 for Notts, 90 of them in the League. Since then, the club's individual record has passed first to Tony Hateley, whose 114 included four in the FA Cup and one in the League Cup, and currently to Les Bradd, whose 137 comprised 125 in the League, four in the FA Cup, seven in the League Cup and one in the Anglo-Scottish Cup.

Sheffield Wednesday needed Sewell and his goals to help them stay in the First Division, to which they had returned only the previous season after an absence of thirteen years. When he joined them they were at the foot of the table with ten games to play – on twenty points with Aston Villa, who had the better goal-average and a match in hand. Immediately above them were Chelsea, on 22 points from two fewer games than Wednesday. Sewell scored in his last game for the Magpies (drawn 2-2 at home to Southampton), and again in an impressive debut for the Owls, though it was not enough to avert defeat by Liverpool at Anfield. Worse still for his new club, Villa edged to a home win against Burnley that afternoon, and Chelsea picked up a point at Sunderland. The situation was further complicated by heavy reverses that sucked WBA and Huddersfield into the relegation reckoning, with Everton hovering uncomfortably on the fringe.

A dropped point at Everton and a loss at Villa Park made Wednesday's plight look desperate indeed, but Sewell revived hopes of escape with the late 'golden' goal, as it was described at the time, that I saw him score to snatch a 4-3 midweek home win against Derby, after the Rams had recovered from two down to share six goals by half-time. He chased a seemingly lost cause when Walter Rickett, a former Sheffield United and Blackpool winger, put over another centre, and screwed the ball inside a post from a difficult angle. It had been against Derby, on successive Saturdays in November 1944, that Sewell had scored the first two of the eight goals he netted for Notts in 28 games before the resumption of League football.

Sheffield Wednesday's hopes of avoiding relegation lingered to the final day, only to be dashed in the cruellest of circumstances. Their only defeat in their last six games was by the only goal at Spurs, whose clinching of the League title the year after being Second Division champions emulated the feats of Liverpool (1905-06) and Everton (1931-32). A week later, Wednesday signed off with a 6-0 home thrashing of Everton, Sewell scoring twice for a total of six goals since his transfer, but it served only to take their victims down with them.

Wednesday made an immediate return as Second Division champions on the back of 46 goals from a gangling young giant of an auburn-haired centre-forward with size twelve boots. Yes, that was Derek Dooley, whose meteoric rise was so soon and so tragically to be curtailed by the amputation of his right leg. That was the result of infection which complicated a double fracture in a second-half collision with the Preston keeper at Deepdale on the murky February afternoon of St Valentine's Day in 1953. Lawton played in Dooley's testimonial match, scoring one of the goals in a 5-1 win for an International XI against a Sheffield team in 1955, in the first game under the new Hillsborough floodlights. There was an attendance of 55,000, with receipts of £7,500. Jackie Sewell scored for the combined side.

Sewell contributed 23 goals towards Wednesday's 1951-52 promotion total of exactly 100, four of them in a home win over Cardiff that enabled Wednesday to wrest the leadership from the Welsh club. And in the November of that season he won the first of his six England caps in a victory gained with two goals from Bolton's Nat Lofthouse against Northern Ireland at Villa Park. Having done well in the Football League's victory over the Scottish League at Hillsborough a fortnight earlier, Sewell joined Gil Merrick, the Birmingham goalkeeper, and Len Phillips, the Portsmouth inside-left, as an international newcomer. He and Phillips were recommended from a talent search specially conducted by an FA committee.

To mark the occasion, Sewell was presented with cutlery, a silver cigarette box and an illuminated address on behalf of the people of Kells, his birthplace. He had played for the Kells Town team after helping Kells Boys to win the Moss Shield, and, as the outstanding member of a footballing family (two uncles played for Kells, two others for Workington), he was the first soccer international produced by that Cumberland village.

Sewell might have kept his place for England's next match, against Austria at Wembley a fortnight after the game with Northern Ireland, but for being given a short break by Sheffield Wednesday. Manager Taylor thought he would benefit from a rest after nearly two years without one, because of his close-season tours of Canada and Australia. As a result he could not be contacted when the FA decided to invite him to the practices arranged in Manchester. He was then excused from the one England training session that remained when he was located, and his place against the Austrians was taken by Manchester City's Ivor Broadis, another new-comer.

As it turned out, however, Sewell still faced Austria when he made his next international appearance, for that was in Vienna the following May. He scored in a 3-2 victory, and also in a 3-0 win over Switzerland in Zurich three days later, when Nat Lofthouse again bagged England's two other goals.

The rest Wednesday offered Sewell the previous winter lasted for four matches, during which he was replaced by Redfern Froggatt, a first-team regular for the past six years who was back in contention after being injured in a pre-season practice match. Four years on, Froggatt was to emulate his father, Frank, in captaining the club to the Second Division title – their third promotion of the decade straight after relegation.

Sewell's next exclusion from the Wednesday line-up arose from his selection against Northern Ireland, drawn 2-2 in Belfast in October 1952. 'I've had a talk with Jack,' said Eric Taylor, 'and he has sportingly agreed that the forward line of the team that beat Stoke in his absence playing for England should have another chance.' That meant eighteen-year-old Albert Quixall, later of Manchester United, kept his place at inside-right, and this time Sewell missed five matches, in which unchanged Wednesday dropped only one point, before Quixall's switch to the right wing, as deputy for the injured Alan Finney, let him back in.

Wednesday won at Blackpool in one game Sewell missed, and it was then that he went to see the manager to clarify his position. 'I think I should be in the team,' he said, 'but there doesn't seem much chance at the moment.' But he had to wait only one more game, won against Chelsea. He finished the season as the club's highest scorer, with the inclusion of the Cup goal in defeat at Blackpool that inched him one ahead of the stricken Dooley.

Relegation again looked to be Wednesday's fate until their final match, in which Sewell did the hat-trick in a 4-0 home win over Sunderland that lifted them clear. They had another close call in 1953-54 after the welcome distraction of an FA Cup run had ended in a semi-final defeat by Preston. Sewell was the club's second highest scorer that season with nineteen goals to left-winger Dennis Woodhead's 21, and earned a recall to the England team after a year's absence. It was not, however, a happy return. He had the misfortune to be involved in a couple of crushing defeats that brought other international careers besides his own to an abrupt end.

On 25 November 1953, the Magyar Marvels of Hungary, the reigning Olympic champions, shattered England's 90-year immunity from home defeat by a Continental team with a 6-3 triumph at Wembley. Sewell was among the scorers that chastening afternoon, but not in the 1-7 crushing defeat in Budapest the following May. In between, he alone of the forwards on those demoralising occasions was in the Football League side that beat the League of Ireland 9-1 at Maine Road. He and Don Revie, then with Manchester City, both did the hat-trick.

Having missed selection against Scotland, Sewell scored one of the Football League's four goals in their win over the Scottish League at Stamford Bridge in April 1954. This gave rise to talk of his being selected for the next full international against Yugoslavia in Belgrade, but it was not to be.

Time was also soon to run out for him with Wednesday. He was their top scorer with fourteen goals in 1954-55, encouraging inquiries by Arsenal and Manchester City, but that was the season in which they again plunged back to Division Two – this time conceding 100 goals. They were also knocked out of the FA Cup by Notts County in a replay following a 1-1 draw at Hillsborough. An ankle injury suffered in the original tie prevented Sewell's reappearance at Meadow Lane, but he was in the side that shared two goals there in the League the following October. It was not, however, a scoring return. Wednesday's point-saver was Redfern Froggatt.

Two months later, after scoring thirteen goals in fifteen games, Sewell was dropped, even though Wednesday were catching up and would win Division Two by three points from Leeds. 'Jackie hasn't missed a first-team match this season,' said Taylor. 'He has always been a great favourite with us, and was intended to play an essential part in our fight to return to the First Division, but this long spell has affected his form slightly, so a change to the Reserves may do him good.' It did. After playing, as his manager conceded, 'brilliantly' in three games in the Central League, Sewell was brought back for a home match with West Ham, drawn 1-1 with a goal from Roy Shiner on the last Saturday of November in 1955.

But that was Sewell's Wednesday farewell. Before the next week was out his transfer took him back to the top flight by a quicker route than that followed by the players he was leaving. It reunited him with the manager who had so reluctantly parted with him at Notts County, and it was still in Sheffield, but over at Bramall Lane, that he again got off to a scoring start. More about that in due course.

CHAPTER FIFTEEN

Renewed clamour for Lawton's England recall

Notts County's struggle to stay in the Second Division intensified after their sale of Jackie Sewell to Sheffield Wednesday in March 1951, and Tommy Lawton to Brentford a year later.. From being eleventh in the table when Sewell left, they sagged to seventeenth, winning only one of their remaining ten matches. After Lawton's farewell appearance they lay tenth, but fell away to finish fifteenth, gaining just two victories in their last nine games. In 1951, they ended nine points clear of the relegation zone. In 1952, that gap was reduced to five.

The heavy reliance Notts had placed on Sewell's goals became uncomfortably clear when they failed to score in six of the ten matches after his departure to Hillsborough. In those games, no fewer than five players were called upon to fill the inside-right position he had vacated: Broome, Billy Evans, Johnston, Simpson and Adamson. In the season after that, six others were among the nine tried there – one of them Lawton, shortly before his departure.

In his last match for Notts, Sewell took his tally for the 1950-51 season to fourteen with one of the two goals that earned a home draw with Southampton, who had recently been Cup winners at Meadow Lane. And that total was not overhauled, though Tom Johnston equalled it with three of the nine County subsequently scored.

Where, you may ask, did that leave Tommy Lawton? Well, he went from 33 goals of the promotion-winning season to a mere nine in his first tilt at Second Division defences. Bad luck was partly to blame. It was estimated that he hit post or crossbar no fewer than thirteen times before getting off the mark as Notts belatedly won for the first time at home, at the seventh attempt, beating Barnsley by 2-1 in late October. Other reasons were the deep-lying role he was at times required to fill, the brilliant saves goalkeepers made at his expense, and his absence from a dozen of Notts' 42 matches.

There was also the fact that Lawton had again relinquished penalties. Although Lee Leuty converted two after taking over from Frank Broome, he failed in a home win over Bury. Consequently, although Broome and Leuty were in the side, Lawton was back to the task, but not for long, in a home win over Barnsley in the first month of the following season.

In his most productive spell of his 1950-51 blight, Lawton answered his mounting critics with two powerfully struck goals in a 4-1 home win against West Ham in late November, equalised two minutes from the end in a 2-2 draw with Hull in the next League game at Meadow Lane, and a week later bagged the brace that broke Coventry's unbeaten home record. Both goals at Highfield Road came in the opening quarter of an hour, starting in the first minute when his marker, Martin McDonnell, mis-kicked on the frozen surface. Relegation was only another season away for Coventry, but at that time they were second in the table.

On the last Saturday of 1950, Notts evoked talk of climbing from Third Division to First in successive seasons by beating Birmingham, another promotion contender, 4-1 at St Andrew's. Notts were then in mid-table, seven points behind Coventry, the new leaders, with a match in hand. Their position was considered comparable to Portsmouth's the previous season. The Fratton Park club had trailed the First Division leaders by five points, with the same number of games played, yet had claimed the championship for a second consecutive year.

The demolition of Birmingham also renewed the clamour for Lawton's England recall. He did not score that bitterly cold afternoon, Sewell and Crookes sharing the four goals, but he led the line in such style that in the *Daily Mail* Roy Peskett again appealed to the selectors on his behalf. He told them that their New Year resolution should be 'to go to a printer, get him to set in big type: "I Must Choose Lawton Against Scotland," and hang the notice where you can see it every day.' He added: 'I have no hesitation in saying that Tommy is still far and away the best and most intelligent centre-forward at England's command. The parrot-cry is still raised that Lawton does not score goals now. He does not need to if he can make three every week, as he did on Saturday. Fit, fast and fearless, he was the only County player to scorn heavily ribbed knee pads on the treacherous surface.'

In the *Sunday People*, Sam Bartram, a goalkeeper whose opinion of opposing forwards demanded the utmost respect, rated Lawton the best of the top ten strikers he faced in his career of some 800 games with Charlton: 'Terrific shot in either foot, could head the ball with as much speed as some players could shoot; excellent positional play; amazing tim-ing; speed in the box.' Behind Lawton in Bartram's assessment came Jimmy Greaves, Arthur Rowley, John Charles, Tommy Taylor, Jackie Milburn, Bobby Charlton, George Best, Trevor Ford and Nat Lofthouse – in that order. He also mentioned Brian Clough, Ted Phillips, Peter Harris, Ronnie Allen, John Atyeo and Pat Glover. To be put first among such a galaxy of talent was an accolade indeed.

But there was still to be no international return for Lawton. Stan Mortensen, recalled after missing all eleven matches England had played since winning at Hampden the previous season, was preferred at centre-forward against Scotland at Wembley on 14 April 1951 – the match the Scots won 3-2 after Wilf Mannion had gone off with a fractured cheekbone early on. Six others had led the line since Lawton won what was to be his last cap: Milburn (Newcastle), Pye (Wolves), Rowley (Manchester United), Bentley (Chelsea), Lee (Derby) and Lofthouse (Bolton).

Although overlooked by the national selectors, Lawton's form at that point temporarily quelled rumours of his impending departure from Notts. These rumours had been feeding on the undercurrent of unrest in the dressing room while the team had been in or around the relegation zone throughout the early months of the 1950-51 season. 'The only time I move from Nottingham is to go to an away game,' he was quoted as saying, but talk of his transfer to a London club was to prove prematurely accurate.

Neither were County's hopes of a happier new year to be realised as they won only four games out of eighteen after the win in Birmingham. That success was their sixth of the season away from home – double the number they had gained at Meadow Lane, and more than any other club in the division had then achieved on their travels – but they failed to add to it in losing five, and drawing three, of their remaining away games.

Two of those away draws in the closing weeks were at Manchester City, heading for promotion as runners-up to Preston, and Blackburn, who finished sixth. There was then a third successive goalless game when Leeds, who would finish fifth – a point behind Birmingham – were the next visitors to Meadow Lane.

The Easter Monday match at Maine Road was thoroughly entertaining despite its lack of goals and the bad weather (a mixture of incessant rain and patches of mist). Roy Smith, enjoying another run in the side, stood between Manchester City and the win their dominance deserved, and Bert Trautmann, the German who had won over those who at first had not welcomed him as a former prisoner of war, pulled off the save of the game to thwart the applauding Lawton.

The return scoreless fixture, rearranged for a Monday evening in late April, was watched by Meadow Lane's smallest League crowd of the season, under 14,000. It was originally to have been played on Good Friday, but had to be postponed when a blizzard turned the heavy pitch into a morass. On their previous visit to Nottingham, in the first post-war season, it had been Forest's ground which the Manchester club had found unplayable. On that occasion, however, it had been possible to switch the match to the County side of the swollen river Trent. The pitch there had drained more quickly, and, in any case, it was further from the river and on slightly higher ground.

An improved home record in the second half of the 1950-51 season steered Notts out of trouble, though only one of their four additional wins was gained after the departure of Sewell to Sheffield. And even then Notts had to hang on grimly to a 3-2 lead after being two up at half-time against Swansea, who ended those two points below them in eighteenth place.

That match with the Welsh club marked the League debut of Geoff Brunt, a Nottingham-born part-time professional who was employed in the city police's forensic department. Brought in on the right wing, he made an encouraging first impression, being involved in the moves that led to all three Notts goals, but he was only infrequently used in the first team over the next two seasons, mostly at wing-half, before going into the Central Alliance with Heanor Town.

The week before Swansea's visit, Ron Mann, a half-back from a boys' club in his home town of Doncaster, made his debut at West Ham, where Notts faded to defeat after going two up through Johnston in the first half. Lawton claimed that Jim Barrett, later of Nottingham Forest, impeded Roy Smith when he stood in front of the goalkeeper and then opened his legs to allow a shot from Bill Robinson to pass through for the third of the home team's four goals. Ted Fenton, the Hammers' manager, afterwards revealed it was a ploy his players had been practising, and neither referee Clough, nor the linesman he consulted, saw any reason to object to it.

With Simpson reverting to left-half from his one-off try-out as a Sewell successor, Mann was omitted from the game with Swansea, never to appear with the seniors again before his move to Aldershot. Two other players also made just the one League appearance for Notts that season. It was a farewell one for Bart Purvis, but the first of more than 200 for Don Roby, a tricky winger who, nevertheless, had to wait four years for his second selection.

Roby, from Billinge, in a Lancashire coal-mining area between St Helens and Wigan, was signed when Bolton, Everton and Manchester United were also interested in him. Given a job on the Meadow Lane groundstaff until he was old enough to become a professional, he had not long turned seventeen when he was introduced into the team for a home match, won 3-0, against Sheffield United on 24 February 1951. With National Service then intervening, he was next seen in the League side in a 2-1 win at Lincoln on 16 March 1955.

For the next six seasons Roby was a familiar name on the Notts team sheet, and he earned a fee of £10,000 when he moved to Derby in August 1961. He missed only one match in his first season with the Rams, playing on both wings, and remained a first choice until having to undergo a cartilage operation near the end of the next one. On his return to fitness, he found Gordon Hughes too well established to dislodge after being signed from Newcastle. After one further first-team appearance, taking him to a career total of 314 in League and Cup, he was transferred to Burton Albion in June 1965.

By that time, Notts County were down in the Fourth Division with home gates often under 5,000. They had enjoyed only one season in the top half of the Second Division before enduring successive relegations. Their decline in 1951-52, the last season with Lawton in their attack, was especially disappointing, considering that they had been among the early pace-setters – briefly leaders in early September and never outside the top six until that Hillsborough humiliation by five-goal Derek Dooley on the first Saturday of November.

The Notts Co team that won 2-1 at Crystal Palace in September 1949 – Back row (left to right): Bill Corkhill, Harry Chapman, Aubrey Southwell, Roy Smith, Norman Rigby, Harry Adamson.. Front row: Fred Evans, Bob Crookes, Tommy Lawton, Billy Evans, Tom Johnston

Bert Loxley (top) and Ken Lawson  Tommy Lawton with Denis Compton (left)

Howard Wilkinson, one of
many Notts County managers

Ken Armstrong, who temporarily
took over from Lawton as leader
of the Chelsea attack

Bill ('Dixie') Dean, another
international centre-forward
who played for the Magpies

England v Sweden (Highbury, November 1947. Lawton's first of four caps as a Notts player. Back: Laurie Scott (Arsenal), Phil Taylor (Liverpool), Ted Ditchburn (Spurs; reserve keeper), Frank Swift (Manchester C), Neil Franklin (Stoke), Billy Milne (trainer). Seated: Stan Mortensen (Blackpool), Tommy Lawton (Notts Co), George Hardwick (Middlesbrough, capt), Billy Wright (Wolves), Harry Johnston (Blackpool). Front: Tom Finney (Preston), Wilf Mannion (Middlesbrough)

Cyril Hatton with QPR after his transfer from Notts Co

Leon Leuty in his Derby County days

Jack Wheeler, Huddersfield's goalkeeper and later a long-serving trainer with Notts Co, advances as if prepared to pounce on team-mate Lawrence Morgan during a match at Highbury

Billy Evans, who was among the signings from Aston Villa

Peter Robinson, whose career was linked with that of Forest's Tommy Capel

Gordon Bradley, a goalkeeper who
was also a professional tennis player

Bill Baxter, who 'swapped'
clubs in a wartime oddity

Harry Adamson, a wing-half from
Jeanfield Swifts who played nearly
250 games for Notts County before
moving to Gainsborough Trinity

Hughie Gallacher, who joined Notts Co
late in his career, pictured while with Chelsea

Ken McPherson,
a footballing former paratrooper

Oscar Hold, who
was briefly with
Notts Co before
leaving for
Chelmsford City

Tommy Lawton on the ball for Notts County

Frank Broome collides with Chelsea's goalkeeper, Harry Medhurst, while playing for Derby County at Stamford Bridge

Jesse Pye in action for England

Jimmy Linton, a Glaswegian goalkeeper

Cecil McCormack, a £23,000
centre-forward from Barnsley

Tony Freeman, a winger
from Melton Mowbray

Aubrey Southwell, a Notts defender
in more than 400 games

Jimmy Jackson, scorer of four
goals in his third League game

Roy Smith, a goalkeeper from
Sheffield Wednesday

Johnny Morris, who was later offered to Notts Co in a suggested exchange deal, looks on as Cyril Sidlow, Liverpool's Welsh international goalkeeper, saves at the feet of Frank Broome in a Derby County attack at Anfield

Leon Leuty (striped shirt) in a heading duel with Ken Plant, Bury's centre-forward

The squad of the 1949-50 season in which Notts County were Third Division champions – Back row (left to right): Billy Baxter, Tommy Deans, Aubrey Southwell, Roy Smith, Eric Houghton (manager), Norman Rigby, Harry Chapman, Harry Adamson. Middle row: Frank Broome, Jackie Sewell, Tommy Lawton, Billy Evans, Tom Johnston. Front row: Fred Evans and Alec Simpson

Tom Johnston, a versatile player and a disciplinarian as manager

'Tot' Leverton, another of the
Notts signings from Forest

Eddie Gannon, a stylish
wing-half capped by Eire

Jack Edwards, one of the many Notts
players who were also with Forest

Notts towards the end of the 1956-57 season, when the club escaped relegation under the acting management of Frank Broome. Back:: John McGrath, Gordon Wills, Gordon Bradley, Jimmy Linton, Aubrey Southwell, Bob Bulch. Middle: Don Roby, Gerry Carver, Frank Broome, Frank Cruickshank, Ron Wylie. Front: Jimmy Jackson, Bert Loxley, Peter Russell, Jack Taylor

Alec Simpson, an adaptable newcomer from Wolves in the 1949-50 promotion season

Bill Corkhill, the second oldest, after
Albert Iremonger, to play for Notts Co

Leon Leuty in action for Derby County

Ray Chatham, a versatile
part-timer whose career was
handicapped by niggling injuries

Bob Crookes, who hit
both posts with one shot

Ian McPherson, a wartime Mosquito pilot
who was awarded the DFC and bar

Joe Mercer, with whom Lawton
was briefly reunited at Arsenal

The Notts Co staff of 1957-58, Tommy Lawton's season as manager. Back: Peter Russell, Gerry Carver, Harry Noon, Cyril Parry, Jack Lane, Hill, Bob Bulch, John McGrath. Middle: Dixon (masseur), Syd Dickinson (scout), Pat Groome, Gordon Wills, Bert Loxley, Jimmy Linton, Gordon Bradley, Frank Cruickshank, Harvey, John Kilford, C H Heath (secretary), Jack Wheeler (trainer). Front: Frank Broome (assistant manager), Jimmy Jackson, Ron Wylie, Frank Sherwood (director), Len Machin (chairman), Bertram Edwards, Len Linnell (directors), John Sheridan, Don Roby, Tommy Lawton (manager). Front: Tom Asher, John Gissing

Eric Houghton, the player and here as manager

Hughie Gallacher, a Magpie with Newcastle and Notts

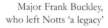

Lord Brabazon of Tara, the chairman, chatting with former referee Arthur Ellis before the first
Football Pools Panel's assessment of the results of postponed matches during the terrible winter
of 1963. Ted Drake is on the far left. Tommy Lawton is second from the right

Peter Doherty, who joined
Notts Co in an advisory capacity

Major Frank Buckley,
who left Notts 'a legacy'

Tommy Lawton in classic action for Notts County

Players in the Division Four promotion season 1959-60 – Back row: Alex Gibson, John Butler, Bobby Forrest, George Smith, Bert Loxley, Tony Hateley, Harry Noon. Middle: Jack Wheeler (trainer), Don Roby, Chris Joyce, John Sheridan, Gerry Carver, Peter Bircumshaw, Frank Hill (manager). Front: Alan Withers, Stan Newsham, Roy Horobin

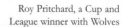

Jackie Sewell in action for Sheffield Wednesday, who made him the game's costliest player when they signed him from Notts Co

Roy Pritchard, a Cup and League winner with Wolves

Jesse Pye, then of Wolves, tries a back flick in an attempt to beat Ted Sagar, the Everton keeper

Tommy Lawton leads
out Notts County

Tommy Lawton in
action for Notts
County

Tommy Lawton in classic County action

The Fourth Division champions of 1970-71 – Back: Mick Jones, Dave Needham, Les Bradd, Barry Watling, Brian Stubbs, Bob Worthington, Jack Wheeler (trainer). Front: Jon Nixon, Richie Barker, Don Masson, Jimmy Sirrel (manager), Tony Hateley, John ('Bill') Brindley, Charlie Crickmore

Jesse Pye, who made a hat-trick start to his League career

George Poyser, a popular manager dismissed after a vote of confidence

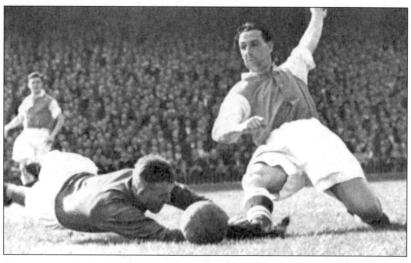

Tommy Lawton challenges Portsmouth's goalkeeper, Norman Uprichard, for possession in one of his games for Arsenal

Alan Brown, a redoubtable defender with Burnley, but failed to settle down at Meadow Lane

Ron Wylie, a schoolboy discovery in Scotland

CHAPTER SIXTEEN

Jackson, Wylie, McCormack, Ken McPherson

In October 1951, a few weeks before that Dooley drubbing in Sheffield, two exciting young Glaswegians were brought into the Notts County attack, either side of Broome (Lawton was out with bronchitis), for a match at home to Doncaster won with a goal from Bob Crookes. One of them was Jimmy Jackson, who had been signed from Mapperley Celtic, a Nottingham club, three years before; the other Ron Wylie, who had been taken on from the Scottish junior club Clydesdale Juniors as a fifteen-year-old amateur in July 1949, turning professional in September 1950.

Wylie was rated by Eric Houghton as the finest young inside-forward he had ever seen. 'When he played in the "A" team,' said the Notts manager, 'he showed that he was a natural footballer.' Before giving Wylie that first League chance, Houghton had made a point of playing in a Midland Midweek League game at Leicester, so that he could give advice on the spot to the schoolboy international for whom he predicted the brightest of futures. Soon after that, in October 1950, Wylie was first introduced into the first team for a game against Chesterfield in aid of the Creswell Colliery Disaster Fund. This was County's line-up: Bradley; Paxton, Purvis; Robinson, Corkhill, Simpson; Evans (W), Sewell, Lawton, Wylie, Johnston.

To begin with, however, it was Jackson who made the biggest impression. He had appeared only once in the League side, without scoring, in a home win over Bristol City towards the end of the 1948-49 season, but he was chosen against Doncaster after top-scoring with ten goals for the Reserves. Notts seemed to have found the perfect answer to the inside-right problem caused by Sewell's exit when, in only his third League game, this slimly built Scot cracked in four goals in a remarkable 5-1 away win against Everton, newly relegated from the First Division.

Injuries soon hampered Jackson's progress, most notably when, a year later, he suffered a double fracture of the jaw in the eighteenth minute of a home defeat by Sheffield United. On the following Good Friday, recalled at centre-forward for a match in which Plymouth were the winning visitors, he was put out of action again, this time with a twisted back.

After that 1952-53 season, Jackson went off to Canada. He returned shortly before Christmas in 1954, and three weeks later, on New Year's

Day, fired in four more goals as Notts sent West Ham packing in another 5-1 spree. It was mainly as a centre-forward, punctuated by further absences through injury, that Jackson completed a half-century of goals in 122 League and Cup games before his move to Headington United, as Oxford United were then known, during the 1958 close season.

Ron Wylie also scored four times for Notts in one match, in a 5-0 home win that ruined the promotion hopes of Birmingham, one of his future clubs, in the last home game of 1951-52, but he was a stylish creator of goals rather than a frequent scorer. He netted 68 in the course of 630 matches in a career he also shared with Aston Villa. For Notts, he scored 38 in 237 games, totals he might have exceeded but for breaking his right ankle in a defeat at Fulham (Roy Dwight, soon to join Forest, scored the only goal) early in the 1957-58 season, by which time Wylie had risen to the captaincy.

Tommy Lawton, who was then Notts' manager, and twelfth man Ken Tucker helped trainers Frank Penn (Fulham) and Jack Wheeler lift Wylie from the field. Refusing to accept a gloomy prediction that his career was finished, Wylie made his comeback in the 'A' team in March 1958, after taking part in several practice matches, and he returned to League action against Liverpool later that month.

It was through a chance conversation between strangers at a match between Partick Thistle and Clyde that Notts County became Wylie's first League club. One of them was Notts' scout in Scotland, who was running the rule over Tommy Deans, the Clyde full-back who was to have Wylie among his team-mates at Meadow Lane. The other was Wylie's father. The scout was immediately interested when he heard that Wylie had played three times for Scotland Boys, and had scored the winning goal against Ireland in Belfast in helping to win the schools international championship. As a result, Notts wasted no time in avoiding the mistake made by Burnley, who had turned down the fourteen-year-old Wylie because they had considered him too small. At the beginning of his senior career, Wylie's slight build was indeed a handicap, causing him to lack stamina in heavy going, but farmwork during the summer quickly built up his physique.

After his rejection by Burnley, Wylie added to his growing reputation in Scotland by winning two Juvenile Cup medals with Clydesdale Juniors. It was a big step for him to take for one so young when he agreed to join Notts County, but shortly before he broke into the first team he had the close support of his parents, who moved to live in Nottingham.

Back in 1951, when Wylie and Jackson were still raw recruits, they were soon followed into the Notts County team by Cecil McCormack, a centre-forward built on Hughie Gallacher lines who was signed from Barnsley for £23,000 – originally in anticipation of a move by Lawton to Hull that fell through.

It was mainly as cover for Lawton that Notts had already acquired Ken McPherson, a 6ft red-haired former paratrooper who was born at West Hartlepool and turned up at Meadow Lane from Horden Colliery. There were high hopes for this strong, sturdy, bustling type of player, but, at inside-right, he got off to a disappointing start in a draw at Bury on the last day of September in 1950, twice missing the target when it seemed easier to score. The nearest approach to a Notts goal that afternoon was made by Lawton, even though he again played behind the other forwards. His shot hit the foot of a post.

There were few other first-team opportunities for McPherson until halfway through the 1952-53 season, when he began a sustained run at centre-forward with four goals, three of them in eight second-half minutes, in a 5-0 home win over Blackburn. That was the kind of form for which Middlesbrough would fork out £15,000 over the summer, but he was unable to help them stay in the First Division. He enjoyed most success on moving into the Southern Section of the Third Division with Coventry, his price reduced to £8,000, two years later. To the 30 goals he had equally shared between Notts and Boro, in over 60 games, he added 40 in nearly 100 appearances for Coventry before having three seasons as a centre-half with Newport County. He was finally with Swindon, retiring at 37 in 1964.

McCormack had played for Gateshead, his home club, during the Second World War and afterwards regularly travelled from Bournemouth, where he was stationed in the RAF, to continue turning out for them. His 150 or so goals in three seasons with Gateshead enticed Middlesbrough into paying £6,000 for him towards the end of the first post-war season, but his opportunities on Tees-side dwindled as his scoring rate fell away. He was transfer-listed at his own request when, in August 1949, now in his mid-twenties, he moved into the Southern League with Chelmsford. That was also the time Oscar Hold joined the Essex club from Notts County, after scoring only nine goals in nineteen League games since his arrival from Norwich.

Barnsley had had a £10,000 bid for McCormack accepted by Middlesbrough, but he preferred the bigger pay packet Chelmsford could offer than the one the Football League permitted in those days of the maximum wage. They got their man, however, for that price during the 1950 close season. He was promptly back in the goals, with five in a 6-1 beating of Luton, and he had more than 40 to his name – 33 of them as the Second Division's top scorer of 1950-51 – when Notts nipped in to sign him.

McCormack made his debut in a home match with Cardiff. that Notts were lucky not to lose after going ahead through Jackson in the first minute. There were only ten minutes to go when Stan Montgomery, the centre-half who played cricket for Glamorgan, headed an equaliser, but the visitors had been victims of a split-second decision on the hour when they got to ball into the Notts net, only for the referee to award them a free kick, which was cleared, for an infringement by Leuty.

Injury kept McCormack out of the next two games, both lost, but he looked the part by scoring in each of three successive victories that ended eight weeks without one, during which the team tumbled from fourth to sixteenth. The first of those overdue successes, against a Coventry side next to bottom, was gained despite being reduced to nine men by injuries to Ian McPherson, who was in his first season back from Arsenal, and Simpson.

The brief revival ended at Bramall Lane on Boxing Day, when one goal by Sheffield United avenged Notts' 3-1 win on Christmas Day, but the new year began in rousing style for the Magpies as they achieved revenge of their own. Ten of the players fielded in the six-goal humbling at Luton back in September were in the team that edged through 5-4 in the return. McCormack for Johnston was the only change in personnel, though right-winger Ian McPherson alone occupied the same place in a reshuffled attack. The in-form Lawton was the only home forward not to score, but that was one of the matches in which he hit the goal frame. The margin of victory would also have been wider but for Luton's goal having a remarkable escape when, from a shot by Bob Crookes, the ball hit the foot of one upright, rebounded across the goal-line, hit the other post, and went behind for a goal-kick.

Crookes ended that season Notts' highest League scorer, but Broome equalled his total of fifteen goals with the inclusion of the two he netted, a week after Luton, in a 4-0 Cup victory over Stockton. By then, Broome had again been entrusted with penalties, first in Lawton's absence from a 3-4 home defeat by Southampton, then with one of the goals he put into Stockton's net. Lawton also scored twice in the Cup, finishing his final season as a Notts player with twelve more in the League.

Half of Lawton's fourteen goals came in his last nine games for the club. Six of those were at home, and in five of them the Meadow Lane attendances dipped below 30,000. Three of those gates were not much more than 20,000. This decline from those heady days leading up to promotion had accelerated with the falling-off in League form, but there had already been an indication of some slump in support. Whereas more than 40,000 turned up when Coventry were the visitors at the start of Notts' first season back in the Second Division, the crowd was down to 34,000 when the same club played at Meadow Lane on the opening day a year later.

Special occasions still pulled the fans in, but there were only two home attendances over 40,000 during 1951-52. The first was the obvious one in mid-September, when Forest's promotion renewed League rivalry with their neighbours. Over 44,000 saw Notts fortunate to draw after going two down just after half-time. Without both Leuty, sent to Skegness to recover from gastric influenza, and the injured Ian McPherson, they were mostly outplayed even though Forest sharpshooter Wally Ardron was slowed by a muscle injury. Yet suddenly they saved themselves by scoring twice in the final five minutes. Broome was allowed to run through to halve the deficit when he looked offside, and Crookes was on the spot to equalise when Harry Walker, in the Forest goal, did well to parry a Lawton piledriver.

There was also an attendance of more than 40,000 at the City Ground the following January, when Forest recovered to win 3-2 after trailing at half-time to goals scored by McCormack and Broome. That was one of the matches in which McCormack led the attack with Lawton alongside him as Ian McPherson's partner, and Broome in the other inside-forward position.

The other bumper gate at Meadow Lane that season was shortly before Lawton's exit. It raised the record to 46,500 for a fourth-round Cup-tie that First Division Portsmouth won 3-1 in February 1952. Lawton broke even in his duel with Jack Froggatt, England's reigning centre-half, and scored the Notts goal. According to Lawton's own reckoning, he scored the 400th goal of his career in the 53rd minute of a match between Everton and Stockport at the Gwladys Street end of Goodison Park on 27 January 1945 (one of his four goals in a 9-2 win). A month after Portsmouth's visit, he reached 200 in the League alone with the first of his two in the 5-1 win at Doncaster.

Those goals, however, were the last Lawton scored for Notts. A week later, on 8 March 1952, he played his final game in a scoreless home draw with, appropriately, his old club Everton. On the same day, incidentally, another former Everton (and Notts) forward, Oscar Hold, scored a first-minute goal on his debut for QPR in a home win over Southampton. Here are the teams for Lawton's first and last matches for Notts County:

At Northampton: Brown; Southwell, Howe; Gannon, Baxter, Corkhill; Houghton, Sewell, Lawton, Marsh, Cumner.

Against Everton: Bradley; Allen, Deans; Robinson, Leuty, Adamson; McPherson (I), Broome, Lawton, Crookes, Johnston.

Lawton did not actually ask for a transfer, but he accepted the club's public announcement that he had insisted on one because of his domestic problems. Chairman Charles Barnes emphasised that he and his fellow directors did not want to lose Lawton, who had been voted the most popular sportsman in the Nottingham area as holder of the Seely Cup hitherto held by Chick Zamick, of the Panthers ice hockey team. 'But,' said Barnes, 'He was insistent, and we had no other choice.'

It was indeed the case that Lawton was only too keen to get away, and he left with no regrets. He also departed emphatically denying rumours that he had 'feathered his nest' while with Notts County. 'I received not one penny illegally during my stay at Meadow Lane,' he said. On the other hand, he did not hesitate to point out, quite justifiably, that he had done much to help the club to promotion and benefit financially from gate receipts, away as well as at home in those days when visitors had their share. Notts also recouped all but £5,000 of the fee they had paid for him when he moved to Second Division Brentford, against whom he had scored in a 5-2 home win the previous month (another game in which Broome converted the penalty awarded).

Without Lawton, Notts County headed straight into a four-goal defeat at Southampton, while he made one of Brentford's goals in their first win for ten weeks, 3-1 at home to Swansea. He was mobbed by delighted fans on his arrival at Griffin Park, and skipper Munro stood aside to allow him to toss for choice of ends. Lawton got off the mark in his third game for the Londoners (discounting a half-time abandonment against West Ham in a spring blizzard), scoring the first of their four goals away to Sheffield United. His other goal that season, taking him to sixteen for the whole season, earned a point in the rearranged match with the Hammers.

Ron Greenwood, a future England manager who was then the Griffin Park club's centre-half, commented on Lawton's arrival: 'Now we are really going places.' Jimmy Bowie, who had played alongside Lawton at Chelsea, said: 'The passes Tommy pushes through make you play better. It's great to be with the big fellow again.' Lawton's debut against Swansea coincided with Bowie's first home appearance for Brentford following his transfer from Fulham.

As at Meadow Lane, however, so at Griffin Park. Life there did not work out as well for Lawton as he had hoped. And, as we shall be coming to in its proper turn, neither had Notts County seen the last of him.

CHAPTER SEVENTEEN

Cup battles with Bolton amid relegation fears

Notts County had Eric Houghton as their manager for only one more full season, 1952-53, after Tommy Lawton's transfer to Brentford. They ended it in nineteenth place, three points clear of Southampton, who went down with Barnsley. Four months later, on the first day of September, Houghton resigned when another door opened for him back with his old club, Aston Villa. George Martin, less successful as manager at Villa Park after steering Newcastle to the First Division in 1948, had left to rejoin Luton, the club for which he had last played, and then also managed, before going to Tyneside.

The 1952-53 season began in cricket weather, but to a background of trade slumps, threatened strikes and a higher cost of living. The cheapest admission price to soccer grounds was increased by 3d, of which enter-tainment tax took 2½d, to 1s 9d (just under 10p), but gates on the open-ing day totalled 1,130,000, only 59,000 below the record of two years ear-lier. There were 29,508 at Filbert Street, Leicester, where Notts had signed off the previous season, but this time instead of a 1-1 draw they lost by three goals. The widest margin of the day in the Second Division dumped Notts at the bottom of the table, yet three matches later, if only temporarily, they were up to the dizzy heights of third.

Two of those games brought victories over Rotherham. In between, on the last Saturday of August for which there was an evening kick-off, Notts draw first blood against Forest in front of a near-40,000 Meadow Lane crowd. McCormack gave them an interval lead, and he and Crookes scored second-half goals to which Scott and Ardron replied for Forest. On the same day, incidentally, Bill Holmes' hat-trick in Blackburn's home win over Everton was the first by an amateur in Division Two since the three scored by J C Burns for Brentford against Notts County in 1934.

There was again only one goal in it when Forest won the return at the City Ground early in the new year, scored by right-winger Alan Moore. By then Notts were in mid-table and set to slump still lower. Welcome relief from an increasingly fraught struggle against relegation was pro-vided by an FA Cup win on their return to Leicester, followed by an eventful battle with Bolton that went to two replays before the First Division club edged through at snowy Hillsborough.

One of three changes made for the third-round tie at Leicester, following Notts' failure at Forest, was enforced because newly recruited Jack Edwards was Cup-tied: he had played earlier for Kidderminster. Wylie was recalled at inside-left, Jimmy Linton, a young Scot, was granted leave from his Army unit to replace Bradley in goal, and Johnston was back at left-half in place of Robinson. Leicester went into the match unbeaten at home, in third place with two games in hand on leaders Sheffield United – so form looked likely to run true when they led at the interval with two goals, including a penalty, from the prolific Arthur Rowley to one by Crookes. In the second half, however, Notts hit back to go through 4-2. Broome scored from the spot, and Ken McPherson, who had only recently plundered his four goals against Blackburn, took his tally to nine in seven games by netting twice.

Notts were kept waiting for the identity of their next opponents because Bolton's home tie with Fulham was postponed by fog. The biggest crowd of the round, nearly 64,000, paid more than £7,000 to see, with some difficulty, eight minutes' play before the abandonment of the match between holders Newcastle and Swansea at St James' Park. Bolton (and Newcastle) duly progressed the following Wednesday, but there was the suggestion of an upset at Burnden Park in the fourth round when McPherson gave Notts a first-half lead. Nat Lofthouse's equalising goal still excluded Bolton from the list of only six home winners in the sixteen ties. The big shock was sprung by Rotherham, wreckers on Tyneside of Newcastle's hopes of winning the trophy for a third successive year, despite falling behind after an hour.

For the replay with Bolton at Meadow Lane, Wylie was replaced as the deputy for Edwards by Jimmy Jackson, back in the side for the first time since breaking his jaw in the defeat at Sheffield United in mid-November. As before, Notts scored the only goal of the first half, and it was Jackson who got it. There was another for McPherson in the second half, but skipper Willie Moir's double for Bolton made another meeting necessary after extra-time, much to the disappointment of most in the 34,000 crowd, 6,000 below what was expected.

A first League defeat for Notts in six games, at promotion-seeking Birmingham, was hardly ideal preparation for the second replay two days later, but Adamson, Leuty, Ken McPherson and Southwell were all rested at St Andrew's with slight injuries. Bolton, too, were having problems – and not only because six of their team, danger-man Lofthouse among them, reported for treatment before leaving for Sheffield. On the Saturday, Bolton lost at Portsmouth in the League, and it was not until 5pm on Sunday that their travel-weary party arrived back in Bolton.

Manager Bill Ridding had booked a plane for the journey home, but the League's secretary, Fred Howarth, although sympathetic, could not give permission for it to be used because of a long-standing resolution of the management committee, of which Norman Banks, a Bolton director, was a member. Ridding then arranged hotel accommodation in London for the Saturday night, only for the train the next day to arrive late. Such an exhausting experience might well have counted in Notts County's favour, but that man Lofthouse dictated otherwise. In scoring the only goal in the second half, he maintained his record of scoring in every round. He carried it through to the final, which Bolton dramatically lost 3-4 Blackpool.

The three ties with Bolton attracted an aggregate attendance of almost 97,000, with receipts totalling £13,700. Most of the injured reported fit for that decisive encounter at Hillsborough, but Jackson was excluded. He was not considered back to his best, despite having scored against Birmingham. These were the teams:

Bolton: Hanson; Hartle, Banks (R); Wheeler, Barrass, Bell; Holden, Moir, Lofthouse, Hassall, Langton.

County: Linton; Southwell, Deans; Adamson, Leuty, Johnston; Broome, Evans (W), McPherson (K), Wylie, Crookes.

From the high point of those praiseworthy Cup displays, Notts faded, winning only four of their remaining fourteen League games. Relegation worries were shaken off only with late victories over Barnsley and Hull, two of the other clubs down in the depths. Barnsley's fate had already been sealed by a home defeat to Southampton, who then joined them in the drop despite wins over Blackburn (6-1) and at Nottingham Forest, both in the top half of the table. Only Bury stood between Notts and the doomed pair in the final reckoning.

Notts' inconsistency was most marked when, on successive Saturdays, they lost by six goals at Hull (who had lost 1-5 at Southampton the week before) and, boosted by Ken McPherson's four, won by five at home to Blackburn. Later, a 4-3 win over Doncaster, after trailing 1-3 at half-time, was sandwiched between conceding five at both Brentford and Swansea. Tommy Lawton was among the scorers for Brentford, and Jesse Pye also contributed to his old club's plight by netting twice in both Notts' losing matches with Luton. The 5-1 victory by the Hatters at Kenilworth Road came a fortnight after the Magpies' defence was breached six times at Fulham.

With McCormack temporarily out of favour, Broome and Ian McPherson transferred to Brentford, and Ken McPherson departed to Middlesbrough, Eric Houghton revealed that he discussed buying the

Hibs centre-forward Lawrie Reilly before Notts opened the 1953-54 season with another six-goal thrashing – when John Charles gave Leon Leuty one of his most uncomfortable afternoons by scoring four times. But that attempt to acquire another international leader had even less chance of succeeding than Houghton's interest in another Scotland forward, Jimmy Mason, of Third Lanark, as a possible successor to Jackie Sewell.

Mason, considered one of the cleverest forwards north of the border, had asked for a transfer, with a £12,000 price on his head, after refusing to re-sign because 'sixteen seasons is too long to spend with one club'. But Brentford, Charlton and Portsmouth, for whom he had guested while on Army service during the 1939-45 War, were to remain the only English clubs for which Mason played. Neither did he move to another one in Scotland. He retired from soccer to become a publican in the Bridgeton district of Glasgow, and he was only 52 when he died shortly before Christmas in 1971.

Houghton's quest for Reilly was a lost cause, not only because others in the queue included Manchester City, who had already offered £30,000, Arsenal, Burnley, Newcastle, Stoke, Tottenham and Glasgow Rangers. Middlesbrough might well have been added to that list if it had been formed earlier. 'He's a fine player,' said their manager, Walter Rowley, 'but we have only just signed Ken McPherson from Notts County.' Frank Hill, the former Arsenal and Scotland player then managing Burnley (and later Notts County), said he had made 'a substantial offer' even though he already had Bill Holden, one of the best centre-forwards in England, on his books. 'I want Reilly for anywhere,' he said. 'Buying Reilly is like buying a forward line.'

Arsenal's manager, Tom Whittaker, was the first to hear the end of the Reilly transfer saga. He was ready for a plane dash to Scotland to sign the 24-year-old, who had been with Hibs since the age of sixteen, but when he answered his phone at his North London home just after 6pm on 16 August 1953, he was told that Reilly would not be joining Arsenal, or any other English club. 'I'll quit soccer rather than leave Scotland,' said the player. As he unpacked his overnight bag, Whittaker commented: 'There's a paradox. We can't pay him more than £15 a week. The Scottish clubs can't offer sufficient money for his transfer.'

So Reilly, like Mason, stayed where he was. He almost quit the game during the 1955-56 season when his row with Hibs after they had refused him a testimonial was eventually resolved by the Scottish FA. As it was, pleurisy and pneumonia caused him to miss most of that season, but it was not until 1958, when he scored his 185th goal, that he made the last of over 250 appearances for Hibs. His 22 goals in 38 games for Scotland gave him an international strike-rate second only to Hughie Gallacher's among those capped more than ten times. He is also remembered as one of the 'Famous Five' (the others Gordon Smith, Bobby Johnstone, Eddie Turnbull and Willie Ormond) who made Hibernian the Scottish League champions of 1951 and 1952. He would surely have made as much of an impression as Lawton himself if Eric Houghton's outlandish dream of signing him had become a reality.

Another forward in whom Houghton was interested during his last months as Notts' manager was John ('Kit') Lawlor, a Republic of Ireland international with Doncaster. Not long afterwards, Notts lost at Belle Vue, and, of course, Lawlor was one of Rovers' scorers. By then he had settled his differences with the club after being suspended for failing to return after being given leave to travel to Dublin following a slight injury in training. He returned at about the time Houghton asked about him, but that was when Doncaster lifted their three-month ban and agreed to allow the player frequent leave to revisit the Republic.

CHAPTER EIGHTEEN

Sewell and Wylie follow Houghton to Villa

Eric Houghton was successful with his next ventures into the transfer market after his impracticable inquiries about Lawrie Reilly and 'Kit' Lawlor, but those were on behalf of Aston Villa.

Notts County were third from the foot of Division Two, with only three points from their first four games, and had just been beaten 1-5 at home by Doncaster (a goal for Lawlor), when Houghton left Meadow Lane on 1 September 1953. Two days later, he took over at Villa Park saying: 'When I first came here as a player they said I'd last a month. I stayed twenty years.' His second coming was to last for just over five – until November 1958, when 'it was mutually agreed that his services be terminated' as Villa lay at the bottom of the First Division eighteen months after he had guided them to FA Cup victory over Manchester United at Wembley.

Houghton was next taken on as chief scout by Forest manager Billy Walker, his former wing partner with Villa and England. After that, he was Rugby Town's secretary-manager, and then a scout for Walsall, with whom he was later a director, before rejoining Villa. His third spell at Villa Park was first to assist with the club's new fund-raising lottery. From September 1972 to December 1979 he was on Villa's board, becoming senior vice-president in January 1983. He was two months off his 86th birthday when he died thirteen years later.

The early signings Houghton made as Villa's manager included three from Wolves – Bill Baxter, Nigel Smith and Les Smith – and Pat Saward from Millwall. He had to wait two years to land the player he had been so reluctant to lose while with County. And even then it was only through his persistence that he signed Jackie Sewell from Sheffield Wednesday on 2 December 1955 for a fee reported as about £20,000. The manager who parted with him was no less sorry than Houghton had been to see him go. 'You can say,' said Eric Taylor, 'that Villa have finally broken down our resistance by the size of their final offer. For weeks now we have been saying "No" to offers from Villa and half-a-dozen other clubs.'

Manchester City were prominent among those Sewell-seekers before Villa stepped in. They had hoped to link him in attack with Don Revie, their appetite whetted by the hat-tricks both had scored in the Football

League's thrashing of the League of Ireland at their Maine Road ground. Arsenal were among the others who made inquiries. Tommy Lawton had by then moved to Highbury, and the prospect of again teaming him with Sewell had some appeal.

It was not only Wednesday, but also Sewell, that Houghton had to persuade. 'I didn't want to leave Sheffield,' said the player, 'but when Eric Houghton came up to see me he started putting the old spell of Villa Park on me! All the time we were together at Notts County, when he was a player shortly after the war and later when he became manager for four years, he never stopped talking about Villa. It was no surprise when Eric finally went back to Villa Park, and I suppose it was inevitable that, after spending so much time telling me about the club, he should persuade me to join him.' An added reason was that trainer Billy Moore, then with Villa, had been at Meadow Lane during Sewell's years with County.

When leaving the Owls, Sewell was their leading scorer with thirteen goals from sixteen games, taking him to a League and Cup total for the club of 92 in 175 appearances. Again he was needed to help ward off relegation, for Villa were fourth from bottom in the First Division, having picked up only thirteen points in winning just three of their nineteen matches. As already noted, he again made a scoring start, putting Villa ahead against Sheffield United, the bottom club, at Bramall Lane. Derek Pace, who joined the Blades two years later and was afterwards with Notts County, increased the lead in the second half, but a first away win was denied as United recovered to draw.

This time, however, Sewell was in a team that stayed up – just, despite being without him for eight of their last ten games. He was so seriously injured in a home draw with Charlton in March, when Villa were rock bottom, that it was at first feared he would not play again that season. 'Two things have helped to give Jackie a chance,' said Houghton. 'He is a sensible lad who has done all that he has been instructed, and the Wolverhampton specialist who has been treating his badly torn groin muscle has done splendid work.' It was out of position on the left wing that Sewell returned with only two games left. He did not add to the two Villa goals he had scored before his injury, but Villa won both matches without having their defence breached, and scrambled clear on goal-average. They and Huddersfield, who went down with Sheffield United, both had 35 points.

A year later, with Villa in mid-table, Sewell was in the team that lifted the FA Cup. He was the only member to have played for England, though he had an international colleague who imposed the decisive, controversial, influence on the 2-1 victory over Manchester United that carried

Villa ahead of Blackburn and Newcastle as winners for a then record seventh time – and also cost United's champions the first League and Cup double of the twentieth century.

This was Peter McParland. It was not his two goals, however, that caused all the rumpus. That occurred after six minutes, when his robust challenge on goalkeeper Ray Wood left him with a fractured cheekbone. Wood returned after half an hour, but for only ten minutes, and then as little more than nuisance value on the right wing. He also, and arguably inadvisably, resumed in goal eight minutes from the end, just in time to see Tommy Taylor head a brilliant consolation goal for United.

Aston Villa's fortunes waned once more after that Wembley success, and at the end of the 1958-59 season, in which Eric Houghton was replaced as manager by Joe Mercer, they found relegation inescapable. As before, they went into their final match against WBA. A draw was insufficient to save them from going down with Portsmouth. An Albion equaliser two minutes from time left Villa one point behind Manchester City, who ended with a home win over Leicester.

Like Wednesday, Villa were promoted as champions at the first attempt – but without Sewell. In the summer of 1959 he refused a move to Doncaster after Mercer had told him Rovers' bid had been accepted, but after leading the attack in the first two games of the following season he was transferred to Hull, his value at the age of 32 reduced to £5,000. His scoring rate with Villa had also declined, to 40 goals from 144 games. Yet again he was pitched into a relegation battle, and Hull failed to survive it despite reuniting him in their attack with Roy Shiner, a centre-forward signed from Sheffield Wednesday for a similar sum. Down they went with Bristol City to Division Three.

In April 1961 Sewell left Boothferry Park to play for and coach the Lusaka City team in what was then Rhodesia, now Zimbabwe. His nine goals in 50 games for Hull had raised his career total in League and Cup to 255 in 562 appearances. Afterwards he had charge of the Zambian national side, and he also coached in the Belgian Congo before returning to England in 1973 and becoming a car salesman in the West Bridgford area of Nottingham.

Sewell was followed to Aston Villa by Ron Wylie, who made the move direct from Notts County on 15 November 1958 – the month of Houghton's dismissal as Villa's manager after only five points had been gathered out of a possible sixteen. Having asked Notts for a transfer because he wanted to play in the First Division, Wylie had been much in demand after scouts had seen him give a brilliant display in a charity game at the City Ground the previous May. Playing for Billy Walker's team against Joe Mercer's, he had helped create four goals and scored the other, in a 5-4 win. Forest were believed to have made an offer of £14,000, which was topped by Birmingham, but Villa were the favourites even though they were at the bottom of the table and had put in a much lower bid.

County had originally hoped for a fee in the region of £20,000, but, with Wylie having expressed his preference, they accepted far less, £9,250 according to one source, because they were urgently in need of the money. Also heading for relegation, they had won only two games out of nineteen in the Third Division, and home gates had dwindled to such an extent (under 5,000 for a recent goalless game with Brentford) that they had launched an appeal for loans. 'I am thrilled at realising my ambition to play in the First Division,' said Wylie. He added: 'I have been happy in my nine years with County, and I'll be happier still at Villa,' but in truth he had not been all that happy at Meadow Lane since Tommy Lawton's brief return as manager, of which more later, had ended that summer.

The deal was completed just before a first-round FA Cup-tie in which Notts lost at home to Fourth Division Barrow, thus making Wylie eligible to play for Villa in that season's competition. He did not score in twenty League games for Villa that season (all but six alongside Sewell), but he did the hat-trick when they caused the biggest surprise of the fifth round by winning 4-1 at Everton. At that stage Villa looked likely to reach Wembley despite struggling in the First Division, but in that respect, too, Wylie had chosen the wrong club. Villa lost their semi-final to a lone goal by Forest, who then overcame the early loss of winger Roy Dwight with a broken a leg to beat Luton in the final.

To his 237 appearances for the Magpies, Wylie added 245 for Villa, the first in a floodlit friendly with Hearts. And although his goals for Villa fell ten below his modest Notts total of 38, he rewarded their investment as an important member of teams that won the Second Division championship in 1960 and carried off the League Cup a year later. In his final season of 1964-65 with the club, during which he was switched to wing-half, he had the double honour of being elected Midlands Footballer of the Year and winner of the supporters' Terrace Trophy.

From Villa, Wylie was transferred to Birmingham, who with other clubs had first been interested in him when transfer listed at his own request during 1956-57 when Notts County narrowly avoided relegation. 'It has needed a lot of thought,' he said at that time, 'but I feel that if I stay my game might suffer. I know some people will call me a fool for giving up my job outside the game [he sold underwear for a Nottingham firm] but since I played for the Scotland youth team, and for County at the age of eighteen, I have hoped that one day I might play for my country. I realise I haven't much chance of that if I stay here.' Sadly, however, that was one ambition not to be realised.

Rumours that Notts would part with Wylie had first arisen during the 1953-54 season. They had been so persistent, with Preston particularly keen to sign him, that Charles Barnes, then both president and chairman, issued an official denial, stating that the board were determined not to encourage any approaches for the player. In 1956, Len Linnell, a director at Meadow Lane by whom Wylie was employed, was against the young Scot leaving, and the transfer request was withdrawn. When Birmingham finally got their man, reportedly paying £15,000 in June 1965 a month before his 32nd birthday, Wylie again joined an ailing club, for they had just dropped out of the First Division.

Wylie was unable to help Birmingham back to the top flight in his four full seasons at St Andrew's, but he skippered them to the semi-finals of both the League Cup and FA Cup before retiring. During that time, in November 1968, he rejected the chance to rejoin Notts as player-manager. That was a post that Les Allen, a QPR forward, also turned down while a successor was sought for Billy Gray, the former Forest player who later became groundsman at Meadow Lane. Wylie felt he still had plenty to offer as a player: 'I am convinced that in eighteen months Birmingham will be promoted, and I want to be there.' Unfortunately, things did not work out that way. The Blues, fourth the year before, finished the 1968-69 season seventh, and they were heading for Division Two's lower regions when Wylie's appearances finally petered out as a substitute the next season. It left him one game short of 150 for the club, in the course of which his role as creator for others restricted him to just two goals.

Wylie then did what Eric Houghton had done, twice rejoining Aston Villa – first as coach to the senior side, then with the second team. Between those returns, he was coach and assistant manager at Coventry, a soccer adviser in Cyprus, and manager of both Bulova, in Hong Kong, and WBA. At the Hawthorns he replaced Ronnie Allen, a former Albion and England forward, in 1982 after the post had been refused by Johnny Giles, who had been the club's player-manager a few years earlier. Giles, however, was the man who took over when Wylie was dismissed, along with chief coach Mike Kelly, early in 1984.

Wylie was community liaison officer and youth development officer in his final spell at Villa Park, but he was ousted when Graham Taylor, later England manager, succeeded former Scottish international Billy McNeill, who returned to Celtic, as manager in 1987 following relegation back to the Second Division.

CHAPTER NINETEEN

Revival with George Poyser as manager

The manager Notts County brought in to fill the vacancy left by Eric Houghton was one of the most likeable and fair-minded characters I have come across in professional football. It has been said that the nice guys never win. Well, placid, pipe-smoking George Henry Poyser was a nice guy who did win. Not always, of course, but often enough as a player – and also as a manager until things eventually began to go wrong after successful starts with Notts County and Manchester City.

In his first season as a full-back with Brentford, 1934-35, Poyser won a Second Division championship medal, and during the Second World War he was in their team that defeated Portsmouth in a London Cup final at Wembley. After ending his playing career, he was manager at Dover and a respected chief coach with Wolves before moving to Meadow Lane. There he first shook off the threat of relegation, then guided the Magpies to the FA Cup quarter-finals. In his first season in charge at Maine Road, Manchester City reached the League Cup semi-finals.

Poyser returned to his Nottinghamshire roots in joining County, for he was born, in 1910, at Stanton Hill, in the Sutton-in-Ashfield area near Mansfield. After playing for Nottingham Boys, he was with his fifth club, Port Vale, before making the League grade. The others were a local colliery team, Wolves, Stourbridge and Mansfield. At Molineux, he slipped through the net that Major Frank Buckley cast widely in his search for young talent. With Mansfield, he did not stay long enough to be in their side elected to the Southern Section of the Third Division in 1931, but then made over 70 League appearances for Vale and 150 for Brentford – plus some 200 more for the Bees in wartime. The last three of almost 430 first-team games were played for Plymouth in the first post-war season of 1946-47, by which time he was into his 37th year.

When Poyser joined Notts County on 22 October 1953, almost two months after Houghton's departure, they were in the position where he was to leave them – at the foot of the Second Division. After fourteen games they had only six points and morale was rock bottom. 'Things got to such a pitch,' Leon Leuty later told me, 'that I seriously began to think of making a move. Believe me, it was not a matter of wanting to desert a sinking ship. I had become dissatisfied, and felt there was nothing else for it but to seek a transfer. We were playing like an already doomed side. This reflected itself in an unhappy dressing-room atmosphere that was aggravated by constant team chopping and changing. No fewer than forty changes were made during that period, and, naturally, we all felt very unsettled. We had been left without a manager since Eric Houghton's departure, and, try as we might, we went from bad to worse.'

Then came George Poyser, and, to quote Leuty again, 'he quickly set about putting the house to order. We soon saw that he was both forthright and extremely fair. He had a difficult job to do, and he made no bones about it. He talked straight from the shoulder, restoring contentment among the players and spreading a welcome air of optimism. He won the respect and confidence of us all.'

As a former defender, noted for the strength of his tackle and surprising turn of speed for someone so sturdily built, Poyser gave priority to tightening up a defence that had leaked 38 goals in those fourteen games. Flaws had been evident from the opening match in which John Charles had scored four of Leeds' six goals. Five had been conceded in home defeats by Doncaster and Bristol Rovers, and also, agonisingly, to Forest at the City Ground – the match from which Leuty was temporarily dropped. The game at Leeds was the only one in which Alec Laird, a right-winger from Corby who had been on Chelsea's books, appeared in the Notts first team. On the same August evening, Frank Broome, main sharer of that position with Ian McPherson the previous season, earned Brentford a point with a debut goal at Stoke, but within three months, after five more games and no more goals, Broome was on the move again. Crewe paid £1,000 for him, and he scored for them in his first match.

Laird was one of seven newcomers to the Notts ranks during the three months before Poyser took over. The others were Fred Lovell; Albert Broadbent, Gerry Carver, Gordon Wills, Billy Coole and 'Tot' Leverton. Lovell, a Crewe-born inside-forward, also failed to establish himself, despite starting with a goal in a 3-3 draw at Bury. Broadbent, signed from Dudley, his home club, came to the fore as a forceful left-winger in the Army side while on National Service before his one season as a Notts regular, 1954-55, led him to quick success as one of Sheffield Wednesday's Second Division champions. He was later with Rotherham and Doncaster. Wills, a winger from Wolves, completed a century of appearances for both Notts and his next club, Leicester, but the best of the bunch for service with the Magpies proved to be Carver.

This constructive inside-forward or wing-half, one of Houghton's last signings for Notts, was spotted playing for Aston Boys. He went to work in Houghton's sports shop at Sutton Coldfield before leaving Boldmere St Michael's and turning professional as soon as he turned seventeen.

Absence on National Service contributed to the delay of his regular first-team selection until his fifth season, 1956-57, but he then survived two successive relegations to help in the escape from Division Four at the first attempt in 1960. He had a final run in the side as late as 1966, after another relegation, and his farewell appearance, in a 3-3 home draw with Rochdale on the last day of that season, was his 297th for the club with the inclusion of seventeen cup-ties. After that he was in the Southern League with Burton Albion.

Six goals were also shared, at Plymouth, in County's first match after George Poyser's appointment. This was the team that ended a sequence of five defeats: Bradley; Southwell, Deans; Adamson, Leuty, Jarvis; Coole, Leverton, Johnston, Wylie, Crookes. It showed one change from that beaten at home by Luton the previous Saturday, Adamson returning in place of Tony ('Tanner') Allen, a part-timer, formerly with Forest, who was an engineering draughtsman. Allen, a local product from Beeston, left for Corby at the end of the season. The concession of three goals to Argyle after being one up at half-time was enough for the new manager to spot the basic fault. His solution was for the full-backs to cover each other, instead of playing so squarely. As Leuty observed: 'Simple, but effective.'

Before that visit to Plymouth, Notts had gained only one point in nine games – at Brentford the day after Tommy Lawton had again caught the headlines with his desertion of the Bees to re-enter the First Division with Arsenal (more about that in its proper turn). The improvement after the return from Devon was remarkable. Only two more points were dropped, and only two more goals given away, as Notts went unbeaten through their next eight games. League games that is, for there was a setback as they paid for being too casual in a friendly with the Austrian team Admira. It was not until the visitors from Vienna had scored their fourth goal, from a penalty, early in the second half that Notts 'woke up'. They then hit back through Leverton, Coole and Johnston in an inspired spell, only for Admira to score again in the last minute.

Another reason for the revival that lifted Notts four places from the bottom of the Second Division in their first nine weeks under Poyser was the fielding of a settled side. Changes were made only for the visit of Leicester, who were held to the 1-1 draw that temporarily cost the Foxes the leadership – and they were enforced by an injury to Harry Jarvis, a wholehearted player who had been discovered by scout Syd Dickinson while with Worksop. McCormack, recalled to lead the attack when Johnston deputised for Jarvis at left-half, opened the scoring in the first half, but that was not sufficient to retain the place he had lost after Notts had gone four successive games without a goal in September. Neither was Jarvis due for an extended return. Soon afterwards he had to step down when Ray Chatham followed Gordon Wills in from Wolves, and although he was taken on by Forest he never appeared in their first team.

Chatham was a cultured and versatile part-timer whose career was handicapped by niggling injuries. Nevertheless, he played in more than 100 senior matches for Wolves, with the inclusion of the 1945-46 transitional season in which he made his debut as a centre-forward. He clocked up another century with Notts County before retiring from League football through injury in June 1958, the month before his 34th birthday. Chatham, who ended his playing days with Margate, was Wolves' top scorer in the League South season that preceded the resumption of normal peacetime soccer in 1946. And although he afterwards had to contend with strong competition for a first-team place, he was such a success at centre-half before his injury jinx struck again that the experienced Bill Shorthouse, for whom he had been deputising, had to be fitted in at full-back. It was at full-back where Chatham played the last of his games for County, which meant that during his career he had appeared in every position except goal.

On their trips by train to and from Wolverhampton for matches at Notts, Chatham and Wills were affable companions for Bob Parker and, on part of the journeys, myself. I went from Derby as a reporter for the local evening paper. For many years, Bob travelled from Wombourne, a village near Wolverhampton, to broadcast running commentaries on Notts and Forest home games to patients in neighbouring hospitals.

County's undefeated League run after Poyser's arrival was ended by three Birmingham goals at St Andrew's on Christmas Day. Gil Merrick, then England's goalkeeper, was carted off unconscious after colliding with Leverton in the final seconds, but no bones were broken and he played in the return game next day (when Notts won 2-1), despite having two black eyes and a cut on the bridge of his nose. With Johnston reverting to the left wing in the absence of Crookes, there was another recall for McCormack that Boxing Day afternoon, and he responded with his 100th League goal. He netted again the following Saturday, but that was in defeat at second-placed Doncaster. He was again omitted when Crookes resumed after an FA Cup exit at Everton and a five-goal trouncing at home to Blackburn, in which Tommy Briggs added a hat-trick to the four goals he had scored against Lincoln in Rovers' previous League match.

Unsettled and feeling that a change of club might be beneficial, McCormack talked with the manager, who granted his transfer request.

'He is a grand footballer,' said Poyser, 'but we want someone with more weight. I'm sure he will do some club a power of good.' Forest showed some interest, but the pale-faced little striker was going nowhere just yet. Although he had further lengthy absences from the side, it was not until 1955 that he left for King's Lynn. On being recalled for the last two of Notts' remaining fifteen matches of 1953-54 (in which they suffered only three more defeats, each by the odd goal), he scored twice on the final day in a 3-1 home win over West Ham. That left the club Poyser had revitalised fourteenth in the table with 39 points – eight clear of Brentford, who went down with Oldham's wooden spoonists.

For the last dozen of those games on the run-in, Notts had a new inside-right. He was Durham-born Jack Taylor, another for whom Poyser went back to Wolves. When Taylor joined Luton from the North-Eastern League club Stockton in February 1949, the journey to complete his signing caused the Hatters' chairman, C D Jeyes, to miss a dramatic 5-5 Cup draw with Leicester in the FA Cup. Two years later, Leicester were again the opposition when Taylor's first Luton hat-trick led Len Shipman, the Foxes' chairman, to describe him as 'even better than Jackie Sewell'. Not long afterwards, the free-scoring Taylor played for England 'B,' and in the summer of 1952 Wolves paid £16,000 for him.

At Molineux, however, Taylor failed to match expectations and soon lost his place – first to Peter Broadbent, then Ron Stockin – and, with Dennis Wilshaw in possession of the other inside-forward position, he spent much of his time in the reserve side after being made available for transfer. On the day, in February 1954, that Poyser turned up at Wolves' training ground with Taylor as his target, he found Lincoln's manager, Bill Anderson, in a quest for another Wolves reserve, left-winger Malcolm Clews. Fees were arranged as the players bathed after training, and both signed. Next day, they again trained at Molineux before setting off to Nottingham together. That Saturday, Taylor, 29, and Clews, 22, were on opposite sides at Meadow Lane, where Johnston saved Notts a point after Lincoln, above them on goal-average in the Second Division depths, had led at half-time.

It was not only in the first team that Poyser's influence wrought an improvement. Results also picked up for the Reserves and the 'A' team. Leuty told me: 'Typical of this rejuvenation is the enthusiasm shown in training. We older heads are not compelled to report for the Wednesday and Thursday afternoon work-outs, but that's a concession of which advantage is rarely taken. More often than not, we do the full sixteen hours – two hours each morning, five days a week, two hours on three afternoons. After the regular lapping and sprinting, the shooting-in by the forwards, and the inter-passing work by the defenders, six-a-side games form a very popular part of our training and help towards its enjoyment. These are played, when the weather permits, on the concrete behind the stands in one corner of the ground. The hard surface makes for good practice in ball control, as does the confined space.'

CHAPTER TWENTY

Record gate, but an FA Cup let-down

The boosting of team spirit and performance under George Poyser's management brought the bonus of an FA Cup run that raised hopes of carrying Notts County all the way to Wembley in 1955.

A trip to Middlesbrough, newly relegated from the First Division, did not bode well for progress beyond the third round, but the Tees-siders were swept aside 4-1 with goals from Wylie (two), Broadbent and Wills. In the continued absence of Taylor through injury, Notts fielded the team that went unchanged through five cup-ties and eight League games following the return of Jimmy Jackson from Canada: Bradley; Southwell, Deans; Adamson, Leuty, Johnston; Wills, Wylie, Jackson, Leverton, Broadbent.

Another away tie in the fourth round took those players to Hillsborough, where Jackie Sewell faced his old club in the First Division opposition. On current form relegation-bound Sheffield Wednesday looked vulnerable. They were at the bottom of the table, already beaten five times at home, and swamped by seven Tottenham goals the previous Saturday. Against that, Notts were third in Division Two, and had had the benefit of an extra week's rest through a League postponement because of bad weather.

The scales tipped further in favour of the visitors when Sewell took a heavy kick on an ankle and was little more than a passenger for the last 40 minutes, yet Notts only just forced a replay. Don Watson, playing in Barnsley junior football only four months before, gave Wednesday the lead in the second half, and the match was into its final minute when full-back Tony Conwell put the ball into his own net for the equaliser.

The replay the following Thursday attracted 35,500 to Meadow Lane, increasing the overall attendance at the two games beyond 88,000. As Sewell was unfit, though no bones were broken, Wednesday brought in Redfern Froggatt, who had only recently resumed training after groin trouble. Again Notts found it hard work, and it was not until extra-time that the deadlock was broken by Jackson, who had passed a late fitness test after treatment for a slight back injury.

Notts went into that replay knowing that the fifth-round draw had presented them with the formidable task of a home tie with Chelsea, a club then in the First Division's top six and on course to become League champions for the first time in their Golden Jubilee year. The Magpies rose to the occasion in reaching what was to be the peak of their season – and of George Poyser's management. Leuty kept a tight grip on Roy Bentley, the Londoners' leading scorer, and Broadbent, an FA tourist of the West Indies that summer, scored the deciding goal in the second half. Newcastle, heading for their third Wembley win in five years, were held to a draw by Forest on the other side of the river, where the City Ground crowd was some 16,000 below the Meadow Lane gate of 41,457. Newcastle were taken to extra-time before putting paid to Forest in their replay, and there was then the possibility that one of the semi-finals would become an all-Magpie affair. Of the six other clubs in the quarter-final draw, four besides Newcastle were in the First Division – Wolves and Sunderland (the top two), Manchester City, and Huddersfield. The number was made up by Birmingham, who were sixth in Division Two, and York, fifth in the Third North.

Leuty and his men therefore appeared to have been presented with their best chance of reaching the last four when they were paired at home with 'little' York. Indeed, complacency was the main enemy they had to guard against, and Leuty vowed in print that 'we intend to treat this match just as if we were playing Wolves themselves; we are not going to make the mistake of under-estimating this progressive Northern Section side.'

There was even talk of Notts completing a Cup and promotion double, which had previously been achieved only by WBA (in 1931), when they defeated Forest 4-1 a week before their shock victory over Chelsea. Notts then lay fourth in the table, with a game in hand over teams above them, but such optimism was tempered by home failures against Liverpool and Middlesbrough in the space of three days before York's visit. To that less than ideal preparation was added the impressive form York had shown in reaching the quarter-finals for the second time in their history – a record for a Northern Section club – while still maintaining a challenge for a rise in the League (they failed, finishing fourth).

After surviving a first-round scare by coming from behind to beat Scarborough 3-2, and then winning 5-2 at Dorchester, York first caught the headlines by knocking out Blackpool, three times Cup finalists since the war, at Bloomfield Road. Their 2-0 triumph, during which Blackpool's Jim Kelly missed a penalty, was the outstanding result of the round, especially as it was achieved by a team that included seven part-timers and had been without a manager since the previous September, when Jimmy McCormick, a former Tottenham forward, had resigned after a dispute with the board over team selection. For an hour York were also under the handicap of having right-winger Willie Hughes hobbling with an ankle injury.

York's next manager, former Charlton goalkeeper Sam Bartram, was not appointed until March 1956. The Cup giantkillers were temporarily in the charge of trainer Tom Lockie, a Scot who had been with the club as a centre-half in the early 1930s, and soon afterwards rejoined them as a member of the training staff – first with the Reserves, then the first team. He held that senior post from 1937 to 1960, when he succeeded Bartram as manager. Promotion from Division Four was achieved in 1965, but York were back there, at the bottom of the League, when Lockie was dismissed two years later. He died a decade after that, on 27 July 1977. Of his 71 years, 31 had been devoted to York City.

In the Cup run of 1955, Lockie had the assistance of York's secretary, George ('Bill') Sherrington, a former civil servant who had been one of the club's five original directors in 1922, and manager in the early 1930s. 'The only advice I gave the lads before they went out at Blackpool,' said Lockie, 'was that they should play their normal game, stick to man-the-man marking, and not be drawn out of position. Even though the York players, I think, were slightly above their normal form, I was very disappointed with the showing of Blackpool.' The Seasiders' five forwards were among eight of the team that had so dramatically snatched victory against Bolton at Wembley two years before. The two Stanleys were firmly shackled by two former Huddersfield players – Matthews by left-back George Howe, Mortensen by centre-half Alan Stewart.

As if that was not sufficient warning for County, York served up another after also winning away in the fourth round, 3-1 against the amateurs of Bishop Auckland. They convincingly claimed another First Division scalp by 'yorking' visitors from Tottenham by the same score, hitting back with two quick goals after falling behind, and then going further ahead in the second half. All that after having their training confined to the local Railway Institute's gymnasium because of the snow and frost that Spurs' manager, Arthur Rowe, perceptively predicted to be 'great levellers' in the match.

Not that all York's players could often get together for training, which made the understanding they developed with so little rehearsing as a unit all the more remarkable. Left-winger Billy Fenton, a draughtsman, did most of his training alone in the evenings; right-half Gordon Brown, a storekeeper, prepared with Mansfield's players; Syd Storey, the inside-left, trained at the ground of the colliery where he worked near Barnsley; and centre-forward Norman Wilkinson tuned up at West Stanley in County Durham. 'I think our secret,' said Lockie as he set out for Nottingham, 'is that we have had an unchanged team since the beginning of October, apart from last Saturday, when Storey was getting married and Wilkinson

needed penicillin injections for a boil on his right hand. I think it is especially important that our half-back line has been the same. Half-backs can
make a team in my opinion.'

York had suffered their first defeat for two months at Darlington the
week before meeting Notts, and Lockie was thankful to be back to this
full-strength line-up: Forgan; Phillips, Howe; Brown, Stewart, Spence;
Hughes, Bottom, Wilkinson, Storey, Fenton.

Some 11,000 York fans travelled to Meadow Lane for the quarter-
final, establishing the ground's existing record of 47,310. After a goalless
first half, Notts had what appeared a good goal disallowed. Leverton's
first shot was blocked by Tommy Forgan, and, although he put the ball
into the net from the rebound, referee Hayworth, of Blackburn, ruled
Wills offside. There was still no scoring until thirteen minutes from time,
when Arthur Bottom got the goal that made York only the third Division
Three side, after Millwall and Port Vale, to reach the semi-finals. It was
his 30th of the season, and he described it as 'the softest of them all'.
adding: 'I only had to tap it in. I thought I was offside.' A tackle by Leuty
seemed fair to many eyes, but the referee awarded York a free-kick. From
this, Hughes lofted the ball into the middle, and Storey's shot was deflect-
ed to Bottom – off a York player claimed the County, but off a Notts
defender ruled the referee.

Bottom said he had no idea who it came off. He was just thankful to
accept it as a gift of such huge significance, a comfortable contribution
to the York record of 39 goals he set up that season. Of that total, 31
came in the Third North, equalling the club's highest for a League campaign created by Fenton in 1951-52, though Bottom could have claimed
it outright but for missing two penalties in a win at Crewe shortly after
knocking Notts out of the Cup.

For York City, in the understated words of Bill Sherrington, progress
to within one step of Wembley made it 'quite a day'. It was one he said
he had 'waited just over 30 years for,' but he also had to admit: 'We were
a bit lucky, weren't we?' For Notts, the dashing of their dream of further
Cup glory was all the harder to accept because of those unfortunate circumstances. I still retain a vivid memory of the great anti-climax of that
windswept March evening as I left Meadow Lane with Leon Leuty.
Although a neutral, I could not avoid sharing his deep disappointment as
we walked along pavements littered with discarded handbills advertising
an article that was to appear under his name in one of the next day's
Sunday newspapers. The words trampled cruelly underfoot mocked the
misery of the departing home supporters: 'Leon Leuty says Notts are
going places.'

Because of the numbering of the clubs in the draw, it did not automatically mean that Notts County, instead of York, would have had a semi-final against Newcastle if they had been the winners, but it might have happened. First, though, Newcastle had a replay with Huddersfield to negotiate before their pairing with York at Hillsborough provided a perfect, if saturated, setting for Bottom's hopes of being tops again at a ground in his home city. He was born in Bramall Lane, only a few yards from where he became a Sheffield United ballboy before playing for the Blades and attracting Jimmy McCormick's attention with his bustling style. In his apprentice days with the Sheffield club, Bottom had been coached by Duggie Livingstone, a former Celtic and Everton full-back who was manager of the Newcastle team that stood between York and Wembley. 'I used to urge him to bang the ball, crack it, hit it, against a specially-built wall,' Livingstone recalled.

Newcastle advanced as Cup favourites from 2-1 to 7-4 after securing their place in the last four, yet they made a meal of getting there and were also uncomfortably near the foot of the First Division. The Tynesiders needed three games and two lots of extra-time to dispose of Nottingham Forest, and more extra-time in their second meeting with Huddersfield. It was therefore no real surprise when York's battlers, though outsiders at 100-7, took them to another replay with a tenacious display on a pitch swamped by more than eight hours of continuous rain.

Bottom, known as 'Nodder' to his team-mates because he could sleep anywhere but on a football field, wiped out the lead Newcastle gained in the thirteenth minute, but York had no answer to the two goals conceded in the replay at Sunderland. Newcastle went on to defeat Manchester City in a final memorable for a rare headed goal by Jackie Milburn in the first minute, but regrettable for the injury that ended the career of Jimmy Meadows, City's England full-back.

Bottom, remembered at York as something of a loner, was the top scorer in each of the three seasons he spent at Bootham Crescent after becoming the club's seventh signing in two months during the 1954 close season – and their costliest up to that time at £2,000. He again equalled the club's League scoring record in 1955-56, and repaid their expenditure with over 100 goals in League and Cup before Newcastle paid £4,500 for him in a rush deal in February 1958, after failing to sign Scottish international Jackie Henderson from Portsmouth. Bottom bagged ten goals in eleven games for the Geordies, scoring twice on his debut against Everton and helping to avoid relegation, yet he was offloaded back to the Third Division with Chesterfield the following November. He was later at Boston, retiring as a player in 1962.

Sadly, life after football was unkind to Arthur Bottom. After working in a bakery, first at Chesterfield and then back home in Sheffield, he took a job on the production line of a cutlery firm, having served an apprenticeship as a silversmith in his younger days. But he was made redundant with a wife, Rita, and four children to support.

Notts County shrugged off their Cup let-down of 1955 by winning six and drawing two of their remaining dozen Second Division games, finishing in a respectable seventh place. Three of their four defeats during that period, which included a national newspaper strike, were inflicted by teams in the top five – among them Luton, who won promotion to Division One for the first time as runners-up to Birmingham. Judging by that season's record, Notts had reason to contemplate the future with some confidence. The opposite, however, proved to be the case. The path ahead led inexorably downhill, to narrow escapes from relegation, an embarrassing Cup exit at the hands of non-League 'minnows,' and the dismissal of Poyser within days of being given a vote of confidence.

CHAPTER TWENTY-ONE

Double dismissal after a Rhyl upset

In the autumn of 1956 there was a boardroom shake-up at Meadow Lane that was to have dramatic repercussions. Charles Barnes, the chairman, and another director, Harry Morley, resigned. Secretary Wilf Fisher left in their wake because, so it was officially announced, he could no longer spare time from the off-licence business he had recently acquired in Nottingham.

The chairman had been associated with Fisher in transfer deals involving more than £150,000 over the past eight years. That was considerable expenditure for those days, yet it had fallen well short of producing the desired effect. After the rise to the Second Division under Tommy Lawton's leadership, and the early promise of further progress under the direction of George Poyser, Notts County had gone into steep decline. In 1955-56, the season following the fanciful talk of a Cup and promotion double, they had finished immediately above the two relegation positions and gone straight out of the Cup at home to Fulham. Now the changes at the very top of their administration came when there was another, and even more dire, threat of a return to the Southern Section of the Third Division. They were next to the foot of the table with only eight points from fourteen games, one ahead of Bury.

The new chairman was Len Machin, a 47-year-old textile manufacturer. He arrived declaring that 'the newly constructed board of directors has every faith in Mr Poyser to lead us out of our troubles'. So confident, it appeared, that they were not content just to leave him with managerial duties that demanded his complete attention if the club were to get out of trouble. He was also saddled with doing the secretary's job until a new man was appointed. 'I've been up to my neck in it,' he told me. 'I reduced the playing staff by eight, and signed only one during the close season. Then we had the bad luck to start the season with six injured.'

Those released included Harry Adamson, to Gainsborough Trinity, Tommy Deans, to Boston United, and 'Tot' Leverton, to Walsall. Jackie Lane, a centre-forward who wore contact lenses, was the new signing. He had scored fourteen goals in 48 League and Cup games for Birmingham, the first of them on Easter Monday in 1953 in a debut against Doncaster for which he had had to wait four years since being taken on from Boldmere St Michael's. For Notts County he scored nineteen in 60 games, with Doncaster again the opposition when he opened his home account on his fifth appearance. By the time he left, for Hinckley in 1959, he was an intermittent member of a team plunging towards a second successive relegation.

Johnny Hancocks, the 5ft 4in Wolves and England winger who wore size 4½ boots, the smallest among players of his day, would have followed Lane to the Lane if Machin had had his way. 'I have not been in the game long,' said the new chairman, 'but I look forward to helping introduce some fresh ideas.' One of those ideas was to set the club's transfer sights on this diminutive scorer of 150 First Division goals, who had recently lost his first-team place at Molineux with the signing of Harry Hooper from West Ham. Chelsea and Charlton were the most persistent of numerous other clubs trailing the little winger. Hancocks, however, hankered only after rejoining Walsall, and when that wish went unfulfilled because of the size of the fee required he stayed on in the Central League side until he eventually moved to Wellington Town (later Telford United).

Whereas the average player used two pairs of boots a year, Hancocks pulled on his fifth pair of the season, when he really needed a sixth, to play for England in November 1950 against Yugoslavia, who salvaged a draw through two defensive errors. 'I just don't seem able to make boots last,' he said. 'The pair I have on have stretched so badly that I am wearing two pairs of socks. I didn't dare risk a new pair for this vital game.' On one occasion when he ordered a new pair, the manufacturers thought they were for a schoolboy and sent him a jigsaw as well.

Notts won only two of those first fourteen matches of the 1956-57 season before the change of chairman. Twice they let in six goals, at Stoke and Leicester, and five to Sheffield United at Bramall Lane. They did show some spirit, however, in replying three times at Leicester against a team at the top of the table. Goalkeeper Gordon Bradley had the satisfaction of putting one of those goals into his old club's net. He gained that opportunity through having to give up guarding his own, and going into the forward line, after suffering an injury that cost him his place for the rest of the season.

Bradley was replaced first by George Smith, a Nottingham-born signing from Dale Rovers, a local club, and then by Jimmy Linton, the Glaswegian from the Scottish junior club Rob Roy. They had deputised in Bradley's absences the previous season. Bradley was never an automatic choice again, making the last of over 200 appearances as a deputy himself, for Linton, before moving to Cambridge United in 1958.

Smith was the man in possession when the Machin regime began ominously with a 1-5 home defeat on the first Saturday of November in 1956 at the unexpected hands of Rotherham, only a few places above Notts in the Second Division basement. A week later, the Magpies fluttered to last place in losing at Lincoln, Bury edging above them on goal-average when extracting a point at Sheffield United. Smith gave way to Linton after being beaten four times in another crushing failure at home to a lowly club, Swansea. Linton remained the No 1 until near the end of a second successive relegation, Smith then taking such a firm grip through eight seasons, in three of which he was an ever-present, that he exceeded 350 League and Cup games before joining Hartlepools United in 1967.

Linton's own move, at the end of 1958-59, took him to Watford, who were displeased by Notts' decision not to allow him to continue training at Meadow Lane. After helping his new club beat the old 4-2 at Vicarage Road in September 1959, Linton was refused access to Notts' ground and arrangements had to be made for him to train with Forest instead. Frank Hill, the former Scottish international who was then the Magpies' manager, said: 'When Jimmy moved to Watford, we explained that we had already had to turn down requests from sixteen other footballers who wanted to train on our ground. But because Jimmy's wife is expecting a baby we said he could train here for a month, either at the start of the season or in November, when the baby is due. He chose to come here at the start of the season. His time is now up.' The Lintons were not intending moving house to the Watford area until after the baby's birth.

In 1956, Linton took over in the Notts goal from George Smith at Fulham, where the Magpies ended November as they had begun it – by conceding five goals. Despite that mauling, he stayed for the remaining two dozen League games of the season, one of only three players to do so. The others were Peter Russell, another of George Poyser's imports from Wolves, and Frank Cruickshank, a Scottish full-back from Nuneaton Borough. Russell alone played in all 42 games, filling the centre-half gap left by the loss of Leon Leuty, apart from one appearance at centre-forward and another at left-half. Ray Chatham was the first to take over as the defensive pivot when Leuty was compelled to drop out, and Scunthorpe-born Allen Wade, a schoolteaching part-timer, then had a few games in that position before Russell's signing on transfer deadline day in March 1956.

On the Saturday after their failure at Fulham, Notts handed last place back to Bury with an encouraging home win over Barnsley in which Gordon Wills, switched from the wing to lead the attack, did the hat-trick. That, however, was to be the last win, only Notts third of the season, under Poyser's management. A beating at Bury dumped Notts to the bottom of the table again, and a double defeat by Huddersfield over

Christmas left them three points astray. Bury saw a remarkable reversal of results with a 7-2 home triumph over third-placed Bristol Rovers on Christmas Day, for they lost the return at Eastville on Boxing Day 1-6. The year ended for Notts with a sixth consecutive defeat, at Doncaster. It was their eighteenth in 25 games, from which they had taken only ten points, and the final humiliation that was to cost Poyser his job was then just another week away.

It was a classic case of dismissal after the 'kiss of death' of a declaration of confidence. On 4 January 1957, the day before the fateful third-round FA Cup-tie against little Rhyl of the Cheshire League, Len Machin looked in at George Poyser's office and, as the manager remembered it, told him that he was the best fellow in the world at his job, and that his salary was to be doubled. Poyser also revealed that even after the shock defeat the new chairman told him that the fault was not his, and firmly expressed the belief that between them they could bring about a revival. Yet how very different everything was to be by Monday morning! The players had still to report for training when Machin again called in at the manager's office. This time, his message was very brief and very much to the point. 'You're fired!' he said. 'Fetch Potts. He's fired too.'

Vic Potts, a former Doncaster and Villa full-back whose playing career had been ended prematurely by injury, was the club's trainer, having been promoted from assistant to succeed Bill Moore. He and Moore, a stickler for discipline, had worked together at Villa Park, and they were reunited in January 1958. Potts left the job he had taken in a Birmingham factory to become trainer for Moore, Walsall's newly appointed manager, following the resignations of Jackie Maund and Jim Southam from the club's training staff. Moore, a former Stoke player, had two spells as Walsall manager, and was England trainer during Walter Winterbottom's reign before retiring to take over a public house in Stafford five years before his death, in January 1978, at the age of 65. Potts lived in retirement until October 1996, when he died aged 81.

A goal by left-winger Peter Bircumshaw kept Notts level with Rhyl by the interval, but they had no answer to the two goals they conceded in the second half. The attendance of 16,000 was a far cry from the days of Lawton and the record gate of only two years before. It was also below that at the City Ground, where 18,000 saw Forest make short work of another non-League club, Goole, by 6-0.

A few years later, Peter Bircumshaw was joined at Meadow Lane by his brother Tony, who became the youngest to play for the club in the League when he turned out at the age of sixteen years and 54 days against Brentford on 3 April 1961. Between them, they made nearly 250 League and Cup appearances before leaving –Peter for Bradford City, Tony for Hartlepool United.

George Poyser, whose three-year contract at Meadow Lane had ended in the October before his dismissal, departed without comment, and with a mere month of his £1,250 annual salary in lieu of notice. 'The present position,' said Machin in offering an explanation, 'is part of the legacy I accepted when I was appointed chairman nearly three months ago. I am determined to make every effort to see that the club's future is assured.' The Supporters' Club held a special meeting at the ground which their secretary, Albert Ward, a 53-year-old painter and decorator, described as 'a tough one'. He added: 'Indeed, it looked like resignations at one time. We consider George Poyser and Vic Potts are first-rate fellows.'

George Poyser did not take long to find another post. His appointment as Manchester City's assistant manager made him responsible for reorganising the club's scouting system, a role that he estimated involved 80,000 miles of travel throughout the country each year. In the summer of 1963 he was promoted to succeed Les McDowall as manager. McDowall, a former City captain, had achieved promotion back to the First Division in his first season in charge, and seen his team to two successive FA Cup finals. In the second of those visits to Wembley, City had won the trophy with the 'Revie Plan', named after the future England manager, who was employed as a deep-lying centre-forward. Since then, however, there had been a big downturn in the club's fortunes. As when he went to Nottingham, Poyser was faced with an unenviable task, for McDowall left after having failed to avert relegation.

Again, Poyser got off to a good start, piloting the team into a promising position by the end of the year, and into a League Cup semi-final with, ironically, a victory over Notts County at Meadow Lane. The only goal of that fifth-round game was scored by big Derek Kevan, one of Lawton's many successors as leader of England's attack, to the dismay of most in a crowd shrunk to 7,000. In the second half of that 1963-64 season, however, things once more began to go wrong for Manchester City. They fell from the FA Cup at Swindon, lost on aggregate over two legs to Stoke in the League Cup, and faded to sixth in Division Two after crucial defeats by the promoted pair, Leeds and Sunderland.

Though remaining a popular figure, Poyser was powerless to arrest a continuing decline. In 1964-65, a crop of injuries contributed to immediate exits from both knock-out competitions, against Shrewsbury and Mansfield of the Third Division, and to the failure to sustain another promotion challenge. City hit a new low with their smallest Maine Road attendance of just over 8,000 for the visit of Swindon (in a stadium with a record gate of 85,569), and at Easter in 1965 Poyser resigned. His team wallowed in mid-table – an unacceptable situation exacerbated by the fact that neighbours United were on course to reclaim the League title.

Poyser lived in retirement until early in 1995, when he died only a few days before his 85th birthday. On 12 April 1965, Notts County, who were then in the Fourth Division, sacked Eddie Lowe, a former Villa, Fulham and England wing-half, and a few weeks before that Les McDowall parted company with Oldham Athletic, who were battling against the relegation from Division Three they only narrowly avoided.

CHAPTER TWENTY-TWO

Caretaker Broome sweeps clean but rejected

Eddie Lowe was Notts County's fifth manager since George Poyser. The first of them, as caretaker, was Frank Broome, a fully qualified FA coach who had rejoined the club as assistant trainer during 1955, shortly after finally retiring as a player in his 40th year, while with Shelbourne.

Broome's entry into the League of Ireland had been quite explosive – though not due to him, nor because of a recovery to draw from a two-goal deficit. One of his new colleagues, Rory Dwyer, had caused a hold-up for repairs after bringing down an upright and the crossbar with an attempt to score that had carried him at full tilt into the back of the Drumcondra net.

Broome had been signed by Shelbourne in February 1955, the month after having his contract with Crewe terminated because of financial constraints that also necessitated the release of manager Ralph Ward, a former Tottenham full-back, and Harry Whitworth, a wing-half who had been transferred from Bury during the previous close season.

Broome's stay with Crewe might have been even shorter. It was only a little longer than that spent with Brentford when, in February 1954, he was suspended for a fortnight because, on the day before a home match with York, he flew to Switzerland for a coaching job interview (he was on a short-list of two) with St Gallen, the country's oldest club. He said he had not been notified that he was wanted against York, and claimed: 'On the Monday before I flew to Zurich I asked Crewe for permission. While I was told it would probably be all right if I went, I understood that a board meeting was to be held to discuss the matter. I expected a call, but Crewe did not contact me, so I went on the trip.'

Reinstated, Broome altogether scored sixteen goals in 36 games for Crewe, taking his overall totals in League and Cup among five clubs to seven short of 200 in 426 appearances over twenty years. There were also his three goals in his seven England games. During the war, he added 88 goals in 133 matches for Villa to the 90 he had scored in 150 in peacetime. He also exceeded 30 in some 50 games as a guest for eight clubs (including fifteen in twenty matches for Notts County, for whom he netted 41 in 114 as one of their own players). Two of his wartime goals for Notts were scored in a 4-11 defeat at Walsall, where Ted Vinall's four goals for the home side included a hat-trick of second-half penalties. At the same ground, Broome scored four in helping Nottingham Forest to a 7-6 win. With Wolves, he was a War Cup winner against Sunderland in 1942.

When George Poyser had left Meadow Lane, Tommy Lawton was promptly sought as his successor. The directors of Kettering, by whom Lawton was then employed as player-manager, met 'to review the position' after receiving an offer from County, and it was predicted that terms would be agreed in time for him to take over the following week. An appointment was deferred, however, when Broome's first game as caretaker, on 12 January 1957, resulted in a shock 5-0 home win over Stoke, who were second in the table and had thrashed Notts 6-0 at their Victoria Ground back in September. With chairman Machin having made it clear that Broome would select the team and be responsible for strategy while the managerial position remained open, seven changes were made for the Potters' visit, compared with the line-up for the Cup-tie against Rhyl that had was Poyser's undoing. Only three players, Linton, Cruickshank and Russell kept their places for both games from the previous League match, lost 2-4 at Doncaster, though three others, Carver, Wylie and Wills, took part in all three, but in different positions.

The team fielded against Rhyl was: Linton; Southwell (who returned in place of Roy Kirkham, a former Ollerton Colliery defender, after the Doncaster defeat), Cruickshank; McGrath, Russell, Loxley; Lane, Wylie, Willis, Carver, Bircumshaw (P). Broome's choice against Stoke was: Linton; Southwell, Cruickshank; Bulch, Russell, Carver; Roby, McGrath, Jackson, Wylie, Wills.

Six of those players, Linton, Cruickshank, Russell, Bulch, Roby and Wills, did not miss any of the remaining sixteen matches of the season. Wylie, having settled the differences that had led him to seek a transfer, was absent once, Carver twice. Ray Chatham was recalled when Southwell, the captain, dropped out through injury. John McGrath, a signing from Aldershot who went to Darlington with north-easterner Bob Bulch during the following season, gave way for the run-in to Jack Taylor, who had almost been driven from Meadow Lane by barracking.

With Wills back at centre-forward when Jackson again dropped out injured, there was a new outside-left for the last eleven games – Ken Tucker from West Ham. There was also nearly a new leader of the attack. Inquiries were made about Leicester's former Glasgow Ranger, Willie Gardiner who, like Tucker, had done the hat-trick on his Football League debut. Gardiner had been the Foxes' joint top scorer with the record-scoring Arthur Rowley the previous season, but he was out of the side heading back up to the First Division. Even so, manager Dave Halliday had no hesitation in saying: 'We're not selling.' Reading were luckier when they made an approach late the next year.

Jackson and Wylie both scored twice in the emphatic defeat of Stoke, McGrath getting the other goal. Although Machin made it known he was not convinced Broome was the right man for the job, Southwell spoke for all the players: 'There is no doubt about the issue. The players want Broome as manager. He planned our victory on Saturday, and we feel we can do well under his guidance.' Notts then drew 0-0 at Middlesbrough, sixth in the table, and at home to Leicester, who arrived with their lead over Stoke extended to six points. At that stage, February 1957, Notts were still last, on goal-average behind Port Vale, who were trounced 1-7 at home by Forest, and one point worse off than Bury, whose defeat by Grimsby was their eleventh out of sixteen home games. Port Vale's manager, Freddie Steele, the former Stoke and England centre-forward, had resigned the week after George Poyser's dismissal. Like Poyser, he had been unable to follow up a successful start, having won promotion from the Third North in 1954 by a record margin and also reached the FA Cup semi-finals.

Despite Notts' improving form under Broome, an attempt was renewed to lure Lawton from Kettering, whom he had led to the Southern League championship since arriving from Arsenal a year before. First a Nottingham journalist who, said Lawton, 'had the ear of the Notts board,' and then Machin himself, telephoned him at his home to ask if he would be interested in returning to Meadow Lane as manager.

Lawton was not among the many applicants for the job (one report put it as more than 100), but it was offered to him after he had been summoned to a hush-hush meeting at Oakham with Machin and two of the club's other directors, Bertram Edwards and Frank Sherwood. The following week, Lawton was called to a meeting of the Notts board, held at Machin's home because the chairman was ill in bed. As Lawton was about to enter the bedroom, Alf Hubbard, another director, hurried out saying he could not agree to the appointment. Inside, another director, Len Linnell, made it clear he was also not in favour, but, after declining to join in the vote, he changed his mind when Lawton threatened to walk out unless Linnell agreed to accept him.

Terms were settled at £2,250 a year, plus £250 expenses, but four days later Lawton had second thoughts. 'I have refused the Notts County job. My reason is simple. The County board is split – and it seems even the city itself is split – over whether or not I should be appointed manager. It is a job I wanted. But I could not take it without 100 per cent support from the board, the team, and the supporters. It is no secret that the board meeting in the chairman's bedroom was a stormy one, for listeners downstairs heard voices raised. I was called upon to defend myself from verbal attack at that meeting. I fought, and I won. But things have changed since then. Dissension in a club is bad enough when the team is doing well. It is fatal when the team is struggling to avoid relegation.'

He added that he had left the club as a player 'under less than happy circumstances', and that resentment still rankled. He felt so strongly about it that he issued the following statement: 'After very careful consideration of the whole situation, and on the principle that all my players must believe in me and my methods, I feel it is only fair to the Nottingham public that Mr Broome and the players have the opportunity to provide them with a successful side. The Kettering players have always believed I could bring them success, and I am determined that both they and myself shall reap the benefit of our labours. When we have completed the job I have been paid to do my situation may well then have to be reviewed. My aim is still to be the manager of a League side, but I will stay with Kettering until the right offer comes along.'

It was only after that uncompromising refusal that the Notts board decided to ask Broome to carry on until the end of the season. In view of those unsettling developments behind the scenes, it was perhaps not surprising that the mini-revival was promptly followed by a mini-slump. Notts lost their next two matches – both in Bristol by 0-3, against Rovers and City – and slipped two points adrift again. On a day of atrocious weather, there was then a crowd below 6,000 for the visit of mid-table Sheffield United, though even that was not the lowest of the season at a ground where the attendance record had so recently been broken. Fewer than 5,000 had seen the defeat by lowly Grimsby on the last Saturday before Christmas – the club's smallest gate for a home League match since the last day of the 1938-39 season, when the clouds of another world war had been gathering.

A third successive loss seemed inevitable when Sheffield United ended the first half two goals ahead, but Notts staged a rousing comeback to salvage a point as Peter Russell scored twice when straying from his defensive duties. On the same February afternoon, incidentally, Stoke, so recently mauled as the new Broome swept clean, piled up eight goals against Lincoln – seven of them from Tim Coleman, a League record for a winger.

County got back to winning ways a week later, when they defeated Queen of the South 3-0 in a friendly because their scheduled opponents, Forest no less, had a quarter-final Cup date with top division Birmingham

(Forest, who were then third in Division Two, forced a draw, but lost at home in the midweek replay). Port Vale were the next visitors to Meadow Lane, and Notts struck a crucial blow for their survival after a scoreless first half, winning 3-1 with goals from Jackson (two) and Russell.

That narrowed the gap behind Vale to one point, and it was closed at the first opportunity, in mid-March, when Notts drew at Rotherham while Vale were losing at home to Liverpool. Notts were then on eighteen points with Vale, but still trailed on goal-average, and with one more game played (33 to 32). Above them were Bury, on twenty points from 36 matches. Two of those three were the likeliest to go down because the next two up the table, Bristol City and Lincoln, had pulled nine points clear with respective home wins over Bury and Bristol Rovers.

Lincoln's next match was at Meadow Lane, and Notts handed last place to Port Vale, who lost to Leyton Orient, by beating them 3-0 with goals from Wills, Tucker and Wylie. Bury's home defeat by Sheffield United left them above Notts only on goal-average, and with three more games played, but at the end of the month Bury drew at Barnsley while Notts failed to do likewise at Swansea, after halving a two-goal deficit. That, however, was the last failure while Broome was in control, and Port Vale were unable to take advantage by losing at home to Huddersfield. Indeed, Vale's defeat at Meadow Lane was to be the first of nine in succession, a bleak spell that left them with the wooden spoon.

The draws at home to Fulham and at Barnsley (between which Broome took time off to play, along with Jesse Pye, in an All-Star XI against Peterborough's Midland League champions) sent Notts into the crucial Easter programme still one point behind Bury, but four ahead of Port Vale. A third consecutive draw at Blackburn on Good Friday took them level with Bury and also enabled Forest who, like Bury, were without a game, to retain on goal-average the second place they had wrested from Blackburn with a home win over West Ham four days earlier. The Hammers were back in Nottingham next day – and well beaten once more as Notts kept pace with Bury, 1-0 winners at home to Lincoln, with a 4-1 victory in which Wills scored twice.

Bury, however, had only one more match to play compared with Notts' three, and on Easter Monday, when the Magpies had no fixture, they lost it, 0-2 at Stoke. Next day, Notts made sure of staying up – and Forest almost sure of going up – by winning at home to Blackburn, also 2-0. Many Forest fans were there to cheer the goals with which Jack Taylor answered his vociferous Notts critics.

From having had only ten points from 25 games when Broome took over, Notts had gained seventeen from fifteen in ensuring safety, yet the modestly paid caretaker was still in the dark. 'I still haven't a clue what is happening here,' he said. I am very happy that we are safe, happy for the lads that they have done so well. Of my own future I know nothing. The directors have said nothing, and I haven't been consulted yet about which players will be retained. I got a very modest rise when I took over. I hope they give me the job, and more money.'

Notts' two remaining games were both away. Two more goals from Wills earned a draw with Leyton Orient in the prelude to an ideal finale. Two more goals from Taylor helped County to a 4-2 upset of Forest, who had ended a 32-year absence from the First Division with a 4-0 win at Sheffield United. In front of a May-Day City Ground crowd of 31,896, Taylor opened the scoring with a calmly placed shot in the 37th minute. He was left unmarked after defenders had been pulled away by a dazzling dribble by Don Roby, who then restored the lead from Tucker's pass after Stewart Imlach's headed equaliser two minutes into the second half. Taylor's second goal, powerfully struck from Wylie's pass with seven minutes to go, was the best of the bunch. The others came in the last minute, Wylie firing home from a Roby cross and Tommy Wilson heading in for Forest from a corner. These were the teams:

Forest: Nicholson; Hutchinson, Thomas; Morley, McKinlay, Burkitt; Wilson, Baily, Barrett, Lishman, Imlach.

Notts: Linton; Chatham, Cruickshank; Bulch, Russell, Carver; Roby, Taylor, Wills, Wylie, Tucker.

And these were the final top and tail positions in the Second Division:

1956-57	P	W	D	L	F	A	Pts
1. Leicester	42	25	11	6	109	67	61
2. Nott'm For	42	22	10	10	94	55	54
3. Liverpool	42	21	11	10	82	54	53
4. Blackburn	42	21	10	11	83	75	52
18. Lincoln	42	14	6	22	54	80	34
19. Barnsley	42	12	10	20	59	89	34
20. Notts Co	42	9	12	21	58	86	30
21. Bury	42	8	9	25	60	96	25
22. Port Vale	42	8	6	28	57	101	22

So, after all the worry and air of inevitability about relegation, Notts ended five points clear of the drop. If anything seemed to guarantee the managerial appointment of the man under whose direction that remarkable recovery had been achieved, surely that was it. But no, Lawton was eventually prevailed upon to change his mind again, this time in favour of a return. And before the year was out so was Broome – his services, even on his reversion to trainer, no longer required 'because of the club's economic situation'. Also jettisoned was Jack Taylor, whose four goals in the last three games had included the pair that had ensured survival. On 17 June 1957 he became Bradford Park Avenue's seventh summer signing.

CHAPTER TWENTY-THREE

Lawton back in First Division
with Arsenal

Chequered was a reasonable word to describe Tommy Lawton's progress between leaving Notts County as a player and rejoining them as a manager. It did indeed 'vary considerably in fortune or character', to quote one dictionary definition.

To begin with, life with Brentford appeared to provide the ideal antidote after the trauma Lawton had encountered at Meadow Lane since leading the team to promotion. In addition to having become happily remarried, he found the Brentford directors 'among the finest people I have been privileged to meet', and was impressed by the sincerity and enthusiasm of their plans for the club's future. He was also content to be under the management of A H ('Jackie') Gibbons, a former Brentford centre-forward and England amateur international who had played once for the full national team during the war, while with Tottenham. That was in the 1942 defeat by Wales at Wolverhampton, where, as recalled earlier, Lawton had had another centre-forward, Ronnie Rooke, on the other side of him in a misfiring experiment.

But that rosy Griffin Park picture too soon darkened. In August 1952, five months after Lawton's arrival, Gibbons resigned because of differences with directors on policy, later coaching abroad. His successor was his assistant, Jimmy Bain, with whom Lawton admitted to disagreements, mainly because he did not rate him as a manager. 'He preferred to let things take their own course,' complained Lawton, 'instead of guiding them in the right direction.'

Bain, a Scot previously with Strathclyde and Manchester United, had been at Brentford since 1928. He arrived as an efficient centre-half, going on to captain of the side that won promotion from the Southern Section of the Third Division in 1933. On giving up playing, he was assistant to manager Harry Curtis from 1934 to 1949 before staying on in that role with Gibbons. He had seen Brentford rise to Division One in 1935, but found his own elevation a problem, being unable to arrest a slide down the Second Division to which the club had returned in 1947. His task was made all the more harrowing if, as Lawton claimed, he also had difficulties with other players, and the team hovered uncomfortably close to the relegation trapdoor when, during the first week of 1953, he reverted to being assistant manager – first to Lawton; then, after only one more season, to Bill Dodgin Senior.

Bain eventually left the club when his contract expired in May 1956, the board having decided to dispense with an assistant manager for financial reasons. He described the end of his 27½ years' service as 'a great shock', and Dodgin said he was 'very sorry' to lose him, adding the obvious: 'He has been 100 per cent loyal to Brentford.' Tangible recognition of that loyalty came when a long-service medal was presented to Bain at the following month's annual meeting of the Football League.

Lawton readily accepted the invitation to become player-manager when Bain was relieved of his managerial duties in January 1953. Lawton was given a free hand, put in charge of coaching as well as choosing the team, and made responsible for 'everything concerned with the field of play'. Furthermore, to quote him again from his book about his rise and fall: 'Nobody interfered with my decision to drop or include a player, sign or sell a player. If I felt a replacement was necessary for any position, I just asked the board what we could afford, which, incidentally, was very little, and they would do everything they could.'

Lawton's first team selection was beset by injury problems, but he got off to a winning start in a home third-round FA Cup-tie against Leeds, scoring the deciding goal himself. First Division Aston Villa were held to a 0-0 draw on their own ground in the next round, and Villa only narrowly won the replay after falling behind to another Lawton goal. In the League, however, Brentford went through their new manager's first four games without a victory, sinking to eighteenth, two points above the relegation zone, after a five-goal mauling by Everton on Lawton's return to Goodison Park.

From that low point, however, the Bees embarked upon a run of four wins that lifted them towards mid-table. It began at home to Doncaster, with a team in which George Bristow became the third youngster in a fortnight to be given his first League chance by Lawton. Of the others, a lad named Bull made little impression before leaving for Swindon, but Jimmy Bloomfield played for England at Under-23 level after costing Arsenal £10,000. The successful sequence also included another 5-0 result against one of Lawton's old clubs, but this time he was among the scorers, with Notts County on the receiving end.

That, though, was as good as it got for Lawton as player-manager. Brentford ended the season seventeenth with 37 points – two places and one point above Notts. After those four wins, only one more was secured in the last ten games, and that by a single goal against a Luton team they knocked out of the promotion race. Five more goals were conceded at

Fulham and, at Swansea, Brentford were victims of Welsh international Ivor Allchurch's first hat-trick for the Welsh club.

Brentford began the following 1953-54 season with Ian McPherson and Frank Broome reunited alongside Lawton in attack through their moves from Notts County. McPherson, who lived in Cambridge, had undergone cartilage surgery in what was his last season with County, but then asked for a transfer after rejecting reduced terms. 'I could not agree to being paid only £7 a week in the summer, or if I were injured.'

Despite that influx of talent, Brentford were next to bottom with just one win and four points from their first nine games – and that was where they lost Lawton. The only club below them was the only one they had beaten, Fulham. Hat-tricks had been scored against them by Jack Lee (Derby), Tommy Briggs (Blackburn) and Geoff Bradford (Bristol Rovers). Considering himself too much of a perfectionist to make a good job of combining playing with managing, Lawton resigned as manager after a loss at Lincoln. Four days later, on the evening of Wednesday, 16 September 1953, he made his last appearance for Brentford, still as captain, in the sixth defeat of those nine matches, 0-3 at Doncaster. It was his 50th League game for the club, in which he had scored seventeen goals – a total to which he had added two in three FA Cup-ties.

Broome and McPherson left the month after Lawton. McPherson, having again asked for a transfer, this time for 'business reasons', joined Bedford Town, the Southern League club of which his former Arsenal team-mate Ronnie Rooke was player-manager. Broome, as previously recalled, went into the Third Division's Northern Section with Crewe Alexandra.

Lawton's departure from Griffin Park developed from the phone call he made home before setting off back from that defeat at Doncaster. He was in the habit of ringing his second wife, Gaye, after each game, and this time she told him that Tom Whittaker, the Arsenal manager, had been on the phone to say that he wanted her husband to sign for him. Lawton suspected that it might be a hoax, but he had the Gunners' interest confirmed when he got back to Griffin Park. Frank Davies, the Brentford chairman, told him that Whittaker had sought permission to approach him for a transfer talk. Arsenal were in deep trouble. Only the previous May they had beaten Burnley on Cup final-eve to become League champions for a then record seventh time, if by only 0.099 of a goal, but now they were in great danger of losing the First Division status they had held since being promoted (from fifth place) after 1914-15.

On the day Brentford lost at Lincoln, Arsenal were bottom with only two points from eight games after suffering their heaviest defeat for 26 years. Whittaker missed the seven-goal avalanche with which Sunderland responded after falling behind – and so did his assistant, Jack Crayston, the former Arsenal and England wing-half. Whittaker was 350 miles away, watching a reserve match at Portsmouth. The quest proved unsuccessful for Jack Froggatt, an England cap at both outside-left and centre-half, who was temporarily out of the first team (he returned for Pompey's next match, and a year went by before he did move, to Leicester). Crayston went to run the rule over Leicester's Johnny Morris, briefly an international inside-forward after joining Derby from Manchester United. Morris was also going nowhere at that time. He twice helped Leicester into the First Division before becoming Corby Town's player-manager. After that, like Lawton before him, he was with Kettering.

Two centre-forwards, Bedford Jezzard of Fulham, and Derek Hines of Leicester, were others linked with Arsenal, but the final target was 33-year-old Tommy Lawton. That, however, was only after Frank Davies had put the idea in Tom Whittaker's head by phoning to ask if he would like to sign him to help Brentford out of what he termed 'a serious financial difficulty'. Lawton was then seen as the sole major asset the Bees had to offer. Whittaker at first thought that a player out of the First Division for six years would not be an answer to his own problems, but he had a swift change of mind on deciding that, after all, Lawton could be a big attraction, and also give the inside-forwards the service they had been lacking, besides scoring a few goals himself. Lawton, too, had some reservations initially, but after going to Highbury for talks with the Arsenal manager he jumped at the chance of a return to the top flight he had so regretted leaving.

When Lawton first realised the approach was serious, he doubted that, with his 34th birthday only weeks away, he could be successful in the First Division after having been out of it for so long. He changed his mind, however, on being convinced by Whittaker that he could supply the experience the team so badly needed. He admitted that it had been one of his ambitions to play for Arsenal, and he told Whittaker, for whom he had 'the deepest regard', that he felt it would be an honour to do so.

There was also the fact that they were no strangers to each other. They had got on well when Whittaker had been the England trainer before the war. Whittaker said later that he would have tried to sign him eight years earlier, had he been Arsenal's manager when Lawton sought a move from Everton (though he also admitted that would have been difficult because the club then owed £160,000). It was because of an Everton connection that the move also appealed to Lawton, for it reunited him with Joe Mercer, the Arsenal captain who had been with him at Goodison Park.

So Lawton put his name to the transfer forms in the Highbury board-room on the Friday lunchtime of 18 September, and Brentford received £4,500 plus left-winger Jimmy Robertson, a young Scot, in part exchange. In marked contrast to when Lawton had signed for Brentford under the glare of newsreel arc-lights in a London hotel, the deal, valued at about £10,000, was done in the utmost secrecy, witnessed only by Whittaker, Crayston and two Brentford officials. The Arsenal manager was taking no chances after the collapse of his negotiations for Froggatt. Consequently, there were constant phone calls from newspapermen seeking the identi-ty of 'this Lawton' when the team for the next day's match was released to the Press Association. 'Oh, he's just a young lad I've just signed,' replied Whittaker teasingly, but it did not take the callers long to realise who the mystery man was.

Arsenal were no longer propping up the table when Lawton joined them. Three days earlier, they moved above Middlesbrough on goal-aver-age by avenging a home defeat by Chelsea with a 2-0 win in the return match. Next day, Boro let slip the chance to reverse those positions, los-ing at home to Manchester United, but Arsenal inappropriately dropped back to last on the day Lawton made his debut. That was on Saturday, 19 September, when the Gunners were held 2-2 at home by Manchester City, Middlesbrough gained a 4-1 victory over Sheffield Wednesday (and Jackie Sewell) at Ayresome Park, and Robertson first played for Brentford in a goalless home game with Notts County.

As J L Manning put it in his Sunday newspaper report, 'Arsenal didn't win, and Tommy Lawton didn't make any difference.' He added: 'England's much-transferred centre-forward put not new life into the team but old life, with which vintage football the Highbury cellars are embarrassingly well stocked already. Lawton is a short-term policy invest-ed with panic which – let's be frank – would appeal to few, if any, other boards of directors in the First Division. While Arsenal are fiddling in this way there's a nasty smell of burning, and Highbury is covered with a heavy ball of smoke.' Trenchant criticism indeed, yet Lawton would leave Arsenal 2½ years later 'content that I helped them remain in the First Division'.

Manchester City arrived at Highbury only a couple of points better off than Arsenal. The crowd of 66,000 was 10,000 bigger than that at the previous home League match, against Chelsea. Both Arsenal goals, the first from a pass by Lawton, were scored by Doug Lishman, a former Marine Commando who had once been an England reserve and was capped once at 'B' level. Lawton went closest to scoring with a header that Bert Trautmann, City's German goalkeeper, only just kept out, but it was 80 minutes before he had a shot at goal in his withdrawn role. Although City did not equalise a second time until two minutes from time, they would have led 2-1 early in the second half if Roy Clarke, their Welsh international winger, had not shot well wide from the penalty spot.

Lawton's inclusion in place of Cliff Holton was Arsenal's only change from the side that had gained a first win at the ninth attempt in beating Chelsea. Holton, known in the 1950s as the man with the hardest shot in football, joined Arsenal from his home amateur club Oxford City as a full-back in October 1947, but was converted into a centre-forward by Whittaker in an emergency. Despite his heavy build, he had an exceptional turn of speed and, like Sewell before him, benefited from the tips Lawton passed on to him. In fact, Holton was the centre-forward Arsenal most used in the 1953-54 season, even after the arrival of Lawton, whose League appearances failed to get into double figures at that time because of what he described as 'the longest spell of injury during my whole career.'

Holton, who died at the age of 67 while on holiday in Spain in 1996, broke both the Watford and Northampton scoring records for one season after netting 88 times in more than 200 games for Arsenal, and his career total of goals, shared between six clubs, was around 300. On successive days in 1960 he did the hat-trick in Division Four games for Watford. Lawton was certainly a good tutor!

A severe ankle injury suffered in the match with Manchester City was the first of Lawton's setbacks while with Arsenal, but he still travelled with the team when he was out of it. Whittaker considered that to be good for morale, in addition to the advice Lawton offered in training. At any rate, form improved. Only four points were dropped in ten games up to the end of November, and, although that was too hot a pace to maintain, the season ended with Arsenal in mid-table. They were thirteen points clear of Middlesbrough, who went down with Liverpool.

Lawton scored two League goals in that first season with the Gunners, both against Aston Villa – but only one of them counted. It earned a draw at Highbury after the clubs' earlier meeting had been abandoned because of fog with Arsenal 3-0 ahead (the two other goals for Holton) after 23 minutes. That rearranged game, on 6 April 1954, came four days before the renewed association between Lawton and Mercer ended in sad circumstances. Mercer had been out of the side injured, but he badgered Whittaker to be recalled for visit of his old friends from Liverpool, on whose ground he trained – only for the curtain to be brought down on his long and distinguished playing career when he broke a leg in kicking at the ball at the same time as Joe Wade, Arsenal's left-back.

Two of the goals in a 3-0 win that day were scored by Derek Tapscott, whom Whittaker described as another 'pupil-learner' alongside Lawton. Tapscott certainly had a rapid rise after joining Arsenal from Barry Town a month after Lawton – at about the same time that Bill Dickson, the exchange 'makeweight' in Lawton's transfer to Notts County, moved to Highbury from Chelsea. Three days after his scoring debut against Liverpool, Tapscott was chosen for the first of his fourteen Welsh caps.

CHAPTER TWENTY-FOUR

Boardroom split by recall from Kettering

Arsenal won one trophy while Lawton was with them – the FA Charity Shield. As reigning League champions, they met Blackpool, the FA Cup holders, under the Highbury floodlights on 12 October 1953, and Lawton scored one of their goals in a 3-1 win. Doug Lishman obtained the two others, in this team: Kelsey; Wills, Barnes; Forbes, Dodgin, Mercer; Holton, Logie, Lawton, Lishman, Roper. There were seven changes from the side which the previous season had made sure of a title that would be Arsenal's last major honour for seventeen years; Blackpool fielded all their Wembley winners except for having Hugh Kelly back in the left-half position he had lost for the final through an ankle injury.

Another highlight of Lawton's stay with Arsenal was the first post-war visit to Moscow by a British soccer team, although it turned out to be a real test of endurance. The journey was made by invitation early in the full season Lawton was to spend at Highbury, but, because of the conditions imposed by the Football League, it had to be fitted in between playing at Leicester on 2 October 1954 and getting back to meet Sheffield Wednesday the following Saturday. Three demanding away games in eight days, involving 3,500 miles of air travel. No wonder Tom Whittaker said afterwards: 'Never again under those circumstances!'

Arsenal drew 3-3 at Leicester (two for Lawton), lost on the Tuesday by five goals to Moscow Dynamo, had the unnerving experience of flying through a snowstorm on the return home, yet still had enough energy and enthusiasm for a 2-1 win at Hillsborough against a club heading again for relegation. One of those goals in Sheffield was scored by Jimmy Bloomfield, the youngster introduced by Lawton into League football who had been transferred from Brentford the previous July.

Lawton was restricted to eighteen League appearances in that 1954-55 season. To the six goals he scored, he added the winner against Cardiff in the FA Cup (Arsenal lost at Wolverhampton in the next round), and one of the six shared with Rangers in a floodlit friendly at Highbury.

On Friday, 6 May, the eve of the Cup final in which Newcastle beat Manchester City, Lawton scored twice as an Old England team of over-30s crushed a Young England side of under 23s 5-0 at Highbury. These were the teams in Lawton's last big representative match:

Old England: Swift (Manchester City); Ramsey (Tottenham), Eckersley (Blackburn); Johnston (Blackpool), Chilton (Grimsby),

Dickinson (Portsmouth); Matthews (Blackpool), Mortensen (Blackpool), Lawton (Arsenal), Baily (Tottenham), Langton (Blackburn). Swift retired with a pulled leg muscle seven minutes after half-time and was replaced by Lawton's Arsenal clubmate Jack Kelsey, a Welsh international.

Young England: Matthews (Coventry); Sillett (Chelsea), Shaw (Sheffield United); Clayton (Blackburn), Smith (Birmingham), Flowers (Wolves); Hooper (West Ham), Atyeo (Bristol City), Hines (Leicester), Haynes (Fulham), Blunstone (Chelsea).

Lawton began the following 1955-56 season with six more goals in four successive matches, Cardiff the victims of his final First Division hat-trick, but his old bugbear of concussion again afflicted him after heading an equaliser against Chelsea. Although by then nearly 37, he felt he could have gone on a little longer with a club in the lower divisions, but he wanted to go out at the top and therefore turned his thoughts to management.

He fittingly scored his last League goal back at his home town of Bolton, on 3 September 1955, though not in victory. It was his 231st, discounting his four in the abandoned 1939-40 season, and there were 25 more in 33 FA Cup-ties. Raich Carter's retirement from playing three years earlier had left Lawton as the only player then still in the game to have scored a double-century of peacetime League goals, though at that time there were four current managers who had also done so: Joe Smith (Blackpool) 315, David Jack (shortly to leave Middlesbrough) 266, Billy Walker (Nottingham Forest) 214, and a former Sunderland colleague of Carter's, Bob Gurney (Darlington) 203.

Lawton finally bowed out of the First Division in his 390th League appearance in a defeat at Sunderland on 24 September. After that 37th game for Arsenal in League and Cup, leaving him with a total of fourteen goals for the Gunners, it was not until February that he moved to Kettering. He left the Football League not only as one of the finest centre-forwards to have graced it, but also with the distinction of never having been booked or sent off.

Meanwhile, Lawton was grateful for the chance to learn from Whittaker to see the game from a manager's perspective. 'Tom showed me how he ran his organisation, and how he dealt with the many problems that arose every day. I saw how he organised his staff and delegated authority to people he could trust. He taught me the value of a good scouting system – in fact, every facet of club management.'

The reason Kettering became Lawton's destination was that an Arsenal director was a Kettering man and in touch with officials of the Southern League club. Through him came the invitation to join Kettering as player-manager, with what he understandably called 'an exceptionally good deal' of £1,500 a year, ten per cent of gate receipts above a certain figure, and expenses. With Arsenal, whom he left with mixed feelings because his stay at Highbury had been 'a particularly satisfying period', he had been on the top basic wage then allowed – £17 a week.

Kettering were not doing that well in the Southern League. They avoided relegation, but action had to be taken if progress was to be made. Accordingly, at the end of the season, he got rid of players he regarded as liabilities and scoured the free transfers from League clubs in search of assets. He went back to Brentford for Jack Goodwin, a former Worcester City and Birmingham winger, and also signed goalkeeper Jack Wheeler from Huddersfield, wing-half Amos Moss from Aston Villa, centre-half Norman Plummer from Leicester, and Bob Thomas, an inside-forward from Crystal Palace. Moss and his brother Frank had followed their father into the Villa team. Plummer, though on the losing side, had played in the FA Cup final of 1949, the year in which Thomas had helped Fulham to reach the First Division for the first time.

Wheeler, who returns to this account in a later chapter, soon moved again, to his home club Evesham Town. Lawton had by then taken Jim Standen on loan from Arsenal, with the agreement that he could return to Highbury whenever Tom Whittaker found himself in urgent need of a goalkeeper. Standen, who also played cricket for Worcestershire – he headed their bowling averages when they won the County Championship for the first time in 1964 – was kept on the wages Arsenal had been paying him, and continued to train at Highbury apart from the one day a week when he travelled to Kettering to keep, as Lawton said, 'in the swim of things.' Standen was later with Luton, but his career did not really take off until he moved to West Ham. In exceeding 200 appearances during his six years at Upton Park, he was in sides that won the FA Cup and European Cup-Winners' Cup, and were runners-up for the League Cup.

With their team strengthened by Lawton's new signings, Kettering swept to the Southern League championship of 1956-57 with a record number of points. Inevitably, despite the Notts players' declared wish to stick with the man who had guided them to safety, that made Len Machin more determined than ever not to leave well alone. In refusing to take 'No' for an answer, he made a further approach to Kettering for Lawton, and was, as he saw it, third time lucky. It turned out to be anything but that, bearing out the strong doubts Lawton still had, and justifying the warning by Kettering's chairman, John Nash, that he was 'taking a foolish step.' Lawton himself came to recognise it as one that 'made subsequent life a fast, uncontrollable, downhill toboggan ride.'

Lawton was still deterred by his belief that the Notts board was as divided about him as when he had left as a player – some in favour, but others violently opposed. And although his return would be welcomed by many supporters, there was also the important fact that he would have to deal with opposition from several players who did not want him back at Broome's expense.

To quote again from his book *When the Cheering Stopped*: 'I argued that the appointment just wouldn't work. I tried to put things in their proper perspective, and asked Machin what would happen if I returned as manager. He seemed not to believe that there were directors who would sooner see me in hell than back at Notts County. He promised me his support, and whatever doubts I had Machin allayed.' The trump card the Notts chairman played was an offer that Lawton found 'too wonderful to refuse'. It comprised an annual salary of £2,500, unlimited expenses, and a house.

The appointment was made on 7 May 1957, but the boardroom split saw the resignations of Hubbard and Linnell, soon followed by Edwards. In an effort to sweeten the bitter pill for Broome, he was retained as Lawton's assistant on the then high salary for that position of £1,000. It was only to be expected, however, that he admitted to being 'a disappointed man, to say the least', adding: 'Football is my life, and I did not, at all costs, want to go back to being a trainer.' His renewed relationship with Lawton was therefore an uneasy one from the start, and it did not last the year as Broome's wage packet fell foul of the board's decision to cut costs.

For a first managerial post in his own right, Broome went, in January 1958, to Exeter City, who had just been beaten 0-6 at Southampton. He succeeded Bill Thompson, a former Portsmouth and Bournemouth defender, who left primarily because he could not agree to being deprived of his secretarial duties. In any case, there was then a feeling at the Devon club that the term 'manager' was 'outdated and obsolete,' leading to Broome's official designation as manager-coach.

Exeter were struggling near the foot of the Third Division's Southern Section, despite expenditure they could ill afford on Johnny Nicholls, a former England forward, from Cardiff, and Gordon Dale, a former Chesterfield left-winger from Portsmouth, who cost their then record fee of £7,000. Consequently, they were well on the way to being among the founder members of Division Four, for that outcome awaited clubs finishing in the bottom half of the Third's North and South sections. In the short time available, Broome was unable to prevent that fate, Exeter plunging to bottom place, but he straightaway steered them to the brink of promotion. The top four made an immediate return to Division Three, and Exeter finished fifth – they needed just two more points.

All, however, was not well behind the scenes. Albert Line, a Cockney who had been a peanut seller at the West Ham ground, was ousted as chairman, and bad feeling in the boardroom was exposed when he replied sharply to a ticking-off from his fellow directors for not attending enough meetings. 'They want me to resign,' he said. 'That's obvious, but they will be disappointed. I'm sitting tight just so long as I can do Exeter City any good. I have lots of supporters behind me. The directors know why I attended no board meetings for three months. I was seriously ill at the time. When I did go back, I was hardly able to talk because of the after-effects of the illness, and the new chairman [hotelier George Gillin] tried to pick a quarrel with me. He didn't succeed, but I'll admit I was discouraged. Most of the directors treated me coldly, even rudely. Later they held an emergency board meeting behind my back. On another occasion they switched the date of the meeting at such short notice that I couldn't attend.'

What a deplorable background for Frank Broome to try to do his job, as if he had not already had enough to complain about from his treatment at Meadow Lane. Line defended him as Exeter slipped down the Division Four table in the closing months of 1959. 'It's not his fault,' he said. 'He isn't the boss any more.' Soon afterwards, Broome handed in his resignation, but he quickly withdrew it when, in October, Line agreed to become vice-chairman, pledging himself to give Broome a free hand. Only five days later, however, Line was voted out again at a special board meeting, which he did not attend. A statement issued by Gillin explained: 'He has not kept his word to keep all reports within the boardroom. By his action he has lost the support of every member of the board. The whole situation is now back in open conflict with Mr Line, and it must be cleared up at the club's annual meeting on October 23.'

Line, who lived in Sidmouth and had timber interests at Coventry, Exeter and Falmouth, made a take-over offer to shareholders: he would repay any money the club owed to Gillin, and any other director, and put in more money for team-building. That, however, he found impracticable. 'It is quite obvious,' he said, 'that I cannot work with the board as it is at present constituted, and therefore can see no alternative but to withdraw my name for re-election at the annual meeting.' He had been a director since 1956, and had become chairman a year later in succession to long-serving Sidney Thomas, who became president, in circumstances as stormy as those in which he departed. Players had petitioned against the dismissal of manager Norman Dodgin, and several directors quit.

Frank Broome stayed on as Exeter's manager until May 1960, having seen them improve to finish ninth. He had an offer the previous month to take over at Carlisle, but was disinclined to move so far north and therefore accepted the chance to stay south when Southend United came in for him. His next move could hardly have taken him further away. Having resigned after only seven months with the Shrimpers, he was manager-coach in Australia with Bankstown in New South Wales and Corinthians in Sydney before having a second spell at Exeter from May 1967 to February 1969. After that he also coached in the Middle East. He was in his 80th year when he died in a nursing home near Exeter on 10 September 1994.

CHAPTER TWENTY-FIVE

Relegated in Lawton's season as manager

Tommy Lawton spent just one season as manager of Notts County – that of 1957-58. They ended it back in the Third Division, from which he had led them as a player eight years before.

Lawton returned from Kettering 'with my eyes wide open', expecting a tough time but feeling that he was sufficiently experienced to cope. However, as he himself said in looking back on that season of turmoil, his confidence was misplaced and his fears were well founded. He had admitted that 'apart from my first marriage the worst day's work I ever did in my career was to leave Chelsea for Notts County'. After such swift relegation had cost him the manager's job back at Meadow Lane, he again felt that he had made a big mistake in going there.

The split view of him on the board was only part of his problems. As he had also anticipated, the division among the players was an even bigger obstacle. It soon became clear that he did not have the support of them all. A few, indeed, so resented his appointment that he regarded them as 'backsliders who just wouldn't play for me'. Neither could he get along with either Broome, during the seven months the former caretaker was his assistant, or Syd Dickinson, the chief scout. 'We didn't see eye to eye at all.' This backroom disharmony was reflected in poor performances on the field that so swiftly led to relegation and his dismissal.

There was one newcomer in the team Lawton first fielded as Notts manager. At 8am on Tuesday, 20 August, four days before the 1957-58 season opened, Stan Newsham, a centre or inside-forward, began a 180-mile car journey from Bournemouth, and that afternoon took part in a full-scale practice match behind locked doors. 'I want the rest of the team to get the feel of Stan Newsham's play,' said Lawton, but it was hardly the ideal preparation for settling into new surroundings. And so it proved as Notts plunged straight into another relegation battle that Newsham was powerless to help them survive.

Newsham came to County's attention because of his prominent part in Bournemouth's run to the quarter-finals of the 1957 FA Cup – shortly after he had earned representative selection for the Third South against the Third North at Coventry, and scored in their 2-1 win. From a home third-round victory against Accrington on the day of Notts' calamitous defeat by Rhyl, the Cherries first attracted national publicity by beating high-flying Wolves at Molineux.

In the fifth round, Newsham was among the scorers in another shock success, by 3-1 at home to Tottenham, who were in second place between leaders Manchester United and Wolves in the First Division. Then, with their odds as outsiders cut from 200-1 to 50-1, Bournemouth were paired at home with United's 5-2 favourites. Never, said Frank Coles in *The Daily Telegraph*, had there been a more intriguing tie in the quarter-finals. And, in front of a record crowd of 28,799, Bournemouth were only a mud-mark on the crossbar away from forcing a replay at Old Trafford when Brian Bedford, their centre-forward, was left regretting that his shot had not been a couple of inches lower. United had to come from behind to win with two second-half goals, one of them a penalty.

As Bournemouth's leading scorer that season, with 30 goals in the League and three in the Cup, Newsham was seen as just the man to pep up the Notts attack. In five years with the Dean Court club he had scored nearly 80 goals in some 150 appearances. But it was a different story at Meadow Lane – to begin with, at any rate. In 1957-58, he managed only eight goals in 32 games and was third in the County's scoring list behind Jack Lane (eleven) and Gordon Wills (ten) in a club total of 44 that was the season's lowest in the whole League.

Newsham's inclusion at No 9 for his Notts debut at Sheffield United on 24 August 1957 was one of four changes from the side that had sub-dued Forest's promotion celebrations back in May. Wills was switched to inside-right in place of the departed Taylor and, with Chatham and Carver unfit, Pat Groome was at right-back and Bert Loxley at left-half. Life with Notts was in marked contrast for those two defenders, both of whom had been signed from Bonsall, a Derbyshire club, as teenagers. The Nottingham-born Groome had found few first-team openings since being given a run in the side during 1955-56, and there would not be many more before he left for Skegness. Loxley, on the other hand, rose to the captaincy as a consistently dependable centre-half in totalling 250-plus League and Cup appearances before his transfer to Mansfield in 1964. From Mansfield he went via Lockheed Leamington to Lincoln, whom he served for 21 years as player, trainer, manager and physiother-apist to 1987. He was 74 when he died in 2008.

Another newcomer besides Newsham under Lawton's management has a special place in the Notts County story. Jack Wheeler, the goal-keeper Lawton had signed for Kettering from Huddersfield, was taken on as trainer in June 1957 – and he did not miss a match in that role until his retirement, through ill health at the age of nearly 64, at the end of the 1982-83 season. He was in his 90th year when he died at Nottingham in January 2009.

On 30 April 1983, with two more games to play that season, Wheeler was on duty for his 1,150th consecutive League match – won at home in the First Division against Brighton. Notts had a dozen managers during Wheeler's 26 years with the club. And one of them was the man himself, as caretaker from September 1968 to November 1969.

It was nothing new for Wheeler to be involved in a rare sequence. Throughout 1952-53, when Huddersfield promptly regained the Division One place they had lost for the first time, he was in an unchanged defence with full-backs Ron Staniforth and Laurie Kelly, and half-backs Bill McGarry, Don McEvoy and Len Quested. All six played in all 42 League games and two FA Cup-ties. Wheeler, who hailed from North Littleton, a village near Evesham in the Cotswolds, fell just short of 200 first-team games as a goalkeeper – the first in 1938 with Birmingham, whom he joined from Cheltenham. He had limited League opportunities with the Blues, however. His path into their side was blocked first by Harry Hibbs, then by Gil Merrick, both capped by England, and he made most of his first-team appearances for the club during the Second World War before Army service took him to Italy.

In my friend Anton Rippon's excellent book *Gas Masks for Goal Posts*, about wartime football in Britain, Wheeler recalled the interruption of matches in London because of air raids. He used to take his ukulele with him, and when the players had to leave the field to seek shelter they had a sing-song in the dressing room until the all-clear enabled them to get on with the game. As was to be expected, considering the instrument he played, he remembered that 'George Formby numbers were particularly popular'. In Italy, the Eighth Army team in which Wheeler played was managed by Andy Beattie, the former Preston and Scotland full-back who was also Huddersfield's manager when Wheeler helped the Terriers to promotion.

Notts did well to restrict Sheffield United to one goal in losing Lawton's first match as manager, but five days later the pattern was set for a dismal season when an unchanged team conceded five at home to Fulham, with just one, by Tucker, in reply. A second-half penalty equaliser by Wills then earned a first point against visitors from Blackburn who would end the season runners-up to West Ham. An improvement was also shown in defeat by an only goal in the return with Fulham, though that was the match in which County lost skipper Wylie with a broken right ankle. He was out of the side until March, returning for the last nine games.

Only Leyton Orient were below Lawton's men after the failure at Craven Cottage, but the positions were reversed the following evening when Orient got off the mark with a home win over Doncaster, the club destined to be the Magpies' companions into Division Three. Defeats at Ipswich and at home to Swansea left Notts still with only one point after six matches. A second point, prised from visiting Huddersfield, handed last place to Doncaster, whose inferior goal-average had been damaged by four-goal Brian Clough at Middlesbrough in midweek.

At that stage, the Notts team included Tom Asher, a Yorkshireman from Wath Wanderers who had followed Jimmy Jackson as Wylie's replacement at inside-left. John McGrath, scorer against Huddersfield, occupied his third position in five games when moved from wing-half to play on the other side of Newsham, and Cruickshank had a new full-back partner in Worksop-born Frank Maddison, his deputy in his few absences the previous season. McGrath's place in a middle line completed by Russell and Carver was taken by John Sheridan, a signing from Linby Colliery who was to make more than 300 appearances before, in 1966, he linked up at Hartlepools with Brian Clough, then that club's manager, and Peter Taylor, his assistant.

After giving up playing, Sheridan worked with Clough and Taylor as a coach with Derby, Brighton and Nottingham Forest. He was in charge of the Rams' reserve side that won the Central League title in 1972 and, after resigning in the stormy wake of Clough and Taylor's departure to Brighton, he became landlord of the Lime Kiln Inn at Breedon-on-the-Hill in Leicestershire. He then had a second spell at Derby as part of Taylor's management team for a few months in 1984. He stayed on when Roy McFarland, the Rams' former England centre-half, briefly took over from Taylor, but left again that summer after another change of manager had brought in Arthur Cox.

On the evening of Wednesday, 18 September 1957 when newly promoted Nottingham Forest became First Division leaders with a 7-0 battering of Burnley, County were deposited back to the bottom of Division Two because Doncaster recovered from a half-time deficit to win their return game with Middlesbrough (no goal for Clough this time). Next day, however, those positions were again reversed, Notts finally winning, at the eighth attempt, 3-1 at Swansea. Hopes of having turned the corner were raised another notch on the Saturday, when a first win at home was gained as Newsham got off the mark with the only goal against Lincoln. That lifted Notts out of the bottom two, in which Doncaster were joined by Cardiff, but a week later Notts returned there after conceding five goals at Bristol Rovers Cardiff, meanwhile, were winners at Doncaster.

There was another new face in the Notts line-up for that game at Eastville. Permission had been obtained from the Chile club Colo-Colo for Eduardo (Ted) Robledo to be taken on a month's trial, and he was brought in at right-half after playing his first game for the club in a 1-3 defeat by Peterborough in the Midland League. Ted and his more famous brother George were born at Iquique, Chile, of a Chilean father and English mother. Ted was only four years old when the family emigrated to Wath-on-Dearne in Yorkshire in 1932 because of the political insta-bility in Chile, and the brothers began their Football League careers with Barnsley. In 1949 both were transferred to Newcastle – the Tynesiders were interested only in signing George, but neither brother would move without the other – and in 1952 they were in the team that defeated Arsenal in the FA Cup final, George scoring the winning goal. They went back to Chile together the following year.

With Sheridan fit to return after the defeat in Bristol, Ted Robledo replaced McGrath at inside-right for Notts' next match, won at home to Derby with another Newsham goal, but that was the last time the Chilean international was seen in the first team. After retiring from football, he worked on an oil tanker and died in mysterious circumstances. It was rumoured that he was thrown off the tanker and drowned. Whatever happened, his body was never found.

The victory over Derby took Notts clear of the relegation places, but only for one more week, and only on goal-average from Cardiff. They and the Welsh club were on eight points with Derby and Bristol City, Doncaster slipping three adrift after a five-goal thrashing at Liverpool. Defeat by two goals away to Grimsby sank Notts to last again, as Cardiff edged home against Derby and Doncaster gleaned a point from Sheffield United. The failure against the Mariners was the first of three in succes-sion, despite which Notts stayed just ahead of Doncaster, but with one match more played. After defeat at Meadow Lane by high-flying Stoke, Lawton's reshuffled pack made another unsuccessful trip to Bristol, cru-cially losing to fellow strugglers at Ashton Gate, while Doncaster's match with Barnsley was postponed because of the flu epidemic sweeping the country.

The drastic changes for the visit to Bristol City, whose recent game at Lincoln had been among others called off for the same reason, included the switching of Peter Russell to lead the attack and the first appearance of John Gissing, a 21-year-old from the local Stapleford Boys' Club, who was brought in on the right wing alongside the recalled Lane. Gissing played fewer than two dozen games before leaving for Chesterfield, and later Arnold in the Midland League, but, indicative of the troubled times the club were going through, he had seven other partners in that brief period.

Russell's only previous try-out as Notts centre-forward had also been against Bristol City. As before, he failed to score, and a week later, when Cardiff were at Meadow Lane on the first Saturday of November, he was omitted for the first time. Over the rest of the season, Lane (mostly), Wills, Jackson and Newsham shared the No 9 shirt, and at centre-half Ken Rawson almost doubled the number of Russell's further appearances. The Ripley-born Rawson's recall against Cardiff bridged a gap of three years, for he had played the last of his previous two League games in December 1954. With Russell subsequently reinstated, and Loxley then settling in as his successor, Rawson had few other first-team chances before joining Ilkeston as player-manager during the 1961 close season.

The match with Cardiff resulted in Notts' biggest win of the season – 5-2 after trailing 1-2 at half-time. Newsham (with the aid of a penalty) and Wills both scored twice, the other goal coming from Lane. At left-back there was another newcomer – Roy Pritchard, from Aston Villa. This former Bevin Boy had been an FA Cup and League championship winner with Wolves, for whom he had exceeded 200 senior appearances since joining them from school in 1941. Villa paid £6,000 in beating both Sheffield clubs for his transfer, but in three years on their books he played only three League games after breaking his jaw on his debut against Arsenal, so strong was the competition with which he had to contend from Stan Lynn and Peter Aldis when fit again.

With Notts, Pritchard was only a little less unfortunate. In his fourth game he cracked an ankle bone and missed the next nine. At 32, he could be no more than a short-term buy in any case, and within a year he moved to Port Vale. Notts tried to recoup £1,000, but the Football League awarded him a free transfer. He subsequently spent several seasons with Wellington, then continued to play in charity games quite late into a life that ended in 1993.

Around the time of Pritchard's arrival, Lawton was also interested in Noel Kinsey, Birmingham's Welsh international forward, and Alex Forbes, the former Arsenal and Scotland wing-half who had also represented his country at ice hockey. But Kinsey took the direct route to Port Vale, and Forbes signed for Fulham, with whom he had been on trial after being given a free transfer by Leyton Orient. Forbes, whose career had been threatened by a knee injury, replaced future Notts manager Eddie Lowe, a flu victim, in the Fulham team against Sheffield United, his first League club, on the day Ted Robledo first played for County.

CHAPTER TWENTY-SIX

Victims of Lincoln's great escape

From their biggest win of 1957-58 under Tommy Lawton's management, against Cardiff, Notts went straight to one of their biggest defeats, unable to reply to the four goals at Anfield that temporarily took Liverpool to the top of the table on goal-average.

Notts were then sandwiched between Lincoln and Doncaster, at the foot of the table, on ten points from sixteen games. Doncaster's victory over Swansea that day was only their third of the season, and a week later, with Lincoln winning against Orient, Swansea's home loss to Rotherham let Notts hand 21st place to the Welsh club by defeating Middlesbrough 2-0. That Meadow Lane match was the first of three in which Asher scored. The other goals helped force a draw at Orient, where Pritchard was injured and Bradley began his final run in the team in place of the unfit Linton, and a home win over Charlton, who were on the fringe of the promotion race.

After that modest revival Notts were fifth from bottom, fifteen points from nineteen games. Below them were Orient, Lincoln, Doncaster and Swansea, in that order. Doncaster edged out of last place with a draw at Lincoln while the Swans were losing again, at home to Grimsby, and next time out Doncaster also climbed above Notts by slamming them 4-0 at Belle Vue. Harry Noon, who hailed from nearby Sutton-in-Ashfield and had been signed from Bentinck Methodists two years before, made his League debut as left-half deputy for Carver. It was his only senior appearance of the season, but he had more than 100 behind him by the time he moved to Bradford City in 1962. He played only once in the Valley Parade club's Fourth Division side, and emigrated to Australia after a spell in non-League football.

The intensity of the Second Division relegation struggle was underlined when a 1-0 home win over Rotherham was sufficient to put four clubs below Notts again. And there was another debutant. Onto the right wing came Cyril Parry, youngest of a Derby footballing family, who had been signed as a fifteen-year-old in May 1953. Two brothers, Jack and Glyn, were on Derby's books (Jack played for them more than 500 times) and a third, Ray, was with Bolton, for whom he made his First Division debut against Wolves in 1951 aged just fifteen years and 207 days.

Ray Parry, later with Blackpool and Bury, was in Bolton's Cup-winning team against Manchester United in 1958. The next year he gained the first of two England caps at Wembley, scoring the winning goal in injury-time against Northern Ireland. Cyril, who had been an inside-forward with Derby Boys and Derbyshire Boys, played in only a dozen League games for Notts – half of them in that 1957-58 season before Don Roby resumed his hold on the outside-right position after being one of six players tried at inside-left in Wylie's absence.

A 1-0 home win over Sheffield United sent Notts into Christmas in their best position all season – six off the bottom, just three points above the relegation trapdoor. Notts also successfully sought the cancellation of Lawton's registration with Kettering, leaving them free to apply to the FA for permission to field him as a permit player in friendly matches – 'without remuneration', as the club's new secretary, C H Heath, explained.

Lawton had officially retired as a player in the Football League after receiving £650 tax free from the Provident Fund, but he was cleared for friendlies as an amateur in aid of charity, and to assist his third team through example on the field. That, however, was only after a parting brush with Kettering. They had retained him as a player on the minimum wage, and they at first blocked his efforts to turn out in unpaid games for Notts by demanding a fee of £860, which was more than the Magpies were prepared to pay. Only after months of wrangling did Kettering agree to cancel his registration and accept Notts' offer of £250 for the player who had once been the costliest in the country.

In taking only one point from two Christmas games with Barnsley, and then losing by three goals at Blackburn, Notts ended 1957 with twenty points from 25 matches – still seventeenth, four points above the last two, Swansea and Lincoln. A week later they had the encouragement of a 2-0 home win against Tranmere in the third round of the FA Cup, only to suffer two more League defeats, against Ipswich and at Huddersfield, and a fourth-round exit at the hands of visiting Bristol City, companions in distress who were between managers. The Robins, a point below the Magpies with a game in hand, were in the caretaker charge of former Charlton manager Jimmy Seed following the departure of ex-Gunner Pat Beasley and the pending appointment of Irishman Peter Doherty.

All three goals in that Cup-tie came in the second half. The scorer for Notts was Roy Pritchard, back in the side for the first time since his injury in November. A frozen pitch earlier in the week had looked likely to delay his return after a successful try-out in the Reserves, but a thaw set in – and that proved Notts' undoing. A back-pass by Chatham stuck in the mud, allowing winger Wally Hinshelwood to nip in for City's 88th-minute winner. Four weeks later, Pritchard himself scored a winner, but into his own net for the only goal of a home match with Leyton Orient.

After the Cup defeat, Linton was back in goal for the return to League fare at lowest-of-all Lincoln, where a 2-2 draw gave Notts, with two more defeats to follow, what would be only their second point in eight Second Division games since the win over Sheffield United before Christmas. Those further setbacks in that sorry sequence – both by the odd goal, at Derby and at home to Orient – came after more bad weather had caused the postponement of the Meadow Lane match with Bristol Rovers. That was in early February, when club flags were flown at half-mast, players wore black armbands, and two-minute silences were observed in memory of those who had perished during the week in the Manchester United air crash at Munich. A disaster of that magnitude certainly put in true perspective the troubles of clubs such as Notts County.

Victory at Stoke with a second-half goal by Lane ended Notts' bleak run on the first Saturday of March, only to be promptly followed by five consecutive defeats that plunged the County back into the relegation zone. Notts went through the first three without even scoring, beginning with a defeat they could ill afford. Bristol City swapped places immediately above the bottom pair by paying another successful visit to Meadow Lane. This time the deciding goal was scored by Bert Tindill, a key signing for whom Peter Doherty had gone back to the Doncaster club he had just left. On the same afternoon, Notts' next opponents, Cardiff, were three goals up at Lincoln when play had to be abandoned in a blizzard at half-time. It was an intervention by the weather that would be of the utmost significance in the relegation outcome.

Cardiff climbed towards safety by beating Notts 2-0 at Ninian Park, a result repeated in County's home match with third-placed Liverpool, in which Ron Wylie made his long-awaited return. The two other defeats that left Notts four points ahead of seemingly doomed Lincoln, but with two games more played, were inflicted at Middlesbrough and, on Good Friday, at leaders West Ham – both 1-3.

Next day, however, hopes of survival were revived by a 2-0 home win over Grimsby, Wylie scoring the clincher. This was how the teams then stood at the foot of the table:

	P	W	D	L	F	A	Pts
17. Rotherham	36	12	5	19	57	87	29
18. Bristol C	37	10	9	18	51	79	29
19. Notts Co	37	10	5	22	39	70	25
20. Swansea	37	8	8	21	57	94	24
21. Doncaster	38	7	10	21	47	60	24
22. Lincoln	35	5	9	21	38	76	19

The Easter Monday results favoured Notts, especially when on the Tuesday they won the return game against West Ham with a penalty by Wills, who had also been their scorer at Upton Park. Lincoln's cause looked hopeless when they were beaten 1-3 at home by Barnsley. Swansea lost at Derby, Doncaster at Blackburn, and Rotherham, heavily defeated at home by Charlton, slipped below Bristol City, home winners against Cardiff.

But Lincoln City were about to pull off one of the greatest escape acts in football history. After winning only five matches in 36 and having gone seventeen games without a victory since early December, they won all their last six fixtures to scrape clear of relegation by one point (although goal-average meant Notts finished two points short of safety). And the triumph that made sure of Lincoln staying up was gained 3-1 in the rescheduled home fixture against Cardiff City which they had originally been well on the way to losing. These were the final positions in Division Two:

1957-58	P	W	D	L	F	A	Pts
17. Bristol C	42	13	9	20	63	88	35
18. Rotherham	42	14	5	23	65	101	33
19. Swansea	42	11	9	22	72	99	31
20. Lincoln	42	11	9	22	55	82	31
21. Notts Co	42	12	6	24	44	80	30
22. Doncaster	42	8	11	23	56	88	27

Nine of Lincoln's sixteen goals in their concluding burst against Bristol City, Doncaster, Rotherham, Huddersfield, Barnsley and Cardiff were scored by Ron Harbertson, one of three forwards manager Bill Anderson signed just before the March deadline for unrestricted transfers. The others, the veteran Harold Brook, from Leeds, and winger Billy Coxon, from Norwich, played less influential roles in their revival. Norwich had been hoping to exchange Coxon for Birmingham wing-half Johnny Watts, and Lincoln had also been foiled in their original quest for a new centre-forward. Harbertson, a £5,000 bargain from Darlington, was sought after Anderson had unsuccessfully pursued Willie Gardiner, the Leicester player unattainable for Notts County. Harbertson, formerly of Newcastle, Bradford City and Grimsby, joined Wrexham after two years at Sincil Bank. He later returned to both Darlington and Lincoln before going out of the League with Grantham.

Another of Lincoln's forwards in that season of their Great Escape was the frail-looking but stylish George Hannah, a scoring Cup winner with Newcastle who was nearing 40 when he spent a season with Notts County before ending his career with Bradford City in the mid-1960s.

Despite Lincoln's astounding finish, Notts could still have saved themselves but for a devastating home defeat by Doncaster. A 1-4 reverse at Charlton, to which they stumbled after accounting for West Ham's coming champions, was hardly surprising considering the Addicks were just pipped by Blackburn for the second promotion place, but conceding five goals at home to doomed Doncaster without reply was the most devastating blow of Notts' traumatic season. It was not only Doncaster's solitary away victory, but also their only win in their last fourteen games. It ended a sequence of six defeats in which their defence was breached six times by Fulham, five by Blackburn and four by Swansea.

With Lincoln having so belatedly found how to win, Notts' three points from their remaining two games were too little, too late. After a goalless home draw with Bristol Rovers, they at least ended on a winning note by beating Rotherham 3-1 at Millmoor with goals from Newsham (two) and Lane. Of the 26 men Lawton called upon in 42 League games and two FA Cup-ties, Gordon Wills alone had an ever-present record – and he was switched about to such an extent that inside-left was the only place in attack he did not fill. Just four players – Linton, Loxley, Newsham and Wylie – finished the season in the positions they had occupied in the first match.

Tommy Lawton suggested to chairman Machin that relegation could 'probably be a life-saver' for the club, providing an opportunity to clear out what he saw as 'the dead wood' and start afresh. Accordingly, he submitted lists of the staff he wanted to retain and release, outlined the policy he wished to adopt in aiming for immediate promotion, and 'sat back hopefully, looking forward to the challenge of turning Notts into a tip-top football club'.

He had not taken the precaution of securing a contract, however, and that left him wide open to the news that soon afterwards left him feeling 'absolutely stunned'. There had, of course, been rumours, but it still came as a great shock when he was summoned on the first day of July in 1958 to a meeting with the chairman and the two other remaining directors, Sherwood and Hudson, and told that they could no longer afford to keep him. Lawton left claiming that he had worked for the club without pay for one period of three months and another of ten weeks, and was owed part of his fixed expenses.

As in the case of George Poyser, Lawton's dismissal represented an about-face by Machin, who, in Lawton's words, 'had moved heaven and earth to get me here.' Within a few months of his 40th birthday, he was out in the cold with a wife and two children to support, bitter and disillusioned with football in general and having no experience of any other form of employment. For the second time, Lawton's ignoring of advice not to go to Meadow Lane had led him to realise what a bad move he had made. Yet, incredibly, Notts County had still not seen the last of him.

CHAPTER TWENTY-SEVEN

'Tiny Tim' and 'Tiger' take over

For a successor to Tommy Lawton, Len Machin and his fellow directors first looked to Bill Anderson, Geordie manager of the Lincoln team whose last-ditch revival had returned Notts to the Third Division. But Anderson, who had first joined the Imps as trainer in 1945, decided to stay where he was.

That approach from Meadow Lane was just one of several lucrative offers Anderson rejected in remaining loyal to Lincoln, latterly as general manager, until October 1966, when he did find his way to Nottingham – as Forest's assistant, then caretaker, manager. It had been against Forest, with whom he had been given a trial as a teenager, that he had suffered the compound fracture of his right ankle that virtually ended his playing career while with Barnsley.

Anderson might well have been the right man for the Meadow Lane job, for he worked wonders at Sincil Bank on a shoestring budget. In 1948, he took Lincoln to the Third North title with a team assembled for only £2,000, and, although they were immediately relegated, he guided them back to the Second Division in 1952. Not until 1961 did they go down again, and that was after a financial crisis that compelled him to sell some of his best players. A further descent into Division Four could not be avoided as he was unable to buy his way out of trouble, and, after he had handed over control of team affairs, re-election to the League had to be sought at the end of the season in which he left.

To tide them over before making a new appointment, County again employed a 'caretaker.' This time he was Ernest ('Tim') Coleman, who after the 1939-45 War had returned to his native Nottinghamshire as player-manager of Linby Colliery in the Central Alliance, following a playing career of more than 300 League appearances shared between Halifax, Grimsby, Arsenal, Middlesbrough and Norwich – after being rejected by Forest. His goals boosted Grimsby's push to promotion to the First Division in 1929, and he won a League championship medal with Arsenal in 1933, the first year of the Gunners' title treble.

Coleman was also tagged 'Tiny Tim' because he was only 5ft 6in tall. While with Linby Colliery (on the edge of Hucknall, a few miles from Nottingham and Mansfield), he and another former Arsenal player, George Drury, were in the team that reached the first round of the FA Cup in 1950 before bowing out to Gillingham, who the previous Saturday had been beaten 2-9 by Forest. Frank Dulson, ex-Forest, was also in that Linby line-up.

Only goalkeeper Linton and right-back Chatham wore the same numbers in the last match under Lawton and in the first match of 1958-59 under Coleman, though four others of that relegated side, Loxley, Wylie, Lane and Newsham, played in different positions. There was a new outside-left, John Langford from Forest, but he would fade from the scene in mid-season with the signing from Lincoln of Alan Withers, a product of Nottingham junior football.

Notts drew at home with Accrington Stanley in that opening match. For the next game, lost at Wrexham, there was also a new right-back, John Kilford from Derby Corinthians. He, too, soon lost his place, and early in the new year was transferred to Leeds in part-exchange for Bob Forrest, a hard-working forward who had had an accidental introduction into League football. Forrest and a friend had gone to watch a match at Retford and were invited to make up the numbers when the home team found themselves two players short. Forrest did so well that he was signed, and soon afterwards attracted Leeds' attention.

Those Notts transfers were conducted by the man appointed to take over from Coleman on 17 October 1958. He was another former Arsenal player – Forfar-born Frank Hill, a combative wing-half nicknamed 'Tiger' who stood 5ft 8in. He won his three Scotland caps before joining the Gunners from Aberdeen. At Highbury, though not a consistent choice, he was in the teams that gained those three consecutive titles. After playing for Blackpool and Southampton, both of whom he captained, he was briefly Preston's assistant trainer until war broke out, then guested for Wrexham before service as an RAF officer service took him to India. He was into his 40s when he hung up his boots as player-manager of Crewe, a post he held for four years to September 1948, when he became manager of Burnley. In the 1954 close season he returned to Preston as manager, but left again two years later when relegation from the First Division was only narrowly avoided. After that he coached in Iraq before the call came from Meadow Lane.

Despite Coleman's best efforts, Notts County were third from the foot of the Third Division when he stepped down to become Hill's assistant. In the past, this would not have been a relegation hot seat. But the Fourth Division was in its first season, and the number of clubs heading up from, and down into, the lowest section of the League would be doubled to four.

After fifteen games with caretaker Coleman in control, Notts had ten points – ahead of Doncaster by two and Rochdale by three. They had moved out of the bottom two by winning at Rochdale with two goals from Newsham, while Doncaster had lost at home to Mansfield. The day after Hill's appointment, Notts were held to a home draw by Doncaster, Newsham again scoring twice, and they went through six more matches – among them a first-round FA Cup home defeat by Fourth Division Barrow – before gaining their first win under him. And for that they had to come from behind to edge through 4-3 at Meadow Lane against a Bournemouth side four points above them.

Two of Notts' goals that late November afternoon were the first for the club by Roy Horobin, a £5,000 signing from WBA who had made his debut the week before in a 3-3 draw at Norwich, along with John Butler, a defender from Bestwood Colliery. Both made more than a century of appearances for the club before leaving – Butler for Chester, Horobin for Peterborough.

Those seven goals in two games equalled the Magpies' output of the previous eight, but that welcome improvement was offset by unrest behind the scenes. Five players were transfer listed – Peter Russell and Stan Newsham (both at their own request), Tom Asher, Cyril Parry and Eddie Russell, an ex-Wolves and Middlesbrough wing-half acquired from Leicester as recently as the month after Lawton's exit.

Ironically, the two who asked to go were among the last to leave. Newsham, indeed, did not play the last of his 103 games for the club until March 1960, by which time he had contributed 23 goals towards promotion from the Fourth Division. Those goals took him to a total of 44, a decent return on the fee paid while Lawton was manager.

Peter Russell also took his appearances beyond 100 before moving to Hereford in 1959. From there he went to South Africa, where his £2,500 switch from Addington, a Durban club, to Durban City in January 1963 broke that country's transfer record. He afterwards moved to Olympia for £1,750. His namesake, Eddie, a schoolteacher who had totalled over 150 first-team games as a part-timer with his three previous clubs, turned out only nine times for Notts before leaving the League and concentrating on teaching. Asher went to Ilkeston Town, the Derbyshire club Ken Rawson would later join as player-manager. Parry did the rounds of several non-League clubs, ranging from Nuneaton Borough through Bourne Town, Lockheed Leamington and Matlock Town to Long Eaton United.

From their overdue victory against Bournemouth, Notts went six more games before winning again, 3-1 in January at home to fourth-placed Reading. The previous Saturday they recovered from three down at the interval to draw 4-4 at home to Halifax, also in the bottom six. One of those second-half goals came from Hucknall-born Keith Brown, a local lad making his League debut. He was the club's eighth centre-for-ward of the season, on a day when his inclusion, and that of Alan Withers on the left wing, increased the number of newcomers since August to eight.

A player who would command £400,000 in transfer fees and end one short of 250 goals and 500 games, shared among seven Football League clubs, was one of those new men. He was among some two dozen play-ers who by that season's end had led the attack since Tommy Lawton. This was Tony Hateley, who was taken onto the Notts staff as an ama-teur while Lawton was still manager, on 13 May 1958. He signed profes-sional forms the next month on turning seventeen, and although he made a scoring debut in a 1-1 draw at Stockport that November, he had only three other chances, without netting, as Notts slid towards their first taste of Fourth Division fare. As we shall see in the next chapter, most of the next season went by before he became a regular, but he then made up for lost time by providing the final impetus for immediate promotion. .

Two more newcomers were introduced into the Notts team during the last few weeks of the 1958-59 descent from the Third Division. Mike Stone, another Hucknall product, kept goal in place of Linton for the last seven matches, and Tony Bates, an amateur, followed Lane, Parry, Newsham, Eddie Russell, Hateley, Loxley, Sheridan, Brown and Forrest in becoming the tenth to be tried as spearhead. Bates, who hailed from Blidworth, a coal-mining village near Mansfield (also the birthplace of 'Tim' Coleman), made just the one appearance at a time when relegation had already been sealed. That was in the penultimate match in which one goal by Colchester was sufficient to inflict a ninth home defeat of a wretched season. The the jaded Magpies finished a mere point ahead of the bottom club, Rochdale. Bates was released to join Sutton Town soon afterwards.

Amid the season's numerous changes, that involved nearly 30 players, Frank Cruickshank, at left-back, alone played in all 46 Third Division games and the one Cup-tie. Don Roby was absent only three times and five others, Linton, Sheridan, Loxley, Carver and Peter Russell, got into the 30s for appearances. Eleven failed to reach double figures.

CHAPTER TWENTY-EIGHT

Hateley and Astle, learners from Lawton

Halfway through the 1958-59 season, morale at trouble-torn Notts sank so low that Len Machin barely survived a call to resign as chairman.

C F Williamson, one of the other directors, said that this would be 'the most beneficial thing that could happen to the club' after Malcolm Macdonald, a wealthy Nottingham industrialist, had refused an invitation to join the board, but Machin stayed on to oversee the immediate return to the Third Division in 1960. His time was to run out, however, during the coming decade, with the appointment of another strong personality – one who rose to the presidency of the Football League. More about him shortly.

Tony Hateley, an agile six-footer, began to make his mark as prompt promotion was attained. Reinstated for the last ten matches of the 1959-60 season, he scored eight goals. One of these came in the only defeat during that period, at Barrow. Another earned the point at Aldershot, with two games to go, that clinched the climb out of the League's depths as runners-up to Walsall. Machin bought the champagne for the celebration on the homeward journey.

For the next three seasons Hateley was a first choice until his £20,000 transfer to Aston Villa in July 1963, leaving with an aggregate of 79 goals in 139 League and Cup games. His 86 in 148 matches for Villa included four against Bradford City on the way to a losing League Cup semi-final against Chelsea, the club to which he next moved, for £100,000 in October 1966. He replaced Peter Osgood, whose broken right leg kept him out for the rest of that season.

Hateley scored the goal against Leeds that took Chelsea to their first FA Cup final at Wembley, but in July 1967, two months after that defeat by Tottenham, he was transferred to Liverpool for £96,000. He scored 27 goals in his one full season on Merseyside, including two League hat-tricks and a four-goal broadside, against Walsall, in the FA Cup. In September 1968 he was sold to Coventry for £80,000, but played only twenty times, scoring five goals, before entering another lean spell (six goals in 30 games) on joining Birmingham for £72,000 in August 1969.

Between Coventry and Birmingham, Hateley enjoyed a return to form on an FA tour of New Zealand, scoring 23 goals in eleven matches. Then, in October 1970, he rejoined Notts for £20,000. In his second spell at Meadow Lane he top-scored with 22 goals in another promotion from Division Four in 1970-71, this time as champions, and increased his total of goals and games for the club to 207 and 114 before departing again, for Oldham, in July 1972.

To Oldham's disappointment, Hateley failed to regain full fitness after undergoing a cartilage operation three months after signing. He made all but one of his five League appearances for them as a substitute, scoring one goal, before being released in May 1974. After that he was with Bromsgrove Rovers and Prescot Town before, as player-coach at Barrow, he briefly linked up again with former Liverpool clubmate Ron Yeats, the club's player-manager.

Two years after retiring from playing in 1977, Hateley was lottery manager at Everton at a time when his Liverpool-born son Mark was with Coventry, following a trial at Stoke. Mark was not such a roamer as his father, but outdid him for the size of his transfer fees. From the £190,000 a tribunal ordered Portsmouth to pay Coventry, after they had offered only £50,000, £1 million moves took Mark to AC Milan and, via Monaco, to Glasgow Rangers. Son also surpassed father in playing for England – 32 times, after ten Under-21 call-ups.

Despite being overlooked by his country, after failing fully to justify his big fee at Stamford Bridge, Tony Hateley had a record of which he could be proud. He was grossly underrated by a lot of people, and constantly criticised. 'It just baffles me why I have to take so much stick,' he once said. 'I'm no troublemaker. Except at Villa, I have never asked for a transfer. People still think I made a fortune. My share from all those moves came to around £25,000, but, remember, that was a gross figure. When the tax man had been I was left with £11,000. Who'd call that a fortune? I'm not embarrassed by the money I've made. The big fees paid for my services do not worry me. Sometimes, I wish people would stop talking about the money that has been spent on me and let me get on with the game. I look after my money as I've got a future to think about, but I'm not ruthless about money. I try to get the best deal I can for myself, and I like to be fair.'

Hateley described his spells at Coventry and Birmingham as 'holes out of my life,' saying that all his years in the game except those were happy ones. 'At Coventry,' he explained, 'there wasn't room for me and their other big-money striker, Neil Martin. One of us had to go – and Neil lived next door to the manager, Noel Cantwell. Stan Cullis bought me for Birmingham, but was sacked soon afterwards. Freddie Goodwin got the job, and that signalled trouble. Goodwin and I never got on.'

Tony Hateley's ability in the air compared favourably with that of Dean and Lawton, and there was nobody of his time better in that respect than, probably, Ron Davies of Southampton. Though somewhat ungainly of style, Hateley was also adept on the ground. Yet a manager as knowledgeable and respected as Harry Storer rejected him as a young-ster. Hateley was born at Derby, and was keen to play for his home club after doing well, then as a centre-half, with Derby Boys and Derbyshire Boys. Storer, manager of the Rams, told him, however: 'Son, you're no use to me. You'll never make a footballer.'

Storer was not alone in seeing no future for Hateley. Thirteen-year-old Tony had been involved in a collision with a bus in Derby and lay uncon-scious in hospital for five days. When he came to he was told he should forget any ideas of a sporting life. It was to his credit that he defied that bleak medical opinion after being almost a semi-invalid for two years.

Tommy Lawton's coaching in his last days as County manager also benefited another forward whose goals topped the double century. Jeff Astle, who was born at Eastwood, near Nottingham, played for West Notts Boys and John Player FC before going to Meadow Lane. It was evi-dent that he was a player of high promise, like Hateley exceptionally good in the air and also no mean performer with the ball at his feet, but Astle had to wait until 23 September 1961 for his chance in the League side – and then he was at outside-right, instead of leading the attack, for a match lost at Reading. In addition to Hateley, players ahead of Astle in the first-team reckoning up to that point included Newsham, Forrest and Peter Bircumshaw (the main scorers in the promotion season of 1959-60), Horobin and Chris Joyce, a Scot signed from Forest, who was later with Nuneaton Borough.

Almost another year went by after that debut before Astle established himself in the first team – in either of the inside-forward positions along-side Hateley or his deputy Joyce, but also occasionally on the left wing. And when Hateley was sold he still played only a few games at centre-for-ward, although he settled into that position before his move to WBA in September 1964. It was a real bargain for manager Jimmy Hagan, the for-mer Sheffield United and England forward.

In the meantime, for the 1963-64 season in which Notts were again relegated to the Fourth Division, Terry Bly was the new attacking spear-head, at a cost of £13,000, in succession to Hateley. Well, in truth, spear-head is hardly the word. Bly, who arrived as Coventry's top scorer, had been particularly prolific for Norwich and Peterborough, but after two cartilage operations he was nowhere near the force he had been in break-ing the Posh's record with 52 goals in the runaway Division Four title tri-umph in their first League season, 1960-61. In over 30 games he scored only five times for Notts before going to Grantham as player-manager.

Astle scored 41 goals in 116 games for County. For Albion, who also fielded him at inside-forward for a couple of seasons before making him their regular attack leader, he scored 174, including six hat-tricks, in 361 games. Two of those hat-tricks came in one week in September 1965; two others in three days near the end of 1967-68. No wonder he quickly became a great favourite at the Hawthorns, hailed as 'The King'.

The Throstles were regular cup finalists while Astle was with them. In 1966, they won the League Cup, beating West Ham over two legs. A year later, they again reached the final, the first to be played at Wembley in that competition, but lost to QPR after going two goals ahead. In 1968, they defeated Everton to carry off the FA Cup, Astle firing the only goal in extra-time to join the select list of finalists to have scored in every round in which they played in one season. In 1970, Albion were again League Cup runners-up, Manchester City beating them 2-1 after falling behind to a goal that made Astle the first to score in the final of both major domestic knock-out competitions.

Astle's England career was less distinguished. He failed to score in winning five full caps, and at the World Cup finals in Mexico in 1970 he lost a great chance to equalise against Brazil after being sent on as a substitute. Regrettably, it is for that glaring miss that he has become well remembered.

On being freed by Albion during the summer of 1974, Astle played for the Hellenic club in South Africa, then was with Dunstable, Weymouth, Atherstone and Hillingdon Borough before quitting the game in 1977 to run an industrial cleaning company. Dunstable, who had finished bottom of Division One South in the Southern League, were said to have offered him a signing-on fee of £8,000 and a weekly wage of £70. The *Daily Telegraph* noted after his death, at the early age of 59 in January 2002, that his van with the cleaning company bore the legend: 'Astle Never Misses The Corners.' His putting away of crosses from left-winger Clive Clark at the back post had been a prominent feature of his career at WBA.

In August 1986, Astle returned to the Hawthorns as president of the club's newly formed Challenge Club. In the 1990s he also came to prominence on the television programme *Fantasy Football League*, hosted by comedian Frank Skinner, an ardent Albion fan, and David Baddiel. Astle's fine singing voice had been a marked asset on *Back Home*, the single recorded by the 1970 World Cup squad, and Skinner asked him to sing over the programme's closing credits. This prompted Astle to tour the country, reminiscing about his career while dressed as Tina Turner. To quote the *Telegraph* obituary again, 'he remained a modest, amiable man who was grateful for what football had given him.' And for that he was indebted in no small measure to the advice he had received from Tommy Lawton.

Notts were in the hands of their third manager since Lawton when Astle followed Hateley out of Meadow Lane. 'Tim' Coleman held the post in his own right for nearly two years after Frank Hill's departure to manage Charlton in the autumn of 1961. Under Coleman's guidance, Notts finished the 1962-63 season seventh in the Third Division, boosted by the goals from their Hateley-Astle combination, but the following summer he stood aside to work in other roles behind the scenes. That was when the post was given to Eddie Lowe, the former England wing-half who had followed more than 100 games for Aston Villa with over 500 for Fulham after joining the Cottagers with his brother Reg.

That imposing record as a player was no true pointer to Lowe's proficiency as a manager, however. His first season at Meadow Lane was the one Notts finished five points adrift at the foot of the Third Division, with only nine wins from their 46 matches.

Lowe got off on the wrong foot even before a ball had been kicked, for in the same month as his appointment he dismayed supporters by parting with Hateley. With Bly failing to hit it off as the replacement, the Magpies sank into the relegation mire. They lost their first five games, the last four without scoring after just one goal, by Bly, on the opening day. The scene was set for an unremitting struggle that intensified with thirteen more blanks – five in succession soon after the turn of the year. The brightest of the few bright spots were a hat-trick by Astle in a victory over Oldham, that avenged a Boxing Day defeat at Boundary Park, and a run to the fifth round of the League Cup that began with the beating of First Division Blackburn.

Matters became so desperate that Lowe was provoked into a playing comeback well into his 39th year:, yet Notts lost at Oldham. With no revival resulting, he made only eight further appearances – the last in the first home match of the following season, when Tranmere were also winners. Notts improved to end that season in mid-table, but Lowe, who by then had also sold Astle, was dismissed on 12 April 1965. He found work in Nottingham as purchasing manager for a central heating company, but kept in touch with soccer by scouting for Plymouth.

Despite better results, based on a new strike-partnership of Jim Rayner, from Grantham, and Derek Pace, an experienced opportunist with Aston Villa and Sheffield United, there were rumours that County were in danger of going out of business. Not long before, their resources had become so stretched that they had not bought anyone for three years before signing winger Keith Fry from Newport. A financial crisis was averted, however, as Coleman resumed control after Lowe's departure – now with unpaid expert assistance of Andy Beattie, the former Preston and Scotland full-back, once a Forest manager, and Peter Doherty, the ex-Irish international who, either side of the 1939-45 War, had been a League champion with Manchester City and FA Cup winner with Derby. Both had managed their national teams.

That trio worked together until March 1966. Beattie stayed on in an advisory capacity, but Coleman finally retired and Doherty became Aston Villa's chief scout, then assistant manager at Preston and Sunderland, before winding up as scout for Blackpool, his first Football League club. Coleman died in Nottingham in 1984, shortly after his 76th birthday, Doherty at Fleetwood in 1990, two months before his 77th.

The next manager of Notts, appointed on 18 March 1966, was Jack Burkitt, who for the past four years had been coaching at Forest since ending a playing career of over 500 games with them. He had captained Forest to promotion to the First Division and victory in an FA Cup final. Fate decreed, however, that Burkitt's time at Meadow Lane would be in stark contrast for length as well as success. Although Notts finished 1965-66 eighth, support had dwindled to such an extent that a new low attendance of 1,927 was recorded for one of his early home matches (won against Chesterfield). The next season began badly, and Burkitt, feeling the strain, suffered a breakdown in health as the team hovered near the bottom of Division Four. In December he was given leave of absence, Beattie taking charge, and in the following February Burkitt resigned.

Seven months later, in September 1967, Burkitt joined Derby, with whom his two years as trainer included the Rams' return to the First Division under Brian Clough and Peter Taylor. He resigned in July 1969 on refusing demotion to the reserve job following the appointment of Jimmy Gordon, a former Newcastle and Middlesbrough wing-half, as trainer-coach. After that, Burkitt ran a post office in Nottingham before retiring to Brighouse, in Yorkshire, where he died in September 2003 at the age of 76.

Another former Forest player, Billy Gray, followed Burkitt as Notts manager after the departure 'by mutual consent' of Beattie, who had a final short spell as general manager before becoming John Harris's assistant at Sheffield United. Beattie, who died in 1983, aged 70, scouted for several clubs before retiring. Since leaving Forest, Gray had been player-manager of Millwall and manager of Brentford. At Millwall, the team plunged into such difficulties that Gray, like Eddie Lowe, brought himself out of playing retirement. He made his last few appearances in 1964-

65, when the Lions finished Fourth Division runners-up to Brighton. They were promoted again a year later, this time as runners-up to Hull, but Gray resigned over adverse comments made about his team by certain directors. At Brentford, he was back in Division Four with a club that, like Notts, sailed perilously close to financial extinction.

Gray's signings while at Meadow Lane notably included Les Bradd, who, as recalled earlier, is the holder of Notts' individual scoring record, and Don Masson, who played for Scotland. Both come more into this account in the next chapter. Gray stayed for only a year as manager, resigning in September 1968 with Notts back at the very bottom of the League. He soon found a new post at Fulham, where his appointment as coach to manager Bill Dodgin Junior reversed the roles they had held at Millwall.

It was for the fourteen months that elapsed before Glaswegian Jimmy Sirrel first arrived as Notts manager in November 1969 that Jack Wheeler stepped up as caretaker. And it was also during that period that Tommy Lawton made what he came to regard as 'another glaringly bad decision' by accepting an invitation to join the club for the third time.

CHAPTER TWENTY-NINE

Lawton suffers crisis of confidence

Tommy Lawton spent four months looking without success for a new job after being sacked as Notts County manager at the beginning of July 1958. His 40th birthday was looming that October, and he had a wife and two children to support with no experience of anything but football. He had a little money put aside, but was approaching what he called 'desperation level'

Then a friend who managed a brewery suggested he should do what so many other former footballers had done – become licensee of a public house. Lawton and his second wife Gaye were not keen on the idea at first, but they came to realise that it could be the best solution. And so it turned out – for a while, at least. They took over the Magna Carta Inn, one of four pubs at Lowdham, a village just outside Nottingham on the road to Newark, and for the next four years they revelled in running it, despite the long and tiring hours. In his own words, 'we took to the licensed trade like ducks to water.'

Eventually, however, they began to feel that a pub was not the ideal place for bringing up their son Tommy and Lawton's step-daughter Carol, who was into her teenage years. They needed to give more time to their children, but to do so they would have to employ extra staff they could ill afford. Their takings, in competition with the three rival inns, were subject to seasonal trade, leaving only a small margin of profit. So they moved out and rented a bungalow at nearby Burton Joyce.

Lawton's search for a new job eventually led to his becoming a representative for a life assurance company, but he also found an unexpected way of getting back into football, for which he had by then shed much of his disillusionment. Having devoured everything he could read about the game, he was well qualified to be a member of the first Pools panel that convened on 26 January 1963.

That Saturday was the fifth of a season on which more than 30 games were called off because of the freezing weather, prompting the Pools firms to set up the panel on the fourth and top floor of the Connaught Rooms in London under the chairmanship of Lord Brabazon of Tara, who arrived in a maroon Rolls-Royce. The other panel members who decided by a majority vote on the 'results' of the postponed games were Ted Drake, the former Arsenal and England centre-forward who had managed Chelsea's League champions in 1955; Tom Finney, the former

Preston and England forward; George Young, the former Glasgow Rangers and Scotland captain; and Arthur Ellis, a former leading referee. With them, but separated by special screens, were technicians, engineers and about 30 BBC and press cameramen. Doors were shut and guarded, and there was no contact with the members of the panel from 2.50pm until 4.45pm, when their findings went on air with an announcer saying that it was 'History in the Making'. He then read out the results – actual and predicted. There were several other occasions on which the services of the panel had to be called upon.

Kettering also provided Lawton with a break back into football, albeit a short one, while he was in the insurance business. The club were struggling in the Southern League's Premier Division when, in November 1963, he accepted their invitation to return as caretaker manager on a part-time basis – but only until the end of that season. Relegation could not be avoided (they finished next to last), but he helped them financially with an FA Cup run in which they knocked out Millwall in a replay at the Den before losing to Oxford United. He was asked to stay on, but declined. Combining his insurance work with travelling to and from Kettering two days a week, in addition to attending matches, proved too much of a strain.

Lawton found selling insurance hard enough as it was, and although his years as a publican gave him many contacts, it led to him drinking heavily. He did not become an alcoholic, but his private life began to suffer through his habit of getting home late almost every night. 'One couldn't walk into a pub and expect to sell a policy to the gaffer without having a drink with him,' he recalled. 'Then this drink would, of course, be returned. Later someone would come in and recognise me, for I was still well known in the Nottingham area, and he would offer me a drink. Whether I refused or accepted, the beer would be served, so I bought one back. In any case, if I didn't drink with the customers I might be considered a miserable devil, or a bit uppity, and as I depended on publicans for the majority of my business I couldn't let this happen.'

To begin with, that business was encouragingly good, but it began to fall off, and Lawton's failure to reach his required quota compelled him to leave after spending four years with that insurance company. He was employed by another soon afterwards, only quickly to feel so uneasy that he resigned. Not long after that, his worst fears were realised when the company went into liquidation.

With money problems mounting, Lawton was next persuaded by an estate agent to go into partnership at a sports shop in Nottingham. Lawton tackled this enterprise with enthusiasm, only to have his hopes of at last finding a path to prosperity dashed after only two months. His partner, who had provided the premises and the capital, told him they would have to close because they were not making enough profit in an out-of-the-way part of the city. For all the effort Lawton had put in, they had been undermined, as small traders, by the refusal of certain large sports manufacturers to supply equipment.

Out of work again, and now with no money in the bank, Lawton suffered a crisis of confidence and was compelled to resort to what his pride had hitherto prevented. He had to stand in the dole queue, ashamed as people who recognised him whispered among themselves and cast him pitying looks. Worse still, he never obtained a job at the unemployment exchange. He now lacked sufficient cash to pay bills, which led him to borrow money from friends he could not always repay.

'If the doorbell sounded,' he wrote in his book *When The Cheering Stopped*, 'we flew into a panic. Nine times out of ten it would be some collector, and sometimes we hadn't a penny to pay him, so we hid behind the curtains, or crouched behind the furniture until the caller had gone.'

Twice their electricity was cut off, and they even had the bailiffs in. The sale of jewellery Lawton's wife had accumulated while married to her wealthy first husband saved them from going under before another lifeline was thrown to them and thankfully grasped. It came from Vernon's Pools company. Lawton was given the job of appointing coupon collectors in various locations, and on Saturdays joined others with the same responsibility in ensuring that the coupons caught the early-morning train from Derby to Liverpool – a task of extreme tension if any collector happened to be late in turning up to deliver his batch.

Lawton was just settling into that new role when he received the invitation to join Notts for the third time. One Sunday night in October 1968 he took a phone call from Bill Hopcroft, then the club's vice-chairman – a post he held until his resignation on doctor's orders eight years later. During that period, Hopcroft put money into the club when extinction threatened, and the Magpies were also in desperate trouble when the call came for Lawton's third coming. They were bottom of Division Four with only two wins in their first dozen games, and were labouring under an overdraft of more than £100,000.

It was a time of gloom for both Nottingham clubs, for Forest were in a decline that within a few years saw their descent from Division One. Indeed, some of County's misfortune could be said to have rubbed off on their neighbours, for Forest failed to win any of the five games they played at Meadow Lane that season after fire had badly damaged the main grandstand at their City Ground during a match with Leeds that had to be abandoned. Notts went without a win and without a goal, through the three home fixtures they fulfilled before Forest were able to return home – an unwanted sequence that left Newport as the only losing visitors to Meadow Lane before the approach to Lawton.

Lawton was asked to help part-time with the training of the first team, coaching of the youngsters, and giving support to Jack Wheeler, who had become caretaker manager the previous month following the dismissal of Billy Gray. Stewart Imlach, a Cup winner with Forest in 1959, had been youth coach and assistant to Gray. He subsequently coached at Everton, Blackpool and Bury before retiring.

Uncomfortably aware of the unhappy circumstances in which he had twice left Meadow Lane, Lawton gave the matter much thought before accepting. In the end, it was his eagerness to return to League football that tipped the balance – with the proviso that Vernon's would allow him to continue working for them. That permission was forthcoming, but not for long. Lawton took to his new duties with such gusto ('this was where I belonged, and once again I felt that I was wanted') that he was soon spending so much time at the ground that his job with Vernon's suffered. It came to the stage where the Pools firm told him that he had to choose between the two. Hopcroft assured him that if he left Vernon's, Notts would make him chief scout as well as part-time coach. That made up his mind. He resigned from Vernon's, if with much regret. Hectic though it could so often be, he had been enjoying his work in being thrown in at the deep end of the Pools.

Back in football, he was really in his element, even though Notts finished the 1968-69 season only six places off the bottom of the Fourth Division. Scoring goals was their biggest problem, the team going without one in 21 of the 46 League games, one FA Cup-tie, and two games in the League Cup. Buxton-born Les Bradd, signed from Rotherham in October 1967, a month before his twentieth birthday, alone got into double figures – just, although he did so before Christmas. Soon afterwards, he temporarily lost his place through an injury that caused Barry Butlin to be loaned from Derby as a replacement. In any case, it was steady accumulation, rather than spectacular bursts, that made Bradd the club's record marksman in almost 450 games before his transfer to Stockport in 1978. Most of his goals came in singles.

Butlin returned to Derby in October 1969 after scoring thirteen goals in 30 League games for Notts, but his first-team appearances for the Rams had not reached double figures when he was transferred to Luton three years later. Even so, the £50,000 fee was the biggest Derby had received for a player to that time, and, having been the Hatters' leading scorer in their return to the First Division, his value was increased to £120,000 when he was sold to Forest in 1974. He was loaned to Reading after losing his place during the 1976-77 season in which Forest also rose to the top flight (four points ahead of Notts, who finished eighth), and he was later with Peterborough and Sheffield United.

The Notts newcomers during the season of Lawton's third and final return most notably included Don Masson, who would be reunited with Bradd fifteen years later as one of Lawton's successors as manager of Kettering. Bradd joined the Northamptonshire club in 1983 after also being with Wigan and, on loan, Bristol Rovers. Masson was at Kettering for only seven months, but during that time another player who exceeded 400 games for Notts (471 in eleven years to be exact) also rejoined him.

This was Dave Needham, a centre-half from the youth club at Blaby, a suburb of Leicester, who, as captain, was the most regular member of the Notts team during the 1968-69 season in which Lawton worked with Wheeler. He was absent only twice. Needham brought in a fee of £90,000 when he moved to QPR in June 1977. Six months later Forest had to pay £50,000 more than that to sign him as an urgently needed replacement for the injured Larry Lloyd. Although Lloyd, a former England defender and future Notts manager, had the prior claim when fit again, Needham still made three figures for Forest appearances, also occupying both wing-half positions.

Masson had played over 60 games for Middlesbrough, whom he joined as an apprentice, before his transfer to Notts in September 1968, along with full-back Bob Worthington. When Needham became the 2010 winner of the club's Former Players Association Achievement Award, Masson, a member of the NCFPA committee, said Needham was one of the reasons why he and Worthington agreed to move to Meadow Lane. 'We looked at the side and our first impressions were that David and Les Bradd were the two players a team could be built around. I also played alongside him at QPR, and had he not had the misfortune to play in an era when there was a surplus of good central defenders, he would have been capped at the very highest level.'

CHAPTER THIRTY

The three managerial reigns of Jimmy Sirrel

A defeat at Darlington, in which Don Masson and Bob Worthington made their Notts debuts, belied the improvement in the club's fortunes they were set to bring about. Along with Bradd and Needham, they were key members of the teams that carried off the Fourth Division championship in 1971 and won promotion as Division Three runners-up behind Bolton in 1973.

On the first of those memorable occasions, Worthington was the only ever-present – a distinction uniquely emulated in the same season by his brothers Frank and Dave with, respectively, Huddersfield and Grimsby. Bob totalled more than 250 games for Notts before leaving for Southend.

In those two promotion seasons, Needham missed only two League matches, Worthington three, Masson six and Bradd a dozen. Masson, the captain, had 294 games and 83 goals behind him by the time he went to QPR for £100,000 before Christmas 1974. Notts would have reported another financial loss without that fee. Although able to announce a profit of £73,619 the following September, they were still £167,680 in debt.

Masson repaid QPR some of their expense by helping them to finish second in the First Division in 1976. They were top after beating Leeds on the last Saturday, 24 April, but the decider was not played until 4 May, when Liverpool edged one point ahead with a 3-1 win at Molineux that sent Wolves down with Burnley and Sheffield United. The Anfield club, who recovered from being a goal down, were champions for the ninth time, then a record.

Masson played fourteen times for Scotland while with QPR, and won three more caps after leaving for Derby in October 1977 – the last of them in the 1978 World Cup finals in Argentina. He had left Notts with the reputation of being 'perhaps the best passer of a ball in the club's history', was rated 'world class' by Scotland manager Ally MacLeod, and became a mainstay of the QPR midfield in more than 100 matches. With Derby, however, he failed to live up to those high ratings, making them miffed because they had signed him in a straight swap for Welsh international Leighton James, a winger who had cost £300,000 from Burnley.

After some two dozen games for Derby, another free-transfer exchange took Masson back to Meadow Lane as player-coach in August

1978, and here again the Rams got the worst of the bargain. Steve Carter, a former Manchester City winger who was the other player involved, had played over 200 League and Cup games for Notts and also been in their promotion-winning side of 1972-73. Yet he made a little more than 30 first-team appearances while with Derby. He, too, returned to Meadow Lane, but only briefly before joining in Bournemouth's final push for the fourth promotion place from Division Four in 1982. Masson, meanwhile, increased his overall totals of games and goals for Notts to over 450 and almost 100, respectively, and in 1981 played a prominent part in their return to the First Division they had left back in 1926. He also scored their only goal in the Anglo-Scottish Cup final they lost to Chesterfield over two legs.

The testimonial Masson received in April 1982, when he was 35, was therefore thoroughly deserved. After leaving Meadow Lane for the last time, he was in the United States with Minnesota Kicks, then in Hong Kong with Bulova, before his short stay at Kettering.

Richie Barker, another player with a Derby connection (doubly so, because he was born there and entered the Football League with the Rams) joined Notts three months after Masson, in December 1968. He was a draughtsman while a Burton Albion part-timer under the management of Peter Taylor, a former Coventry and Middlesbrough goalkeeper. In the autumn of 1967 Barker was at the advanced age of almost 28 for a League newcomer when Taylor, by then the talent-finding assistant to Clough at the Baseball Ground, was again responsible for signing him. Barker scored valuable goals in a team being rebuilt after many lean years, but was allowed to leave for Meadow Lane when he was himself replaced following the arrival of Willie Carlin from Sheffield United. The diminutive Carlin, already a promotion winner with Carlisle, from the Third Division in 1965, promptly exerted a big influence on Derby's return to the First Division, and he had two more promotions in store – with Leicester's Second Division champions of 1970-71 and in the Notts side that climbed out of Division Three in 1973.

Barker was also in a team that won promotion. His thirteen goals made him the third highest scorer, behind Hateley (22) and Masson (fourteen), in Notts County's 1970-71 escape from Division Four. The following season, having scored nearly 40 goals in 120 games for the Magpies, he moved to Peterborough, but a broken leg precipitated his entry into management – first as assistant to Alan Durban, a former Derby clubmate, at Shrewsbury. He subsequently succeeded Durban as manager at both Shrewsbury and Stoke when the Welshman moved first to the Potters, then Sunderland. He was also assistant manager of Wolves before going back to Notts as Larry Lloyd's managerial successor in November 1984.

It was an ill-fated return, however. Barker was dismissed five months later with the club at the foot of Division Two, five games from a second successive relegation. After that, Barker coached in Greece and Egypt, was again assistant manager, with Sheffield Wednesday, and scouted for WBA. His final taste of League management was for one match – as Albion's caretaker after the departure of Ray Harford in 1997.

The man who followed Barker as Notts manager – chosen from more than 40 applicants – was also the man whose appointment led to Tommy Lawton's third and final parting. This was because those were two of the three occasions on which Jimmy Sirrel, son of a Glasgow grocer, took over the managerial reins at Meadow Lane. He had been a beam-boy in a carpet factory on leaving school at fourteen, and two years later was apprenticed as a coppersmith. At seventeen, his form as an inside-forward with Renfrew Juniors persuaded Chelsea to sign him as a professional, but then came the war, which he spent helping to repair ships from Cairo to Mombasa. Afterwards, a sciatic nerve restricted a playing career that took him to Bradford, Brighton and Aldershot.

Sirrel first joined Notts, in succession to Jack Wheeler, in November 1969, after spending nine years with Aldershot as their trainer-coach, and then showing his worth as a manager at Brentford – a post he obtained despite not being among more than 30 applicants. It was after Sirrel's appointment at Meadow Lane that Jack Dunnett, who had taken over as Notts chairman in 1968, called Lawton into his office and told him he was no longer required. The club's scouting system was being rearranged, with the post of chief scout made redundant. 'This time,' said Lawton, 'my departure was not totally unexpected.' There was, however, to be one last special occasion for which he returned to Meadow Lane. In 1995, he was back there for his official opening of the Tommy Lawton Bar.

With Brentford, Sirrel had worked long hours filling the roles of chief scout, coach, physio, groundsman, baggage man and general dogsbody in his successful efforts to reduce debts that had gone close to driving the club out of business (there had been talk of a takeover by QPR). The inability to spend on new players had made it impossible for him to get the club out of the Fourth Division, but in his two years at Griffin Park he had reduced the overdraft by £80,000 to £20,000.

That was an aspect of his work that especially appealed to Jack Dunnett, the solicitor and MP who had acquired first-hand knowledge in having previously been Brentford's chairman. With receipts from home gates averaging just £4,700, County reported a loss of £40,000 in

December 1969, increasing the total deficit to £140,000. Considerable as that amount was for those days, it bore favourable comparison with the £1.8 million that threatened the future of the club in 1986, and again early in the 21st century when it went into administration. Survival on both those occasions was due in no small measure to the backing of fans and players – most notably when, on 15 September 1986, 1,500 packed the Astoria Ballroom in the city, with hundreds locked outside, to attend a meeting called to cope with the crisis. Lawton was among those who addressed that gathering, along with Masson and Sirrel, and support was pledged by all the current players, led by the then captain, Steve Sims.

Notts would almost certainly have folded beforehand but for financial support provided by Jack Dunnett, who served on the Middlesex, Enfield and Greater London councils while with Brentford, then was the Notts chairman until 1987 following his election as Labour MP for Nottingham Central in 1964. He held that seat until it was abolished in boundary changes for the 1974 election. He became MP for the new Nottingham East constituency until 1983, when he did not stand again. Two years before, he was elected President of the Football League on a second ballot from John Smith, the Liverpool chairman; Ernie Clay (Fulham) and Jack Wiseman (Birmingham) had been eliminated in the first ballot.

Dunnett was succeeded as Notts chairman in June 1987 by Derek Pavis, a wealthy local plumber who was paid £500,000 of the £3 million with which an anonymous supporter bought Meadow Lane. This was part of the deal that, in December 2003, took the club out of the administration which had lasted eighteen months. The other influences on the saving of the club were down to the Supporters' Trust and three local businessmen. Pavis received the £500,000 because that was the amount he had paid in 1999 for the lease of the ground's West Stand, for which the club had been paying a peppercorn rent to Dunnett's company, Park Steet Securities, since May 1987. In return for financing the building of the stand, Dunnett had rented the use of its executive boxes back to the club, and hired rooms inside the stand to a social and sports club. Pavis negotiated similar payments, even while the club faced extinction.

Such complicated financial arrangements were far from Jimmy Sirrel's mind when he relieved Jack Wheeler of managerial responsibilities, though he was to become a member of the Notts board in June 1984. It was under Sirrel's direction that Notts soared from Fourth Division to Second in three seasons in the early 1970s, the rise from the Fourth earning him that section's Manager of the Year award. The club had come close to another promotion, finishing fifth, when Sirrel, then 53, left in October 1975 to follow Ken Furphy as manager of Sheffield United, but it was a move he came to regret. He was sacked two years later after the Blades had been relegated from the First Division with only 22 points.

Only a fortnight elapsed, however, before Sirrel was back at Meadow Lane for his second spell, this time in place of Ron Fenton. The team was bottom of the Second Division after nine games without a win in the 1977-78 season. Fenton had also joined Notts from Brentford, as youth coach, and had stepped up to succeed Sirrel after helping in the club's revival. With Colin Addison, a former Forest forward, initially his assistant before leaving to be manager of Newport, Fenton twice had Notts challenging for a third promotion before the rot set in that cost him his job. He refused to stay on as assistant manager, a post filled by Colin Murphy, but, like Sirrel, soon found another post. He worked with Brian Clough at Forest until 1993, leaving when Clough resigned.

Sirrel steered Notts to fifteenth place in 1977-78, when Forest became First Division champions and winners of the League Cup (they knocked out their neighbours on the way to beating Liverpool in a replayed final). Three seasons later, Sirrel was again the guiding hand in Notts' rise to the Division One as runners-up to West Ham, but one year later, in August 1982, he stood aside to become general manager. Team affairs were handed to Howard Wilkinson, who had become his assistant after Murphy's departure to manage Lincoln. Wilkinson, an England Under-21 manager who later coached the England senior side, kept Notts in the top sphere, but he would enjoy his greatest successes in gaining promotion to the First Division with Sheffield Wednesday (one of the clubs for which he had played) and Leeds, whom he also piloted to the League title.

Wilkinson's one season in control at Meadow Lane was followed by relegation in 1984 with Lloyd at the helm. Then came the further decline under Barker, from whom director Sirrel took over in April 1985 for his third spell as manager following a tenth home defeat of the season. Of their remaining five matches, Notts lost only the last – at Fulham, but they would still have gone down to the Third Division with Cardiff and Wolves even had they won. Middlesbrough, the club immediately above them, pulled three points clear with a 2-0 win at Shrewsbury and also had a superior goal-difference.

Promotion and relegation issues were made to seem unimportant, however, for that was the day, 11 May, when Bradford City's Valley Parade went up in flames, causing 56 deaths.

The previous Saturday, Notts County's last home game had been held up while police had struggled with rioting Manchester City supporters. Nearly 18,000 (three times the average) saw the Magpies win 3-2. 'The effect Jimmy Sirrel had on the players during our last five matches was remarkable,' said Dunnett. 'While both Larry Lloyd and Richie Barker did their best, they could not be as successful as Jimmy.'

Sirrel kept Notts in the top half of the Third Division before hand-ing over to former Forester John Barnwell in 1987. The play-offs were attained the following season, but Notts were unable to overturn a 1-3 first leg home defeat by Walsall, who beat Bristol City in the final. Neither could Barnwell sustain the momentum. In December 1988, after eighteen months in the job, he was dismissed with the club embroiled in another battle against relegation. His assistant, John Newman, an FA Cup finalist with Birmingham in 1956, was put in charge until the appointment in January of Neil Warnock, who had taken Scarborough into the Football League, the first to be promoted automatically from the Conference.

Warnock lifted Notts to the respectability of ninth place, and pointed them to promotion in both the next two seasons via the play-offs. In 1990, they were third in Division Three and defeated Tranmere 2-0 in the final at Wembley. In 1991, they not only beat Brighton 3-1 on their return to the national stadium , having finished fourth in Division Two, but also went close to the FA Cup semi-finals. In their televised quarter-final tie at Tottenham, the lead they gained in the first half was wiped out by an own goal conceded by Craig Short, who a year later earned them their record fee when transferred to Derby for £2½ million, and only seven minutes were left when Paul Gascoigne scored Spurs' winner.

Thereafter the Warnock magic wore off as he found working with limited resources too big a handicap back among the big boys. Notts pitched up next to the bottom of the First Division in 1992, missing involvement in the birth of the FA Premier League, while ironically stay-ing in the revamped First Division. They were again in trouble when Warnock was dismissed early in 1993. Relegation was narrowly avoided, but not for much longer. Further descents in 1995 and 1997 returned them to the lowest rungs of the League ladder. Although promoted as Division Three champions in 1998, they descended again in 2004. They remained in Division Two only because that was what the old Division Four had become through more restructuring of the League.

Jimmy Sirrel, meanwhile, did some scouting for Derby after stepping down at Meadow Lane, and lived on in retirement until September 2008, when he died in Nottingham, four months before Jack Wheeler, in his 87th year. He has gone down in Notts County history as legendary a fig-ure as a manager as Tommy Lawton has been as a player. The big differ-ence, however, is the manner in which their three spells ended. Unhappy as Lawton's other exits had been, the final one led him to the most trau-matic and depressing period of his whole life.

CHAPTER THIRTY-ONE

Horrendous problems after Lawton's third departure

The inability to repay money he had been forced to borrow from people he knew was only the start of the horrendous problems that weighed Tommy Lawton down after his final break with Notts County.

At just 50, he was at an age when it was increasingly difficult to obtain new employment, and he soon found himself unsuited to the new jobs he did find. Consequently, he spent more time on the dole than off it, driving him to swallow his pride and seek those favours from friends in order to give his family some measure of the support to which they had become accustomed in the good times.

Those emergency sources of supply quickly petered out, however, when the debts remained outstanding, making him fortunate to be fixed up with work that promised the required solution before his financial situation became desperate. This arose, after Christmas 1970, as the result of a newspaper publishing a picture of him in the dole queue. A furnishing company in Wales offered him a decent wage, a company car and expenses as one of their representatives. He was taken on after attending a sales course, and all seemed well when, as he thought, he began to do good business in the Nottingham area. It was therefore much to his consternation when the firm said they were not satisfied with the number of orders he was securing. He could only assume that some of those he had posted had gone astray, but that was not accepted as an excuse, so once again he was on the unemployment scrapheap.

On being told to return the car to Colwyn Bay, he feared the cost of taking the train back home and the possibility of an overnight stay. Could not, he suggested, a spare driver be sent to collect the car when a delivery was next made to Nottingham? As no reply was received, he continued to use the car, but that resulted in another setback. The vehicle would not start when he and his wife prepared to return home after accepting a friend's invitation to have a short stay at his caravan at Sutton-on-Sea, a resort adjoining Mablethorpe in Lincolnshire, with the intention of relieving their renewed depression. In trying to give the car a push start with Gaye at the wheel, Lawton collapsed and was rushed to hospital in Louth, where a suspected thrombosis was diagnosed. He was discharged a fortnight later with strict instructions to take a complete rest.

'Apparently I was exhausted physically and mentally,' he said in the chapter of his book headed SLIDING, SLIDING, SLIDING. 'This fact I found as hard to believe as I did to follow the hospital's instructions. I had lived such a fit and active life, and to be told in effect that I was worn out was a bitter pill to swallow.'

This breakdown in his health obviously made Lawton's prospects of further employment even more remote, and he was not long in learning that his troubles were not to come singly. A few days after returning home he had a visit from the police, to whom he had been reported for being in possession of a stolen car. His explanation was of no avail. Neither was his contention that he was entitled to keep the car as security against the wages he was owed. The car was taken to the local police station, which he had the unpleasant experience of having to attend late at night to make a statement, and from there the vehicle was claimed back by the company.

Besides being cast into ever-deepening gloom, Lawton was embittered by the fact that very few of those he had helped financially when he had been in a position to do so were now inclined to return the favour. 'Instead,' he said, 'they seemed to prefer to look down on me, and to gloat at my fall from grace.' He was back on the dole with an ever-pressing need for more than the weekly £19.50 then handed out, but another door opened for him after his plight had been publicised in an interview with the television presenter Eamonn Andrews for the *Today* programme. The offer again came from a furnishing concern, a larger one. And again he felt that this was the perfect chance he was looking for. The proposal was to form a subsidiary of the company, labelled Tommy Lawton Ltd, with himself on the board of directors at an annual salary of £2,500. As before, there was a company car and an expenses account. In addition, Lawton's son had a share issue of 38 per cent, but, as he was still a minor, Lawton signed the certificates.

At the outset, all seemed as ideal as Lawton had hoped. The early contract he secured to furnish Derby County's 600 Club was worth almost £5,000. The regular payment of his wages, expenses and commission enabled him to meet some outstanding bills and once more to have a bank account. But, as before, it was all too good to be true. The flow of money from the parent company soon began to dry up – so much so that Lawton had to apply for an overdraft. There was another warning sign when he had to hire a car after his own vehicle had been damaged in an accident. Contrary to what he had expected, the bills he signed for the hire, repairs, petrol and servicing were not met by the main company, and it all came to yet another dead end when Lawton arrived home one night to hear his wife had been told in a telephone call that Tommy Lawton Ltd had been put into liquidation.

Consequently, Lawton did not have enough funds to meet cheques he had signed. It was a severe enough blow when, at an uncomfortable interview with the bank manager, overdraft facilities were withdrawn. Worse was to follow when two CID officers visited his home and escorted him to the police station at Arnold, a suburb of Nottingham, where he was charged with issuing dishonoured cheques and of obtaining a car by false pretences. A few dud cheques were destroyed by the recipients, but not by others. This meant that six charges remained for the case to be dealt with at the Shire Hall in Nottingham, and Lawton was convinced that he would have been sent to prison but for the strong plea on his behalf put forward by his solicitor. Instead, he was put on probation for three years, a verdict he still considered 'pretty hardish' because he felt he had not committed his offences deliberately. He put his troubles down to his own foolishness in persisting in the belief that the money he was owed would eventually turn up.

Some small relief was offered by the landlords to whom he had fallen behind in paying rent on his house. They allowed him some arrears on the understanding that he would eventually be able to square his account. But the fact remained that he was now again out of a job with debts mounting. On top of that, there was the publicity his court case had aroused – especially in Nottingham, where front-page reports were carried with big headlines and photographs. He could not pay the price of a good standard of living, but was paying the price of his past fame. To quote again from his book: 'I left the court judged a criminal, although all my life I had made a point of honesty and straight dealing. The shame I felt after the hearing was unbelievable. I was scared to move out of the house. For the first time in my life I was ashamed to look anyone in the face. My nerves were in a terrible state. I couldn't sleep very well, had no appetite, and my confidence had vanished completely.'

The lone bright spot at that lowest point was that his family never failed to give him support. Then, arising from the prosecution, another lifeline was thrown to him by John Mabbutt, the managing director and owner of a Nottingham company called Floor Maintenance Services. Lawton had done him a favour while still playing for Notts by arranging for two local teams to play at Meadow Lane as a fund-raising effort for their newly formed league, and with which Mabbutt was involved. Lawton had presented a cup, named after himself, to the winners, and the money raised had enabled the league to get off on a sound footing. Now the favour was returned. Lawton was offered a job as a representative for the company. He accepted with heartfelt thanks, and, as the business prospered, the regular wage again coming in at last enabled him to regain some of his self-respect.

Around this time, in 1972, Lawton received some more good news. The idea of a testimonial had been suggested before, but he had reluctantly not gone ahead – even though League secretary Alan Hardaker had given permission, and Notts had agreed to the use of their ground – because he had viewed arranging it single-handedly too daunting. The difference now was that Sir Matt Busby, by then a Manchester United director, Andy Beattie, and his old friend Joe Mercer had formed a committee to organise it. The secretary of the committee was Coventry's secretary, Eddie Plumley. Those who served on it were Lawton's other former footballing colleagues Cliff Britton, Harry Catterick, Stan Cullis and Bill McGarry. Others who promised help included managers Clough, Revie and Shankly. It all made Lawton fully aware, and everlastingly thankful, for the comradeship and loyalty of old friends.

The match took place not in Nottingham but at Goodison Park, on the night of Monday, 6 November 1972. Rain poured down half-an-hour before the kick-off, but there was still an attendance of 12,209, producing receipts of £6,300 for a contest between Everton and a Great Britain XI. It resulted in a 2-2 draw, Everton denied victory after leading by the brilliance of one of their own players, goalkeeper Gordon West, who stood in at short notice for the injured Peter Shilton in the representative team. This was how they lined up:

Everton: David Lawson; Tommy Wright, Henry Newton; Howard Kendall, Roger Kenyon, John Hurst; Alan Whittle, Mike Bernard, Ron Belfitt, Colin Harvey, John Connolly.

Great Britain XI: Gordon West (Everton); Keith Newton (Burnley), Willie Donachie (Manchester City); Bruce Rioch (Aston Villa), Ron Yeats (Tranmere), Bobby Moore (West Ham); Mike Summerbee (Manchester City), Colin Stein (Coventry), Francis Lee (Manchester City), Willie Carr (Coventry), Bobby Charlton (Manchester United).

George Best was a late withdrawal from the Great Britain XI. Early that month, death threats had forced Manchester United to pull him out of the Northern Ireland squad for a match with Spain in Belfast.

Lawton was especially grateful to Bobby Moore, the England captain, who drove to and from the match after missing his train from London. Here, as Lawton observed, was a man who had never seen him play, had heard about him only at second-hand, yet had gone to all that trouble.

Before the match, Lawton, who was accompanied by his son, ate with the Great Britain team. After it, he revelled in a get-together in the club-room with friends from the old days – among them several players with whom he had helped Everton win the League championship in 1938-39, and, above all, 'Dixie' Dean, who was then 65. 'Many, many wonderful memories returned. Memories which brought tears to my eyes.' Lawton's only regret was that he had been unable to take part in the game. 'I would have loved to have put a strip on, but it would have been ludicrous for a 53-year-old man, out of condition, to have kicked about with the cream of British football.'

A week later, Lawton had another day to remember. At the invitation of the *Daily Express*, he attended the celebration lunch given to mark the Queen's Silver Wedding anniversary at the Savoy Hotel in London. He and Billy Wright, who was the first to play 100 times for England, were football's representatives for 1947, the year of her majesty's wedding. The Pathe newsreels showed Lawton's transfer to Notts County, plus snippets of the international against Sweden in which he first played for England after dropping into the Third Division. Both items were given a warm reception, as was Lawton, as people went up to talk about the old days. 'It did my ego good to think that so many were still interested in me. It was a wonderful week altogether.'

Lawton's troubles did indeed seem behind him at that point, yet only two years later he was once more on the wrong side of the law – this time for obtaining £20 by deception from 'a trusting friend'. He was sentenced to 200 hours of community service. In 1977, he underwent major stomach surgery and in 1985 was again in financial difficulties. This time the *Nottingham Evening Post* came to his rescue. The chance to contribute a regular column helped both their circulation and his pocket, allowing him to air his views on a wide range of soccer subjects. He was a constant source of interesting stories, expressing opinions and thoughts based on his long experience of the game as both player and manager.

Help was also received by the Brentford club, who arranged a match in aid of Lawton in May 1985. Lawton, by then living in a rented house in Nottingham without a telephone, said: 'When I heard what they were doing for me I was really choked. Yet I feel Brentford are the club I did least for.'

His later years were clouded by the death of Gaye, but he was ever ready to make appearances in aid of charity. On 4 August 1998, he was on the list of 100 Football League Legends, based on the votes of fifteen journalists, that was issued by the League to celebrate its 100th season, and in 2003 he was inducted into the English Football Hall of Fame at the National Football Museum at Preston.

CHAPTER THIRTY-TWO

The final tributes

For all the disruptions with which his three spells with Notts County ended, Lawton looked back on the good times as a player there: 'Believe me,' he said, 'there were far too many happy memories to pick out one above another. I made Nottingham my adopted city. That says enough about my feelings for the place. We broke all records, both home and away, with support at the time.'

Tributes to this footballing great flowed into the offices of the *Evening Post* after his death from pneumonia at his home in Nottingham on 6 November 1996, a month after his 77th birthday. His ashes were lodged at the National Football Museum. These are just a few of the glowing terms in which former colleagues remembered him:

Jackie Sewell: 'Tom was the best centre-forward I ever saw, no problem. Not only was he the best there'd been in the air, he also had two exceptionally good feet. The man had incredible presence and brought a tremendous amount of pleasure to spectators. I couldn't speak highly enough about the man. I'm very, very sad.'

Sir Stanley Matthews (Stoke, Blackpool and England): 'It's a very sad day. He was one of the great centre-forwards. He also had a wonderful personality. He was full of jokes, full of humour. He never lost his temper and he always took things in his stride. I was very fortunate indeed to have played with him. He was sharp, he was quick, and if he had a chance in the goalmouth you could guarantee, before you blinked an eye, it would be in the back of the net.'

Wilf Mannion (Middlesbrough and England): 'Tommy was a truly great player, one of the best centre-forwards there has been anywhere. As a bloke he fitted into the set-up like anyone I have known. There was always a good camaraderie and atmosphere among the players in those days when we played for the love of the game.'

Denis Compton (Arsenal and a wartime team-mate with England): 'I had all the time in the world for Tommy, both as a player and as a person. Tommy was a great, great centre-forward – the best I've seen or played with. What is the reason for his greatness? I should say perfect balance, anticipation, and, above all, patient practice. No man could hope to become as talented as he was without putting in a good deal of hard work. Tom, believe it or not, could actually "steer" a ball with his head, and when you sent over a cross that you felt worthy of a goal it was more than likely, if it was any good, that Lawton would nod it into the back of the net.'

Tom Finney (Preston and England): 'I played with some terrific centre-forwards, but Tommy was the best of the lot. He was a Lancastrian lad like myself, with a lovely sense of humour. He helped in the dressing-room camaraderie as much as anybody did. Just look at his record of scoring 22 goals in 23 games for England – and that's overlooking the fact that he probably lost his best years due to the war. He was very talented indeed, one of the greats.'

Jimmy Armfield (Blackpool and England): Tommy was the archetypal England centre-forward – a one-off. The transfer fees he commanded beggar the mind – £20,000 in 1947 was an absolute fortune. In his first-class career he scored 510 goals. That's 50 a season over ten years, an incredible strike rate.'

Keith Wiseman (FA chairman at the time of Lawton's death): 'He's one of the legendary figures of the game, from a vintage era that produced some of the greatest players.'

Noel White (FA International Committee chairman): 'The first star I can remember. He was a name everyone connected with Everton when I was a kid.'

Gordon McKeag (Football League President): 'He was the first player I saw who had the ability to hang in the air and wait for the ball. He was a great player.'

David McVay (a former Notts player who was also a columnist with Lawton on the *Nottingham Evening Post*): The one thing Tommy Lawton earned was respect, and that's a commodity money can't buy in these days of multi-million transfer fees and wages. He never ducked an issue or flinched a controversial challenge. He was prepared to call a spade a spade and say what he thought about the high and mighty and the humble. Tommy Lawton remains a giant of the beautiful game. His death means another vital link with the game and a way of life has gone forever. I fancy the memory of Tommy Lawton and his days of soccer innocence will remain. We'll be looking for you at the far post, Tommy.' (McVay, who hailed from Workington, made 130 first-team appearances as a Notts midfielder from 1973 to 1978 before joining Peterborough).

And there was also the tale Sam Bartram, Charlton's long-serving goalkeeper, never tired of telling – of how he waited on his line while Lawton rose for a centre: 'Tommy kept on climbing as his marker began to fall, arched his neck, and shouted: "Top left corner, Barty." A thud, and a split second later the ball found its chosen spot. And I didn't move a muscle.'

The final quote comes from Lawton's obituary in the *Daily Telegraph*: 'The Lawton story, however, was one of two halves. As a player he was lauded on Merseyside and then in London [and Nottingham]. As a manager, scout and later publican, sports shop owner, insurance salesman and pools representative he was – by his standards – a failure. It was a mark of the man that he was able to discuss his fallen circumstances and even to admit that his spirits were once so low that he seriously contemplated taking his own life. He blamed no one but himself.

'Lawton, however, deserves only to be remembered as the player he was: handsome, funny, outrageously gifted, a player's player, a man's man, someone for boys to dream about and their dads to worship. His name and reputation reach down through the years. He was a lion of English football.'

And that says it far better than I ever could. Here's to you, Tommy!

DATE		SCORE	OPPONENTS	SCORERS	ATT	POS
Aug	23	A 0-2	Ipswich		13,000	
	28	H 1-2	Bournemouth	Sewell	14,000	
	30	H 3-1	Bristol C	Sewell, Houghton, Evans (F)	18,950	15th
Sept	3	A 0-2	Bournemouth		16,800	
	6	A 1-3	Reading	Sewell	13,000	21st
	11	H 1-1	QPR	Lyman	19,315	21st
	13	H 1-0	Walsall	Cumner	18,000	18th
	18	A 1-4	QPR	Keeble	14,500	19th
	20	A 1-2	Leyton Orient	Sewell	11,000	20th
	27	H 1-1	Exeter	Lyman	19,000	20th
Oct	4	A 1-3	Newport	Marsh	14,000	21st
	11	H 2-1	Port Vale	Cumner, Gannon	20,124	20th
	18	A 1-1	Swindon	Marsh	18,000	19th
	25	H 0-0	Torquay		23,096	19th
Nov	1	A 1-1	Crystal Palace	Marsh	16,350	19th
	8	H 0-2	Aldershot		20,766	19th
	15	A 2-1	Northampton	Lawton, Marsh	18,300	19th
	22	H 4-2	Bristol R	Lawton 2, Sewell 2	29,437	18th
	29	H 9-1	Horsham	Lawton 3, Marsh 2, Sewell 3, Freeman	24,815	FAC1
Dec	13	H 1-1	Stockton (aet)	Sewell	30,156	FAC2
	20	N 4-1	Stockton	Cumner, Lawton 3	34,261	FAC2R
	26	H 5-1	Swansea	Lawton 2, Freeman, Marsh, Sewell	45,116	16th
	27	A 1-1	Swansea	Marsh	28,000	18th
Jan	3	A 0-1	Bristol C		35,287	18th
	10	A 2-0	Birmingham	Corkhill, Marsh	53,000	FAC3
	17	H 5-1	Reading	Sewell 3, Marsh, Lawton	34,732	15th
	24	A 0-1	Swindon		27,000	FAC4
	31	A 1-2	Walsall	Lawton	20,383	17th
Feb	7	H 1-4	Leyton Orient	Lawton	28,875	18th
	14	A 1-0	Exeter	Parks	20,000	17th
	21	H 4-1	Newport	Lawton, Sewell 2, Lyman	17,953	15th
	28	A 2-1	Port Vale	Lawton, Sewell	18,000	14th
March	6	H 2-1	Swindon	Marsh 2	27,629	12th
	13	A 2-2	Torquay	Lyman, Marsh	10,000	13th
	20	H 1-0	Crystal Palace	Lyman	31,508	12th
	26	H 2-1	Southend	Lawton 2	35,038	12th
	27	A 0-1	Aldershot		10,000	13th
	29	A 2-1	Southend	Cumner, Sheard og	24,000	10th
April	3	H 3-2	Northampton	Lawton 2, Lowery og	30,853	10th
	7	A 3-1	Watford	Cumner, Sewell, Marsh	12,432	10th
	10	A 0-2	Bristol R		12,094	10th
	15	H 0-1	Ipswich		33,515	10th
	17	H 1-2	Norwich	Sewell	18,580	10th
	22	H 4-0	Brighton	Pimbley, Sewell, Marsh, Cumner	19,633	
April	24	A 3-1	Brighton	Lawton 2, Cumner	19,344	6th
	28	A 1-0	Norwich	Lawton	37,847	6th
May	1	H 3-3	Watford	Lawton, Freeman, Sewell pen	23,076	6th

P42. Home W12 D5 L4. Away W8 D10 L4. Goals F68 A 59. Pts 46

LEAGUE APPEARANCES: 42 – Southwell; 41 – Sewell; 40 – Brown, Gannon; 39 – Corkhill; 37 – Howe; 32 – Baxter; 31- Cumner, Freeman; 30 – Marsh; 21 – Lyman; 19 – Lawton; 14 – Pimbley; 12 – Parks; 7 – Evans (F); 6 – Dickson, Houghton; 4 – Keeble; 3 – Bagnall; 2- Orgill; 1- Adamson, Jayes, Molloy, Rigby. GOALS: 18 – Lawton; 17 – Sewell; 12 – Marsh; 6 – Cumner; 5 – Lyman; 2 – Freeman, own-goals; 1 – Evans (F), Houghton, Gannon, Keeble, Parks, Pimbley.

FA CUP APPEARANCES: 5 – Brown, Corkhill, Cumner, Freeman, Howe, Lawton, Marsh, Sewell, Southwell ; 4 – Baxter, Gannon; 1 – Bagnall. GOALS: 6 – Lawton; 4 –Sewell; 3 – Marsh; 1 – Corkhill, Cumner, Freeman.

DATE			SCORE	OPPONENTS	SCORERS	ATT	POS
Aug	21	A	1-3	Torquay	Sewell	9,000	
	26	H	2-0	Walsall	Male og, Johnston	36,766	
	28	H	4-1	Bristol R	Marsh, Sewell, Johnston, Lawton	35,480	8th
Sept	2	A	2-3	Walsall	Sewell 2	16,000	9th
	4	A	3-3	Newport	Sewell, Houghton, Marsh	19,000	8th
	9	H	9-2	Ipswich	Lawton 4, Sewell, Bell og, Marsh, H'ton, J'ston	32,820	6th
	11	H	1-1	Swansea	Lawton	36,322	7th
	15	A	2-3	Ipswich	O'Mahoney og, Lawton	21,262	10th
	18	A	4-1	Reading	Houghton, Evans (F), Johnston	23,265	7th
	23	H	1-2	Swindon	Marsh	18,594	7th
	25	H	5-1	Crystal Palace	Johnston, Marsh 2, Sewell 2	23,933	6th
Oct	2	A	1-1	Watford	Evans (F)	22,340	8th
	9	A	0-3	Norwich		29,764	7th
	16	H	9-0	Exeter	Hold, Sewell 4, Lawton 4	37,547	3rd
	23	A	2-3	Millwall	Sewell, Johnston	45,000	7th
	30	H	2-0	Aldershot	Sewell, Johnston	35,498	6th
Nov	6	A	1-3	Leyton Orient	Hold	16,500	7th
	13	H	2-1	Port Vale	Johnston, Hold	29,464	7th
	20	A	1-3	Bristol C	Johnston	29,126	9th
	27	H	2-1	Port Vale	Lawton 2	36,514	FAC1
Dec	4	A	2-3	Brighton	Johnston, Hold	24,750	10th
	11	H	3-2	Barrow	Lawton, Johnston 2	36,710	FAC2
	18	H	5-0	Torquay	Hold, Sewell 2, Johnston, Lawton	26,000	7th
	25	A	2-1	Northampton	Johnston, Sewell	17,200	7th
	27	H	2-0	Northampton	Lawton, Sewell	38,000	6th
Jan	1	A	2-3	Bristol R	Johnston, Hold	11,981	7th
	8	A	1-0	Plymouth (aet)	Sewell	40,000	FAC3
	15	H	11-1	Newport	Sewell 4, Johnston 2, Lawton 4, Houghton	27,017	7th
	22	A	1-3	Swansea	Johnston	30,000	9th
	29	A	0-1	Liverpool		61,003	FAC4
Feb	5	H	1-0	Reading	Sewell	34,000	8th
	12	H	0-0	Southend		29,290	8th
	19	A	5-1	Crystal Palace	Johnston 3, Evans (F), Lawton	30,500	7th
	26	H	4-0	Watford	Johnston 3, Evans (F)	32,069	6th
March	5	H	2-1	Norwich	Lawton, Evans (F)	34,465	5th
	12	A	1-3	Exeter	Clark og	14,000	6th
	19	H	1-3	Millwall	Houghton (pen)	31,642	9th
	26	A	1-0	Aldershot	Johnston	10,500	7th
April	2	H	2-1	Leyton Orient	Houghton (pen), Johnston	29,287	6th
	9	A	0-1	Port Vale		12,000	8th
	15	A	1-2	Bournemouth	Hold	24,237	9th
	16	H	2-1	Bristol C	Sewell 2	27,313	9th
	18	H	2-3	Bournemouth	Evans (F), Lawton	28,132	9th
	23	A	0-3	Swindon		18,000	9th
	30	H	1-1	Brighton	Lawton	19,478	10th
May	7	A	2-3	Southend	Sewell, Hold	14,500	11th

P42. Home W15 D3 L3. Away W4 D2 L15. Goals F102 A68. Pts 43

LEAGUE APPEARANCES: 42 – Sewell; 41 – Johnston; 39 – Southwell; 36 – Lawton; 33 – Adamson;
31 – Houghton; 29 – Gannon; 27 – Baxter; 22 – Smith; 21 – Purvis; 19 – Hold; 17 – Brown (H); 15 – Howe;
13 – Brown (A); 11 – Marsh; 10 – Chapman. Evans (F), Freeman; 8 –Pimbley; 7 – Corkhill; 5 – Rigby;
3 – McCavana, Mowl, Praski, Stone; 2 – Russell (R); 1 – Macdonald, Jackson.
SCORERS: 26 – Sewell; 24 – Johnston; 20- Lawton; 9 –Hold; 7 – Evans (F); 6 – Houghton, Marsh;
4 – own-goals.

FA CUP APPEARANCES: 4 – Baxter, Gannon, Hold, Houghton, Johnston, Lawton, Sewell, Southwell;
2 – Adamson, Brown (A), Howe, Purvis, Smith ; 1 – Brown (H), Mowl.
SCORERS: 3 – Lawton; 3- Johnston; 1 – Sewell.

DATE		SCORE		OPPONENTS	SCORERS	ATT	POS
Aug	20	H	2-0	Southend	Evans (F), Sewell	33,490	
	24	A	3-4	Norwich	Lawton, Evans (W), Sewell	32,130	8th
	27	A	3-0	Bristol R	Lawton 2, Johnston	24,794	5th
Sept	1	H	5-0	Norwich	Evans (F) 2, Evans (W), Johnston, Lawton	35,149	3rd
	3	H	2-0	Bournemouth	Lawton 2	34,456	1st
	8	H	3-3	Exeter	Johnston 2, Lawton	32,167	2nd
	10	A	2-1	Crystal Palace	Evans (W), Johnston	30,000	1st
	17	H	1-0	Watford	Sewell	33,962	1st
	24	A	1-0	Reading	Evans (W)	29,091	1st
Oct	1	H	7-1	Leyton Orient	Sewell 2, Evans (W) 2, Lawton 2 Johnston,	36,332	1st
	8	A	1-1	Newport	Sewell	22,000	1st
	15	H	4-1	Bristol C	Sewell 2, Southwell, Lawton	37,978	1st
	22	A	3-2	Brighton	Lawton 2 (1 pen), Johnston	17,222	1st
	29	H	1-1	Walsall	Lawton (pen)	42,576	1st
Nov	5	A	3-1	Millwall	Lawton, Sewell 2	19,495	1st
	12	H	3-0	Swindon	Lawton 3 (2 pens)	37,121	1st
	19	A	0-0	Torquay		14,000	1st
	26	H	4-0	Tilbury	Lawton, Sewell, Broome 2	28,584	FAC1
Dec	3	A	2-1	Nott'm Forest	Lawton, Broome	37,903	1st
	10	A	2-1	Rochdale	Johnston, Lawton	24,231	FAC2
	17	A	0-2	Southend		13,000	1st
	24	H	2-0	Bristol R	Broome, Evans (F)	31,995	1st
	26	H	2-0	Ipswich	Sewell, Johnston	40,192	1st
	27	A	4-0	Ipswich	Sewell, Lawton 2, Johnston	22,983	1st
	31	A	0-3	Bournemouth		22,585	1st
Jan	7	H	1-4	Burnley	Johnston	44,000	FAC3
	14	H	0-1	Crystal Palace		31,303	1st
	21	A	1-2	Watford	Evans (F)	17,393	1st
	28	H	3-1	Aldershot	Broome, Evans (F), Sewell	27,024	1st
Feb	4	H	4-0	Reading	Sewell, Broome, Lawton, Johnston	36,183	1st
	18	A	4-1	Leyton Orient	Sewell, Johnston 2, Broome	22,000	1st
	25	H	7-0	Newport	Sewell 3, Lawton 2 (1 pen), J'ston, Evans (W)	28,427	1st
March	4	A	0-4	Bristol C		29,795	1st
	11	H	4-2	Brighton	Tennant og, Chapman, Lawton, Johnston	34,322	1st
	18	A	3-3	Walsall	Lawton, Johnston, Simpson	19,589	1st
	25	H	2-0	Millwall	Simpson 2	31,024	1st
April	1	A	1-1	Swindon	Simpson	18,000	1st
	7	H	3-1	Port Vale	Boyes, Lawton, Simpson	32,021	1st
	8	H	1-1	Torquay	Lawton	43,906	1st
	10	A	1-3	Port Vale	Lawton	15,000	1st
	15	A	0-2	Aldershot		10,000	1st
	22	H	2-0	Nott'm Forest	Sewell, Lawton	46,000	1st
	27	H	2-0	Northampton	Lawton 2	31,843	1st
	29	A	1-5	Northampton	Broome	9,940	1st
May	6	A	2-2	Exeter	Broome, Crookes	10,000	1st

P42. Home W17 D3 L1. Away W8 D5 L8. Goals F95 A50. Pts 58

LEAGUE APPEARANCES: 42 – Adamson, Smith (R); 41 – Evans (W); 39 – Chapman; 37 – Johnston, Lawton; 36 – Rigby; 33 – Baxter; 32 – Sewell; 29 – Deans; 24 – Broome; 20 – Evans (F); 18 – Southwell; 16 – Simpson; 3 – Boyes, Crookes, Purvis; 2 – Robinson; 1 – Brunt, Corkhill, Freeman, Pimbley, Stone. GOALS: 31 – Lawton; 19 – Sewell; 15 – Johnston; 7 – Broome, Evans (W); 6 – Evans (F); 5 – Simpson; 1 – Boyes, Chapman, Crookes, Southwell.

FA CUP APPEARANCES: 3 – Adamson, Chapman, Evans (W), Johnston, Lawton, Rigby, Sewell, Smith (R); 2 – Baxter, Broome, Deans; 1 – Freeman, Simpson, Southwell. GOALS: 2 – Broome, Johnston, Lawton; 1 – Sewell.

DATE		SCORE	OPPONENTS	SCORERS	ATT	POS
Aug	19 H	0-2	Coventry		41,023	
	24 A	0-1	QPR		16,000	21st
	26 A	0-2	Cardiff		36,000	22nd
	31 H	3-3	QPR	Evans (W), Crookes, Broome	33,404	21st
Sept	2 H	0-1	Birmingham		34,648	22nd
	4 A	1-1	Leicester	Johnston	36,069	21st
	9 A	4-1	Grimsby	Broome, Johnston, Sewell 2	20,000	19th
	16 H	1-2	Doncaster	Broome	39,381	19th
	23 H	1-3	Preston	Simpson	44,195	21st
	30 A	0-0	Bury		21,328	21st
Oct	7 A	2-1	Sheffield U	Sewell 2	30,000	20th
	14 H	2-2	Luton	Sewell, Johnston	34.054	19th
	21 A	0-1	Southampton		25,905	20th
	28 H	2-1	Barnsley	Johnston, Lawton	39,335	19th
Nov	4 A	3-1	Brentford	Broome 2, Johnston	26,399	17th
	11 H	1-1	Blackburn	Broome	35,487	18th
	18 A	1-0	Leeds	Sewell	30,000	17th
	25 H	4-1	West Ham	Lawton 2, Sewell, Evans (W)	27,073	13th
Dec	2 A	1-2	Swansea	Broome	25,000	15th
	11 H	2-2	Hull	Leuty, Lawton	32,708	15th
	16 A	2-1	Coventry	Lawton 2	25,114	14th
	23 H	1-2	Cardiff	Johnston	27,434	15th
	25 A	0-0	Chesterfield		19,148	15th
	26 H	1-0	Chesterfield	Leuty (pen)	35,035	15th
	30 A	4-1	Birmingham	Sewell 2, Crookes 2	33,000	12th
Jan	6 H	3-4	Southampton	Broome, Leuty (pen), Simpson	29,260	FAC3
	13 H	3-2	Grimsby	Johnston, Broome, Sewell	24,849	11th
	20 A	2-3	Doncaster	Sewell, Johnston	25,000	14th
Feb	3 A	1-3	Preston	Johnston	32,000	15th
	17 H	4-2	Bury	Lawton 2, Evans (W), Johnston	21,005	15th
	24 H	3-0	Sheffield U	Sewell 2, Johnston	31,290	11th
March	3 A	1-1	Luton	Crookes	17,398	11th
	10 H	2-2	Southampton	Sewell, Leuty	25,712	11th
	17 A	0-2	Barnsley		12,756	13th
	24 H	2-3	Brentford	Broome, Johnston	24,936	16th
	26 A	0-0	Manchester C		31,948	16th
	31 A	0-0	Blackburn		17,600	15th
April	7 H	0-0	Leeds		23,466	16th
	14 A	2-4	West Ham	Johnston 2	26,000	17th
	21 H	3-2	Swansea	Broome, Crookes, Adamson	17,789	16th
	28 A	0-1	Hull		24,190	16th
	30 H	0-0	Manchester C		13,873	16th
May	5 H	2-3	Leicester	Crookes, Lawton	24,092	17th

P42. Home W7 D7 L7. Away W6 D6 L9. Goals F61 A60. Pts 39

LEAGUE APPEARANCES: 39 – Simpson; 38 – Robinson; 37 – Deans, Johnston; 35 – Evans (W); 33 – Broome, Leuty; 31 – Crookes; 30 – Lawton; 26 – Sewell; 22 – Bradley; 21 – Corkhill; 20 – Smith (R), Southwell; 14 – Adamson; 5 – McPherson (K); 4 – Brunt, Chapman, Rigby; 2 – Baxter, Evans (F), Paxton; 1 – Mann, Purvis, Roby.
GOALS: 14 – Johnston, Sewell; 10 – Broome; 9 – Lawton; 6 – Crookes; 3 – Evans (W), Leuty; 1 – Adamson, Simpson.

FA CUP APPEARANCES: 1 – Bradley, Broome, Corkhill, Crookes, Deans, Johnston, Lawton, Leuty, Robinson, Sewell, Simpson.
GOALS: 3 – Broome, Leuty, Simpson.

Date			Score	Opponents	Scorers	Att	Pos
Aug	18	H	2-1	Coventry	Crookes 2	34,001	
	25	A	1-1	Swansea	Lawton	16,000	9th
	30	H	4-0	Barnsley	Lawton (pen), Broome 2, Johnston	15,507	2nd
Sept	1	H	2-1	Bury	Lawton 2	30,915	2nd
	6	H	4-0	Hull	McPherson (I), Lawton, Johnston, Broome	38,203	1st
	8	A	0-6	Luton		24,411	3rd
	12	A	1-2	Barnsley	Crookes	16,090	4th
	15	H	2-2	Nott'm Forest	Broome, Crookes	44,087	5th
	20	A	3-1	Hull	Lawton 2, Johnston	35,700	2nd
	22	H	0-0	QPR		23,185	2nd
	29	A	0-2	Blackburn		25,000	4th
Oct	6	A	0-1	Brentford		29,500	6th
	13	H	1-0	Doncaster	Crookes	33,087	6th
	20	A	5-1	Everton	Crookes, Jackson 4	49,604	4th
	27	H	3-4	Southampton	Jackson, Broome (pen), Crookes	31,540	4th
Nov	3	A	0-6	Sheffield W		46,571	9th
	10	H	1-2	Leeds	Jackson	25,307	14th
	17	A	0-2	Rotherham		21,000	14th
	24	H	1-1	Cardiff	Jackson	19,452	12th
Dec	1	A	0-2	Birmingham		27,000	14th
	8	H	2-3	Leicester	Crookes 2	27,065	16th
	15	A	2-0	Coventry	Broome, McCormack	20,224	15th
	22	H	2-0	Swansea	Broome, McCormack	22,175	12th
	25	H	3-1	Sheffield U	McCormack, Adamson, McPherson (I)	30,019	11th
	26	A	0-1	Sheffield U		39,721	12th
	29	A	1-2	Bury	Broome	14,942	14th
Jan	5	H	5-4	Luton	McC'k, McPh'n (I), Crookes, B'me, Owen og	22,808	12th
	12	H	4-0	Stockton	Broome 2 (1 pen), McCormack, Lawton	22,805	FAC3
	19	A	2-3	Nott'm Forest	McCormack, Broome	40,005	14th
	26	A	4-1	QPR	Lawton 2, McCormack, Crookes	18,782	12th
Feb	2	A	1-3	Portsmouth	Lawton	46,500	FAC4
	9	H	0-1	Blackburn		26,177	14th
	16	H	5-2	Brentford	Broome 2 (1 pen), Lawton, J'ston, McPh' (I)	22,503	13th
March	1	A	5-1	Doncaster	McPherson (I), Lawton 2, Crookes 2	22,000	12th
	8	H	0-0	Everton		29,380	10th
	15	A	0-4	Southampton		20,604	12th
	22	H	2-2	Sheffield W	Crookes, Broome	32,230	13th
	29	A	0-1	Leeds		12,867	13th
April	5	H	0-3	Rotherham		13,161	15th
	11	A	1-2	West Ham	Crookes	23,000	16th
	12	A	0-1	Cardiff		30,000	16th
	14	H	1-0	West Ham	Robinson	16,306	16th
	19	H	5-0	Birmingham	Wylie 4, Adamson	24,360	14th
April	26	A	1-1	Leicester	McPherson (I)	21,318	15th

P42. Home W11 D5 L5. Away W5 D2 L14. Goals F71 A68. Pts 39

LEAGUE APPEARANCES: 40 – Deans; 38 – Crookes, Leuty, Robinson; 34 – McPherson (I); 32 – Broome, Southwell; 29 – Lawton; 23 – Smith (R); 20 – Johnston; 19 – Bradley; 17 – Adamson, McCormack, Simpson; 11 – Allen, Brunt, Jackson; 10 – Baxter; 7 – Brown (R), Evans (W), Wylie; 2 – McPherson (K); 1 – Corkhill, Mitchell.
GOALS: 15 – Crookes; 13 – Broome; 12 – Lawton; 7 – Jackson; 6 – McCormack, McPherson (I); 4 – Johnston, Wylie; 2 – Adamson; 1 – Robinson, own-goal.

FA CUP APPEARANCES: 2 – Adamson, Bradley; Broome, Crookes, Lawton, Leuty, McCormack, Southwell; 1 – Baxter, Brunt, Deans, Jackson, McPherson (I), Simpson.
GOALS: 2 – Broome, Lawton; 1- McCormack.

Tommy Lawton's League and FA Cup career statistics

Season	Club	League Apps	League Goals	Total Apps	Total Goals	FA Cup Apps	FA Cup Goals	Overall total Apps	Overall total Goals
1935-36	Burnley	7	5						
1936-37		18	11	25	16			25	16
1936-37	Everton	10	3	35	19	1	1	36	20
1937-38		39	28	74	47	2	0	77	48
1938-39		38	34	112	81	5	4	120	86
1939-40		3	4	(not included; season abandoned at start of war)					
1946-47	Chelsea	34	26	146	107	5	4	159	116
1947-48		8	4	154	111			167	120
1947-48	Notts Co	19	18	173	129	5	6	191	144
1948-49		36	20	209	149	4	3	231	167
1949-50		37	31	246	180	3	2	271	200
1950-51		30	9	276	189	1	0	302	209
1951-52		29	12	305	201	2	2	333	223
1951-52	Brentford	10	2	315	203			343	225
1952-53		34	13	349	216	3	2	380	240
1953-54		6	2	355	218			386	242
1953-54	Arsenal	9	1	364	219			395	243
1954-55		18	6	382	225	2	1	415	250
1955-56		8	6	390	231			423	256

Lawton also scored one goal for Arsenal in 1953 Charity Shield victory over Blackpool.

FOR ENGLAND

	Apps	Goals	Apps	Goals (Totals)
Peacetime	23	22		
Wartime	18	24	41	46
Victory internationals	5	1	46	47

FOR EVERTON DURING THE 1939-45 WAR

	Apps	Goals	Apps	Goals (Totals)
1939-40	20	18		
1940-41	21	30	41	48
1941-42	11	14	52	62
1942-43	12	15	64	77
1943-44	25	40	89	117
1944-45	17	28	106	145
1945-46	5	3	111	148

Lawton guested for Aldershot, Chester, Greenock Morton, Notts County and Tranmere. He also played in many Army games.